# THE ENCYCLOPEDIA OF
# BASEBALL MANAGERS

# THE ENCYCLOPEDIA OF

# BASEBALL MANAGERS

## 1901 TO THE PRESENT DAY

Thomas Aylesworth and Benton Minks

John S. Bowman: General Editor

**CRESCENT**

The 1990 edition published by Crescent Books, distributed by Crown Publishers, Inc. 225 Park Avenue South New York, NY 10003

Produced by Brompton Books Corp. 15 Sherwood Place Greenwich, CT 06830 USA

Printed in Hong Kong

ISBN 0-517-67909-4

h g f e d c b a

**Page 1:** *Yankee manager Joe McCarthy chats with Babe Ruth during spring training in 1933.*

**Page 2:** *Connie Mack and Joe McCarthy featured on a 1929 Cubs souvenir scorecard.*

**Pages 4-5:** *Casey Stengel leads the cheer after the Yanks won the 1949 pennant.*

# CONTENTS

# INTRODUCTION

**Above:** *Old No. 14, Manager Pete Rose, comes out to talk with Reds pitcher Ron Robinson. Rose was later to take himself permanently out of the lineup.*
**Opposite:** *Pirates Manager Chuck Tanner in a contemplative mood.*

This encyclopedia lists the names and describes the careers of all the men who have served as regular or interim managers of major league baseball teams since 1900.

Although it might at first seem that the most obvious way to do this would be to list the managers, along with their biographies, in alphabetical sequence, that is not the way this book has been organized. The straightforward alphabetical arrangement may serve well enough in purely statistical works, but it is less satisfactory for an encyclopedia, which must be concerned with contexts as well as with stats. The primary context in which managers operate is the nature of the team they are directing, and no two teams are alike. Some managers have been dimissed for failing to direct a team to a pennant or even a National Championship. Others have been gladly retained for advancing a team from fourth place to third. Much depends on what a manager has to work with, as well as on the expectations of the owners and the fans.

Also, managers are, by and large, a peripatetic lot. A few, like Connie Mack, may spend long periods of time managing a single team, but many more spend a good deal of their lives jumping in and out of jobs. Billy Martin's case may be a little extreme, but it is not for that reason an exception. In fact, it is not uncommon for a team – especially a team in trouble – to have two or three managers in a single season. In an encyclopedia arranged alphabetically by managers, every time a given manager switched teams the status and character of the new team would have to be described. And for the sake of coherence, it would have to be described again in the entry dealing with his replacement, and then again in the entry for *his* replacement and so on. Yet during the period covered by a number of these repetitions the team itself might not have changed much. Indeed, we might still even be talking about the same season.

So this encyclopedia is first organized by leagues and teams, and only then by managers. The National League, by virtue of seniority, comes first, then the American. Under the league headings the teams appear (under their best-known names) in alphabetical order, and for each team the managers appear in chronological order. We have tried to indicate in all cases where a manager came from (*ie* where he was managing or playing before) and where he went after he left the team, so threads of continuity run throughout the book. Details of managers' early lives appear in the entries devoted to their first managing jobs, but readers seeking the full biographies of managers who have been associated with more than one team will doubtless wish to consult the index.

Does this encyclopedia reveal any eternal truths about what it takes to be a great manager? No, but it may help to dispel some myths. For example, though a great many fine players have gone on to managerial careers, experience playing in the majors seems to be neither a prerequisite nor a guarantee of managerial success. Casey Stengel had a distinguished outfielding career, but Joe McCarthy had no major league playing experience whatsoever. Red Schoendinst did amazingly well managing for St. Louis, but Ty Cobb bombed when he took over the reins in Detroit.

Nor is there any single obviously successful managerial style. It is difficult to think of personalities more different than, say, Leo Durocher, John McGraw and Tommy Lasorda, yet few people would be tempted to minimize the contributions that each made to his teams' winning ways.

Does a successful manager always have to have a special kind of sympathetic

**Above:** *Charlie Grimm of the Cubs.*
**Right:** *John McGraw of the Giants (l.) and Wilbert Robinson of the Dodgers in 1914.*
**Opposite top:** *Managers Mel Ott (Giants), Bill McKechnie (Reds), Leo Durocher (Dodgers) and Frankie Frisch (Pirates).*
**Below right:** *A rhubarb between Manager Tommy Lasorda of the Dodgers and Umpire Dick Stello in 1987.*
**Opposite below right:** *Left to right: Managers Bucky Harris (Senators), Joe McCarthy (Yankees), Lou Boudreau (Indians) in 1942.*

bond with the members of his team? Apparently not. Some victorious managers have been benign father figures to their teams, but others have had such tempestuous relations with their players and bosses that it is sometimes difficult to remember that they, too, were solid winners. Billy Martin, for example, may not be everyone's favorite, but it is worth remembering that only once has he managed a team that failed to win a pennant sometime during his tenure.

For readers who insist on drawing general conclusions from the evidence there may, however, be one rule that can be proposed with some confidence: in the volatile world of baseball managing you have to assume that direction is always more important than position. If you move your team one notch up from the cellar you are more likely to have your job next season than if you move the team one notch down from the pennant. Whether this is entirely fair is moot, but that is the way it seems to work. Most people think that Casey Stengel, after one of the most spectacular managing careers in history, was fired in 1960 just for losing a World Series.

Finally, there is one generalization that we can certainly make after reading all these stories of managers who won, lost or drew. It is in a sense obvious, yet it remains more the assertion of a mystery than its explanation. It is simply that managers *can* make an enormous – often crucial – difference in the fortunes of a ballclub. The quality of leadership may take many forms, may be infinitely elusive and subtle, but, by Heaven, it *is* real.

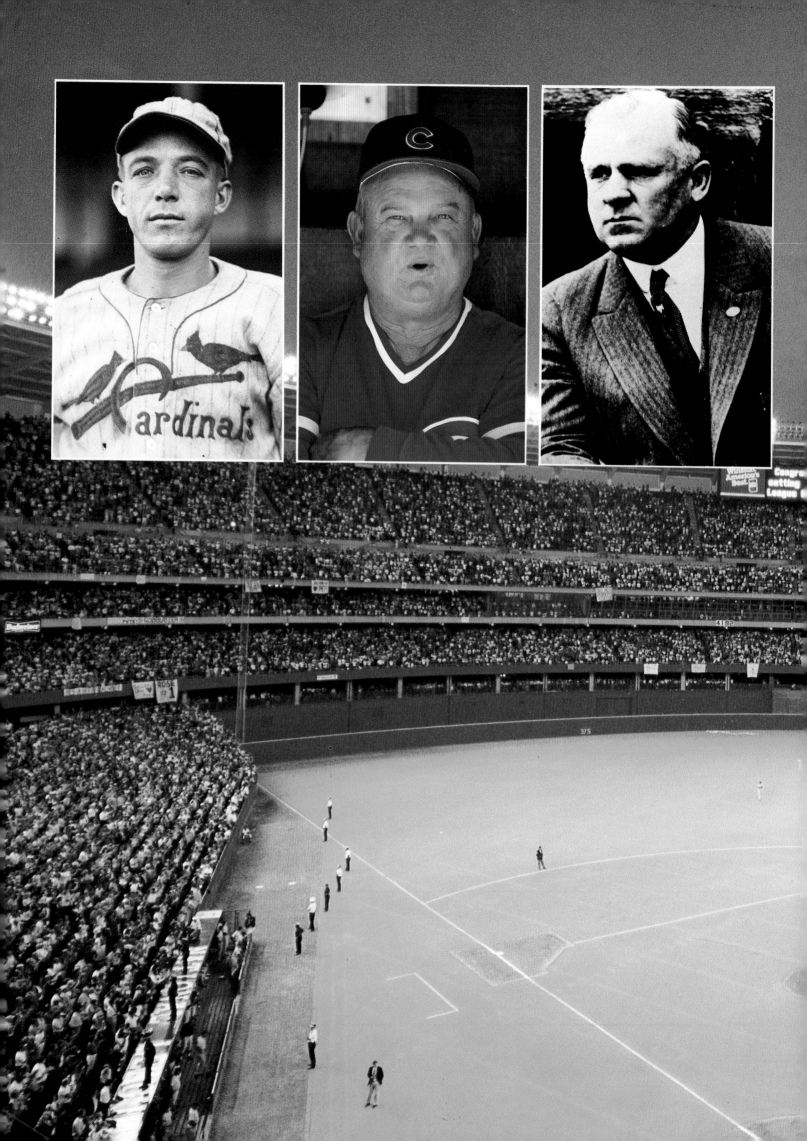

# The National League

### Called **COLT .45s** (1962-1964)

### 1962-1964 Harry Francis Craft

Nineteen sixty-two was a year of expansion, as the National League grew to ten teams by adding two brand-new clubs. One of them was the Houston Colt .45s, and Craft was selected to be their first manager. He had managed the Kansas City Athletics (1957-1959) and had then been hired by the Cubs in 1961, a year when he became a part of an ill-conceived plan of having several Cub coaches manage by committee. In 1962 he was able to lead Houston to an eighth-place finish (64-96) – not very good, but at least he finished six games ahead of his previous team. In 1963 the club fell to ninth place (66-96), and in 1964, with the team in ninth place (61-88) after 149 games, he was fired. He did not manage thereafter.

### 1964 Chalmer Lumen "Lum" Harris

Harris had been the manager of the Orioles for a mere 27 games when he was called in to finish the season for the Colt .45s with only thirteen games left in the season. He won five and lost eight, and the club stayed in ninth place (66-96 overall).

### Called **ASTROS** (1965-    )

### 1965 Chalmer Lumen "Lum" Harris

Harris was brought back for the 1965 season, but he could not improve the club's fortunes and led them to another ninth place (65-97) finish. He was fired and re-appeared as the manager of the Braves in 1968.

### 1966-1968 Grady Edgebert Hatton

Born on October 7, 1922, in Beaumont, Texas, Hatton was a good third baseman for the Reds (1946-1954), the White Sox (1954), the Red Sox (1954-1956), the Cardinals (1956), the Orioles (1956) and the Cubs (1960). In 1966 he did manage to lead the Astros to eighth place (72-90), but in 1967 it was ninth place (69-93) again, and in 1968, with the team in last place (23-38) after 61 games, he was fired.

### 1968-1972 Harry William "The Hat" Walker

Walker had been the manager of the Cardinals (1955) and the Pirates (1965-1967) and had done rather well with those teams. He took over with the Astros in tenth place (23-38) in 1968, but by winning 49 and losing 52 he could not get them out of the cellar, and they ended up with a 72-90 record. Things began to look up in 1969, as Walker managed a fifth-place (81-81) finish, and then he led them to fourth place (79-83) in 1970. The next year, 1971, was a repeat of the year before, and the Astros came in in fourth again, with an identical 79-83 record. He was let go in 1972, with the team in third (67-54) after 121 games.

### 1972 Francis James "Salty" Parker

Parker had been the manager of the Mets for 11 games in 1967 and was brought from the coaching ranks to manage one game for the Astros in 1972, which he won, and that was enough to move the team to second place (68-54).

### 1972-1973 Leo Ernest "The Lip" Durocher

Durocher took over the Astros in 1972 after a long career as manager of the Dodgers (1939-1946, 1948), the Giants (1948-1955) and the Cubs (1966-1972). He inherited the team in second place (68-54) and kept them there by winning 16 and losing 15 (84-69 overall). The next year, 1973, was a disappointment. The Astros finished fourth (82-80), and Leo was fired.

### 1974-1975 Preston Martinez Gomez

Gomez had been the manager of the Padres (1969-1972) and came to Houston in 1974, bringing the team in fourth place (81-81). After 127 games in 1975, with the team in sixth place (47-80), he was let go. In 1980 he became the manager of the Cubs.

### 1975-1982 William Charles "Bill" Virdon

Virdon, who had been the manager of the Pirates (1972-1973) and the Yankees (1974-1975), took over when the Astros were in sixth place (47-80) in 1975. Even though he split the last 34 games (17-17), he was only able to keep them in sixth place (64-97 overall). Then came two straight years in third – 1976 (80-82) and 1977 (81-81). The Astros fell to fifth (74-88) in 1978, but in 1979, with pitcher J.R. Richard striking out 313 to set a league record for right-handers, it was second place (89-73).

The 'Miracle' came in 1980. With three games to go in the season, the Astros were ahead of the Dodgers by three games, but they still had to face the Dodgers in a final three-game series, which Los Angeles swept. This forced a playoff game, and the Astros won, finishing in first place (93-70). The League Championship Series went the full five games, and the Astros lost to the Phillies three games to two. In the strike-split 1981 season the Astros finished in third place (28-29) in the first half and in first (33-20) in the second half. In the Divisional Playoff Series the Astros were beaten by the Dodgers three games to two. In 1982, with the team in fifth place (49-62) after 111 games, Virdon was let go, only to turn up as the manager of the Expos in 1983.

### 1982-1985 Robert Perry "Bob" "Flea" Lillis

Lillis, born on June 2, 1930, in Altadena, California, played shortstop for the Dodgers (1958-1961), the Cardinals (1961)

and Houston (1962-1967). He inherited the Astros in fifth place (49-62) and kept them there (77-85 overall), although he did win 28 while losing 23. It was third place (85-77) in 1983, and second (80-82) in 1984. Lillis brought the club in at third place (83-79) in 1985, and then he was gone.

**1986-88 Harold Clifton "Hal" Lanier**
Born on July 8, 1942, in Denton, North Carolina, Lanier had been a shortstop-second baseman for the Giants (1964-1971) and the Yankees (1972-1973) before coaching for the Cardinals and then coming to

Houston to take over the Astros. In his first year he brought them in in first place (98-66), finishing ten games in front, but the Astros then lost to the Mets 4-2 in the playoffs. Lanier, however, was named Major League Manager of the Year by the Associated Press, and National League Manager of the Year by the Baseball Writers Association of America. But Lanier's fiery, aggressive style didn't work in 1987, when the Astros lost 26 of their last 37 games and finished in third place (76-86). In 1988, although many predicted they would at least take their division, they also

went into decline at the end, after being only one-half game behind the Dodgers as late as August 9. They ended up in fifth place, 82-80, and Lanier was dismissed.

**1989- Arthur Henry "Art" Howe, Jr.**
Born on December 15, 1946, in Pittsburgh, Howe had been a utility infielder for the Pirates (1974-75), the Astros (1976-82) and the Cardinals (1984-85). He had then moved on to serve as a coach with the Rangers. He was given his first managerial post with the Astros in 1989.

14

**Above:** *Manager Art Howe had some things to be concerned about.*
**Opposite:** *Bill Virdon was a successful manager of the Astros for seven years, and often had a reason to smile.*

**Left:** *Hal Lanier was the Houston manager for three years.*

15

# BRAVES
## Boston (1901-1952)

Called **BEANEATERS** (1883-1906)

### 1890-1901 Frank Selee

Frank Gibson Selee, who was born on October 26, 1859, in Amherst, New Hampshire, had never played in the majors, but he had managed in the minors before he was called up to pilot the Beaneaters in 1890. During the 1890s he led the team to five first-place finishes, finished second once, third once, fourth once and fifth once. In 1900 his club won 66 and lost 72, for a fourth-place finish, and in 1901 the Beaneaters came in fifth, with a 69-69 record. Selee was soon on his way to Chicago to manage the Cubs.

**Above:** *Frank Selee of the Beaneaters.*
**Above right:** *Fred Tenney.*

### 1902-1904 Albert "Al" Buckenberger

Albert "Al" Buckenberger, another manager who had never played in the majors, followed Selee as the Beaneater manager in 1902. Buckenberger, who was born on January 31, 1861, in Detroit, Michigan, had had a fairly undistinguished record of managing since 1889 at Columbus of the American Association and Pittsburgh and St. Louis of the National League, lasting out the season only twice. When he came to Boston, after being out of the managerial ranks since 1895, things continued to go downhill. He finished third in 1902 (73-64), sixth in 1903 (56-80), seventh in 1904 (55-98) and then left the club. He died in Syracuse, New York, on July 1, 1917.

### 1905-1906 Frederick "Fred" Tenney

Fred Tenney, born on November 26, 1871, in Georgetown, Massachusetts, became the Beaneaters' player-manager in 1905. He had been a catcher, an outfielder and a second baseman with the club, but his specialty was first base. This diminutive athlete (5′ 9″ and 155 lbs.) had a .295 lifetime batting average and amazingly few strikeouts – a mere 43 in 17 years, beginning in 1894. But in his first three years of managing the Boston club he showed little improvement over the previous managers – a seventh-place finish in 1905 (51-103) and an eighth in 1906 (49-102).

Called **DOVES** (1907-1908)

### 1907 Frederick "Fred" Tenney

In 1907 the Doves were in seventh place (58-90) again, and Tenney was on his way to play for the Giants at the end of that season.

## 1908 Joseph James "Joe" Kelley

Joe Kelley was born on December 9, 1871, in Cambridge, Massachusetts. Best known for his abilities as an outfielder, this Hall of Famer (1971) had a career average of .319 batting for several National League clubs. After managing the Cincinnati Reds from 1902 to 1905 he was called to become player-manager of the Doves in 1908, where he carried on the losing tradition by finishing sixth (63-91). He was gone at the end of the season, at which time the team decided to change its name again – this time to the Pilgrims. Kelley was finished with baseball for good. He died in Baltimore, Maryland, on August 14, 1943.

## Called PILGRIMS (1909-1911)

### 1909 Frank Eugene "Mike" Bowerman

Bowerman was born on December 5, 1868, in Romeo, Michigan. He had spent most of his playing days as a catcher, beginning in 1895 with Baltimore of the National League, then with several other clubs, and finally coming to the Doves in 1908. His tenure as manager in 1909 was brief – only 79 games (23-55) – and he was demoted

**Above:** *Joseph James Kelley, the manager of the Doves in 1908.*

with the club in eighth place. Bowerman died in Romeo on November 30, 1948.

### 1909 Harry Thomas Smith

Smith, born on October 31, 1874, in Yorkshire, England, took over the reins from Bowerman for the rest of the 1909 season. His contribution was a 22-53 record, and the Pilgrims ended in last place, with a 45-108 overall tally. Smith, who had been a major league catcher since 1901, went back behind the plate in 1910. He died in Salem, New Jersey, on February 17, 1933.

### 1910 Frederick Lovett "Fred" Lake

Fred Lake was born on October 16, 1866, in Nova Scotia, Canada, and had had a rather odd career as a player. He was a catcher-outfielder-second baseman-shortstop-first baseman with several clubs, and often sat out whole seasons. He had played for Boston (1891), Louisville (1894), Boston (1897), Pittsburgh (1898) and Boston again (1910). He had managed the Boston Red Sox in 1908 and 1909, and he was called to the Pilgrims in 1910, where he carried on the losing tradition by finishing eighth (53-100). Lake died November 24, 1931, in Boston.

## Called BRAVES (1911-1935)

### 1911 Frederick "Fred" Tenney

Tenny was called back from the New York Giants to be Boston's player-manager in 1911. He, too, carried on the tradition by finishing last (44-107). Tenney died on July 3, 1952, in Boston.

### 1912 John "Johnny" "Noisy" Kling

Kling, who was born on February 15, 1875, in Kansas City, Missouri, had been an outstanding catcher with the Chicago Cubs since 1900. He was traded to the Braves in the middle of the 1911 season, and he took over the managerial reins in 1912. He did no better than his predecessors, finishing last with a 52-101 record. At the end of the season he was traded to the Cincinnati Reds, for whom he played for one year. He died in Kansas City on January 31, 1947.

### 1913-1920 George Tweedy "The Miracle Man" Stallings

Who would have ever guessed that George Stallings would become the man who would bring respectability to the Braves? Born on November 17, 1867, in Augusta, Georgia, he had had a minuscule career as a big league player. As a catcher, he had played four games for Brooklyn in 1890, and, as an outfielder and first baseman for Philadelphia, he had played two games in 1897 and one in 1898, accumulating a career batting average of .100. Before he came to the Braves he had managed the Phillies, the Tigers and the Yankees for five years, all with only modest success. But in his first year with the Braves he led them out of last place and finished the season in fifth (69-82).

Then came the "Miracle Braves" of 1914. At the beginning of the season Stallings had said, "I have 16 pitchers, all of them rotten." But slowly he began to bring order out of chaos via such shrewd maneuvers as using two sets of outfielders, one for right-handed pitchers and one for left-handers. Nevertheless, the Braves were in dead last place on July 19. But then came the miracle. The team won 60 of its last 76 games to take the pennant, 10½ games ahead of the New York Giants. Then the Boston Braves, in their very first World Series, shut out the Philadelphia Athletics in four games.

That was easily Stallings' finest year, but he still managed to finish second in 1915 (83-

69) and third in 1916 (89-63). After that the team began to collapse. The Braves were sixth in 1917 (72-81), seventh in 1918 (53-71), sixth in 1919 (57-82), and seventh in 1920 (62-90). After the 1920 season Stallings left. He died on May 13, 1929, in Haddock, Georgia.

### 1921-1923 Frederick Francis "Fred" Mitchell

Mitchell, who was born Frederick Francis Yapp in Cambridge, Massachusetts, on June 5, 1878, came to the Braves after managing the Chicago Cubs for four years. This combination pitcher-catcher-first baseman-third baseman-outfielder-short-stop-second baseman had played for several teams sinced 1901, and he brought the Braves back to the first division, finishing fourth in 1921 (79-74). But then it was last place in 1922 (53-100) and seventh in 1923 (54-100), his last year as a manager. He died in Newton, Massachusetts, on October 13, 1970.

### 1924-1927 David James "Dave" "Beauty" Bancroft

Bancroft, born on April 20, 1891, in Sioux City, Iowa, was a distinguished shortstop for 16 years in the National League, playing for the Phillies, the Giants, the Braves, the Dodgers and the Giants again. He would be

*Above: Dave Bancroft, Frankie Frisch.*

elected to the Hall of Fame in 1971, but as a player, not as a manager. As player-manager of the Braves, he merely perpetuated the team's second-division performance, finishing eighth in 1924 (53-100), fifth in 1925 (70-83), seventh in 1926 (66-86) and seventh in 1927 (60-94). After the 1927 season he left for the Dodgers, and his last playing season was in 1930 with the Giants. Bancroft died on October 9, 1927, in Superior, Wisconsin.

### 1928 John Terrence "Jack" Slattery

Slattery, who was born on January 6, 1878, in Boston, had had an off-and-on career as a catcher (and sometime first baseman) with the Red Sox (1901), the Indians (1903), the White Sox (1903), the Cardinals (1906) and the Senators (1909). His career as manager of the Braves was short, since he left in the middle of the 1928 season, with the team at 22-53 and in seventh place. He died in Boston on July 17, 1949.

**Opposite top:** *George Stallings (center).*
**Opposite bottom:** *The 1914 Braves.*

*Above: Left to right: Hughie Jennings, John McGraw and Dave Bancroft, 1925.*

## 1930-1935 William Boyd "Bill" "Deacon" McKechnie

This Hall of Fame (1962) third baseman, after managing Newark in the Federal League and Pittsburgh and St. Louis in the National League, was brought to Boston to manage the Braves. But in his long tenure with the club, he never finished higher than fourth. He was sixth in 1930 (70-84), seventh in 1931 (64-90), fifth in 1932 (77-77), fourth in 1933 (83-71), fourth in 1934 (78-73) and last in 1935 (38-115).

## Called BEES (1936-1940)

## 1936-1937 William Boyd "Bill" "Deacon" McKechnie

In a move possibly made to change its luck, the team changed its name to the Boston Bees in 1936. It didn't help. McKechnie finished sixth (71-83) in 1936 and fifth (79-73) in 1937. After that season he was off to manage the Reds, where he was much more successful.

Left: *Rogers Hornsby – 1928.*
**Opposite top:** *Stengel – The Old Perfessor.*
**Opposite bottom:** *Manager Billy Southworth.*
**Below:** *Manager McKechnie (l.).*

## 1928 Rogers "Rajah" Hornsby

Hornsby, who had been the manager of the St. Louis Cardinals in 1925 and 1926 (the Cards won the pennant in 1926), was brought to the Braves during the season of 1928 to see if he could turn them around. He had no more luck than Slattery, and the team stayed in seventh place (50-103) after Hornsby had gone 39-83. He would next appear as manager of the Cubs in 1930.

## 1929 Emil Edwin "Judge" Fuchs

Fuchs was brought in as manager in 1929 with the same mission that Hornsby had failed to accomplish the year before. But he was a much less likely choice. He had had no major league playing experience – and was to have very little managing experience. The 51-year-old Fuchs (born on April 17, 1878, in New York City) brought the Braves in at their accustomed eighth place with a 56-98 record. That signaled the end of his managing career. He died in Boston on December 5, 1961.

### 1938-1940 Charles Dillon "Casey" "The Old Perfessor" Stengel

Stengel had been the manager of the Brooklyn Dodgers from 1934 to 1936 and was brought in to help out the Bees in 1938. He did no better than his predecessors, finishing fifth in 1938 (77-75), seventh in 1939 (63-88) and seventh in 1940 (65-87).

### Called BRAVES (1941-1952)

### 1941-1943 Charles Dillon "Casey" "The Old Perfessor" Stengel

In 1941 the team changed its name back to the Braves again. It didn't help. Stengel finished seventh (62-92) in 1941, seventh (59-89) in 1942 and sixth (68-85) in 1943. After that season Stengel went to the minors, where he had great success as the manager of the Oakland Oaks of the AAA Pacific Coast League. He would return in 1949 as manager of the Yankees.

### 1944-1945 Robert Hunter "Bob" Coleman

The Braves' next manager, Bob Coleman, was born on September 26, 1890, in Huntingburg, Indiana. As a catcher, his playing career had been short, covering only 116 games in three years with Pittsburgh and Cleveland. But his managerial career was even shorter. After 27 years away from the headlines he took the Braves to a sixth-place finish (65-89) in 1944 and left the club in seventh place (42-49) in 1945. Coleman died in Boston on July 16, 1959.

### 1945 Adelphia Louis "Del" Bissonette

Bissonette was born on September 6, 1899, in Winthrop, Maine, and spent five years as a first baseman for the Brooklyn Dodgers. Leaving them in 1933, he was hired by the Braves to finish out the 1945 season. He took the team from seventh to sixth place (67-85) by posting a record of 25-36. He died in Augusta, Maine, on June 9, 1972.

### 1946-1951 William Harrison "Billy" Southworth

In the five years before 1946 Southworth, as manager, had brought the St. Louis Cardinals to the top of the National League three

**Above:** *Billy Southworth – the new manager of the Braves – in 1946. He was to stay with them until 1951.*

## 1951-1952 **Thomas Francis "Tommy" Holmes**

Coming in to replace Southworth was Tommy Holmes, born on March 29, 1917, in Brooklyn, New York. Outfielder Holmes was truly a superstar as a player, hitting .302 in his ten years (1942-1952) with the Braves and his one year with the Dodgers. He did improve the club a little, with a 48-47 record that brought them up to fourth place (76-78) in 1951, but in 1952, when the Braves were 13-22 and in sixth place, he was replaced as manager. He did not manage thereafter.

## 1952 **Charles John "Charlie" "Jolly Cholly" Grimm**

With their players losing and fans leaving, the Braves brought up Grimm, who had won two pennants in two separate stints with the Chicago Cubs. He didn't help much, since the team finished in seventh place (64-89). He was the last manager of the Boston Braves, for the team's owners stunned the sports world by announcing at the end of the season that the franchise was moving to Milwaukee.

**Below:** *Charlie Grimm brought the Braves in in second place in 1953 and was named manager of the year in the National League.*

times and finished second twice. In an effort to improve their lot the Braves brought him to Boston, and he did what he was supposed to, putting them in the first division with a fourth-place finish (81-72) in his first year. It was third place in 1947 (86-68), and, wonder of wonders, the club won its second pennant in 1948 (91-62). Except for two superstars, Warren Spahn (24 wins) and Johnny Sain (15 wins), Southworth had a pretty pedestrian pitching staff that year, which led to the bit of doggerel, "Spahn and Sain, and pray for rain." Unfortunately, the Cleveland Indians won the World Series four games to two.

The Braves were fourth in 1949 (75-79) and 1950 (83-71). In 1951 they were in fifth place, with a 28-31 record, when Southworth was let go after about one-third of the season was over. He died on November 15, 1969, in Columbus, Ohio.

### 1953-1956 Charles John "Charlie" "Jolly Cholly" Grimm

The switch from Boston made many of the Milwaukee players a bit nervous, but they were heartened by the comments of Andy Pafko, the fine outfielder (for the Cubs and the Dodgers) who had just joined the team. A Wisconsin native, Pafko told them about the way he expected the city of Milwaukee to take the team to its heart, and, as it happened, he was right. By their first 13 games of the new season the Braves had surpassed their total 1952 attendance of 281,278 in Boston.

Under Grimm the Braves experienced a metamorphosis in 1953, finishing second (92-62). Indeed, they were contenders for the next two years, finishing third in 1954 (89-65) and second in 1955 (85-69). But in 1956 Grimm had them only in fifth place, with a 24-22 record, when he was let go. He would manage again, for the Cubs, in 1960.

### 1956-1959 Fred Girard "Pudge" Haney

Haney, who had managed the Browns and the Pirates with little success, was brought in to finish the 1956 season, and he went 68-40 to push the club up to second place (92-62). He provided a greater miracle in 1957, winning the pennant (95-59) and the World Series four games to three over the Yankees. His record slipped to 92-62 in 1958, although the Braves did finish first. But they fell to the Yankees four games to three in the World Series. Haney led the Braves to a second-place finish (86-70) in 1959 and left the club. He was to die in Beverley Hills, California, on November 9, 1977.

### 1960-1961 Charles Walter "Chuck" Dressen

Dressen had had an up-and-down career as manager of the Reds, Dodgers and Senators before he was brought in to replace Haney. In 1960 he kept the Braves in second place (88-66), but when they fell to third place late in the 1961 season, with a 71-58 mark, he was let go. Dressen later showed up as the manager of the Tigers in 1963.

**Above:** *Charlie Grimm in 1953.*
**Left:** *Grimm suffers a rainout.*
**Left center:** *Fred Haney.*
**Left bottom:** *Chuck Dressen.*

### 1961-1962 George Robert "Birdie" Tebbetts

Tebbetts, who had had a so-so record as the manager of the Reds, was brought in to replace Dressen. In 1961 he could manage only a 12-13 mark, and the Braves ended the season by falling from third to fourth place (83-71). It was worse in 1962. With an 86-76 mark, the team finished fifth, and Tebbetts was out. He was to manage the Indians the next year.

### 1963-1965 Robert Randall "Bobby" Bragan

Bragan had been let go as manager by both the Pirates and the Indians, and he didn't do much better with the Braves. He led them to a sixth-place finish (84-78) in 1963, and then to two fifth-place finishes in 1964 (88-74) and 1965 (86-76). In 1966, once again, the Braves owners confounded the sports world by selling the team to broadcasting magnate Ted Turner, who moved them to Atlanta. The reason given for the change was that they would have more television exposure, since in Milwaukee they were hemmed in by telecasts of the Cubs, the White Sox, the Indians and the Twins.

# BRAVES
## Atlanta (1966-    )

### 1966 Robert Randall "Bobby" Bragan

After 111 games into the 1966 season, with the team still in fifth place (52-69), the Braves management let Bragan go. He did not manage in the majors thereafter.

### 1966-1967 William Clyde "Billy" Hitchcock

Hitchcock was brought in to replace Bragan. He had previously managed the Tigers and the Orioles with little success, and he had a worse time in Atlanta. He finished the 1966 season with a 33-18 record, but the team stayed in fifth place (85-77). In 1967 he was let go after 159 games, with the team in seventh place (77-82). This ended his managing career.

### 1967 Kenneth Joseph "Hawk" Silvestri

Silvestri, who was born on May 3, 1916, in Chicago, had been a decent catcher for the White Sox, Yankees and Phillies from 1939 to 1951. He was brought in to finish off the last three games of the Braves' 1967 season, and he led the team to three straight defeats. The Braves finished seventh (77-85). Silvestri was offered no further managing jobs.

### 1968-1972 Chalmer Luman "Lum" Harris

Things began to look up when Harris, who had coached in Houston in 1964-5, took over the club. In 1968 he brought the team up to a fifth-place finish, with a .500 record (81-81). Then, in 1969, Harris led the team to a first-place finish (93-69) in the National League West, but lost to the Mets, three games to none, in the League Championship Series. In 1970 the Braves finished fifth (76-86), and in 1971 they were third (82-80). After 104 games into the 1972 season, with the club in fifth place (47-57), Harris was let go. He has not managed in the majors since.

### 1972-1974 Edwin Lee "Eddie" Mathews

Mathews had long been a hero to Braves fans. Born on October 13, 1931, in Tex-

arkana, Texas, this third baseman began with the Braves in Boston in 1952, lasted all the years in Milwaukee and played in 1966 in Atlanta. He later played in Houston and Detroit for a total of two years, but this man, who was to be elected to the Hall of Fame in 1978, would always be a Brave.

He took over the Braves as manager to finish up the 1972 season and had a 23-27 record, which was enough to lift the team to fourth place (70-84). But the team fell to fifth place (76-85) in 1973, and when they were 50-49 in 1974 and in fourth place, Mathews was fired, thus ending his brief managing career.

**Above:** *Lum Harris (r.), Eddie Mathews.*
**Below:** *Eddie Mathews in 1952.*

### 1974-1975 Clyde Edward King

King had had some success managing the San Francisco Giants in 1969 and 1970, and he was brought in to finish the Braves' 1974 season. He led them to a record of 38-25, which was enough to lift them to third place, but his success was short-lived. In 1975, 125 games into the season, the Braves were in fifth place, with a record of 59-76, and King was let go. He was later to resurface as manager of the Yankees (1982).

### 1975 Cornelius Joseph "Connie" Ryan

Ryan, who was born in New Orleans on February 27, 1920, had been a better-than-average second baseman for 12 years with the Giants, Braves, Reds, Phillies, White Sox and the Reds again. He was brought in to finish the 1975 season, but with a mere 26 games to go there was not much that he could do. The team went 8-18 and finished fifth (67-94). Ryan was later to manage the Texas Rangers (1977).

### 1976-1977 James David "Dave" Bristol

Bristol had had seven years of managerial experience with the Reds and the Brewers when he was appointed manager of the Braves in 1976. It was not a good year, and the club finished in sixth place (70-92). In 1977, with the team in sixth place (8-21), Bristol was asked to step aside for one game in one of baseball's oddest maneuvers.

### 1977 Robert Edwards "Ted" Turner

Turner, who was born on November 19, 1938, in Cincinnati, had no real baseball experience apart for the fact that he owned the team. Yet, after a 17-game losing streak, he insisted upon inserting himself as manager for one game, which he lost. And that is how Turner's name came to be permanently listed in baseball history's official Manager Register, along with such others as Casey Stengel, Connie Mack and Joe McCarthy.

### 1977 James David "Dave" Bristol

After Turner's single game Bristol came back to finish the season. The Braves finished last again (61-101), and he was on his way out. In 1979 he became the manager of the Giants.

### 1978-1981 Robert Joe "Bobby" Cox

Cox had had a very short playing career in major league baseball. Born on May 21, 1941, in Tulsa, Oklahoma, he had been with the Yankees for only two years at third base in 1968 and 1969. He came to the Braves as manager in 1978 and led them to a last-place finish (69-93). They finished last again in 1979 (66-94) and then climbed to fourth in

*Previous page: Joe Torre in 1982, when he brought the Braves in in first.*
**Above:** *Bobby Cox in 1980.*
**Above left:** *Russ Nixon.*

1980 (81-80). In the famous split season of 1981 they finished fourth in the first half of the season (25-19) and fifth in the second half (25-27). Then Cox was off to manage the Blue Jays. He would eventually become the Braves' general manager.

### 1982-1984 Joseph Paul "Joe" Torre

In 1982 Torre was called over from his job as manager of the New York Mets. Amazingly, he led the Braves to a first-place finish (89-73) in his first year, but the Braves lost to St Louis three games to none in the League Championship Series. The team fell to second in 1983 (88-74) and 1984 (80-82), and Torre was gone.

### 1985 George Edwin "Eddie" Haas

Haas was next in line in the long stream of Braves managers. Born in Paducah, Kentucky, on May 26, 1935, he had spent only three years as a major league player, appearing in 55 games for Chicago and Milwaukee. He managed the Braves for 121 games in 1985, winning 50 and losing 71, and left while the team was in fifth place.

### 1985 Robert Paul "Bobby" Wine

Wine, born in Norristown, Pennsylvania, on July 13, 1962, had played shortstop for 12 years in the majors, first with the Phillies and then with the Expos. He came to Atlanta just to finish the 1985 season and led the team to a 16-25 record. They finished in fifth place (66-96).

### 1986-1988 Charles William "Chuck" Tanner

Tanner was brought to the Braves in 1986 because of his success as the manager of the White Sox, Athletics and Pirates. In his 16 years of being at the helm in the big leagues, he had finished first or second five times. But in 1986 he led the Braves to a sixth-place finish (72-89) and was only able to get them to fifth in 1987 (69-92). In 1988, on May 22, with the team in last place and with the worst record in either league (12-27), he was fired.

### 1988 Russell Eugene "Russ" Nixon

Nixon, who had managed the Red for part of 1982 (when they finished sixth) and all of 1983 (when they also finished sixth), was called in to replace Tanner. Things did not improve much, and the Braves finished the season 54-106 and in last place in the Western Division.

# CARDINALS
St. Louis (1900- )

### 1901-1903 **Patrick Joseph "Patsy" Donovan**

Patsy Donovan was, in fact, the third Cardinal manager of the twentieth century. The first was Oliver Wendell "Patsy" Tebeau. Patsy Tebeau directed the Cardinals to fifth place among 12 teams in 1899, his first year with St. Louis. In his second year with the Cardinals, however, Tebeau (born on December 5, 1864, in St. Louis) won only 48 of the 104 games he managed before losing his job and retiring from managing with his team in seventh place. He died in St. Louis on May 15, 1918. Relieving Patsy Tebeau for the remaining 38 games of the 1900 season, Louis Heilbroner, a native Hoosier (born on July 4 in Ft. Wayne) led the Cardinals to 17 wins – enough to advance the team in the final standings from seventh to fifth. Heilbroner did not manage in the major leagues after 1900. He died in Ft. Wayne on December 21, 1933.

Donovan, who was born in County Cork, Ireland, on March 16, 1865, started managing in Pittsburgh in 1897. The year before he received his appointment as manager of the Cardinals, Donovan played for the team as an outfielder, batting .316 and stealing 45 bases, best in the league. He continued playing while working as manager the next three years and in his last season batted .327. His first year of managing in St. Louis was most satisfying, resulting in a fourth-place finish, one notch above that of 1900, but with 11 more wins. St. Louis also set the League attendance record that year, with 380,000. The Cardinals dropped to sixth in Donovan's second year and finished last in 1903. He did not return to St. Louis after the 1903 season, but he turned up managing the Senators in 1904.

### 1904-1905 **Charles Augustus "Kid" Nichols**

Inducted into the Hall of Fame in 1949, Kid Nichols won his accolades more for his pitching than for his work as manager. The hard-working Nichols had won 30 or more

**Right:** *Kid Nichols in his pitching days.*

games in seven of his 12 playing seasons before coming to the Cardinals. In 1904, his first year with the Cards, Nichols (born on September 14, 1869, in Madison, Wisconsin) won 21 of the 34 games in which he pitched and helped move the team from the last place of the year before to fifth in his first year managing. After 19 wins in the first 48 games of his second year, however, he lost his managing job. He moved on to the Phillies, for whom he pitched through 1906. He died at the age of 84 on April 11, 1953, in Kansas City.

## 1905 James "Jimmy" "Sunset Jimmy" Burke

Second of three managers to try to deliver the Cardinals from mediocrity in 1905, Jimmy Burke (born in St. Louis on October 12, 1874) was able to claim even fewer wins than his predecessor (17 of 49 games) and was gone before the end of July, with the team even deeper in sixth place (of eight teams). He would turn up managing the Browns in 1918.

## 1905 Matthew Stanley "Matt" Robison

Unable to advance the Cardinals from the sixth place they occupied when he relieved Jimmy Burke, Matt Robison nonetheless prevented their falling behind the Boston Beaneaters. Robison, born on March 30, 1859, in Pittsburgh, Pennsylvania, did not manage in the major leagues afterwards. He died on March 24, 1911, in St. Louis.

## 1906-1908 John "Honest John" McCloskey

Two years of managing in Louisville (1895-1896) had familiarized John McCloskey with the major league competition he faced when he came to the Cardinals in 1906. Furthermore, his experience in Louisville had prepared him for the discouraging prospects he confronted in St. Louis. In his five years managing major league teams, McCloskey directed only one to a better-than-last place finish – the 1906 Cardinals (seventh of eight). A native Kentuckian (born on April 4, 1862, in Louisville), he was unable to improve the team's winning record in 1907 (52 games) – last place again. McCloskey's last season with the Cardinals was even more despiriting (49-105). He did not manage in the big leagues again and died on November 17, 1940, in his home town of Louisville.

## 1909-1912 Roger Philip "The Duke of Tralee" Bresnahan

Roger Bresnahan came to the Cardinals at little risk – at least in one respect – for the woeful performances of the previous two years had resulted in last-place finishes and a combined 101-206 record. Acquainted with winning, the Duke of Tralee (elected to the Hall of Fame in 1945) had played on John McGraw's 1905 World Champion Giants as catcher and had received acclaim for his speed; but his familiarity with winning could not substitute for the necessary wherewithal absent from the Cardinals.

To his credit, Bresnahan (born on June 11, 1879, in Toledo, Ohio) moved the team out of last place during his first year and closed the season with the first winning record since 1901, strong enough to win fifth spot (only two and one-half games behind the fourth-place Phillies). In his final year with the Cardinals, though, the team dropped below .500 again and ended in sixth place. Bresnahan would turn up managing the Cubs in 1915.

## 1913-1917 Miller James "Hug" "The Mighty Mite" Huggins

The steadiness which distinguished Miller Huggins as a second baseman from 1910-1916 was apparent in his work as manager as well. In his first four years directing the Cardinals he also played (in 1914 he batted .304 in 148 games and led the league in bases on balls with 105). In his first year of managing the Cardinals remained in their familiar last-place position, but the next year they improved in the win column by 30 games and abruptly became a team of respectability, ending in third only two and one-half games behind John McGraw's second-place Giants.

Huggins (born on March 27, 1879, in Cincinnati, Ohio) continued playing and managing the next two years, but the team again drifted toward last spot, with a sixth-place finish in 1915 and seventh the next season. In his final year in St. Louis, before being enticed away to lead the Yankees, the taciturn but wiley "Mighty Mite," whose manner and size belied his stalwart character, exacted peak performance from a team of modest talent, and the Cardinals finished third again, the second time in four years. Huggins, who had begun playing baseball in 1899 against his Methodist father's wishes and had prepared to practice law (he passed the bar examination in 1902), was the Cardinals' first manager to direct a team even close to being a contender. When he left St. Louis for New York at the end of the 1917 season he was on the brink of a managing career that would put him in the Hall of Fame in 1964.

**Above:** *Miller Huggins.*
**Top:** *Roger Bresnahan wearing the tools of ignorance in 1909.*

## 1918 **John Charles "Jack" Hendricks**

Unable to maintain the kind of performance that had enabled an essentially frail team to finish in third place the year before, Jack Hendricks from Joliet, Illinois (born on April 9, 1875) managed the 129 games which constituted a 1918 season shortened by the War. Hendricks' Cardinals won only 51 games and dropped to last place. He would go on to manage the Reds, beginning in 1924.

## 1919-1925 **Wesley Branch "The Mahatma" Rickey**

Third place in the league was the best performance the Cardinals could boast of in their first 18 years in the National League. What they didn't have in cash (the advantage that continued to produce winners for the Giants, for example), they tried to compensate for in frugal planning and use of available resources. In 1916 the team was $185,000 in debt when its original owner decided to sell. Branch Rickey was persuaded to leave the position of president-manager of the St. Louis Browns to become the new president of the Cardinals. Rickey, who had prepared himself to practice law, was a baseball theorist as well as a practitioner.

One of his first important decisions was to acquire Rogers Hornsby, whose .327 in 1917 was second best in the league. A second important decision by Rickey occurred in 1919, the year of the "Black Sox Scandal," when he bought shares in the Houston team in the Texas League with the intention of developing a farm system which would eventually feed the talent-starved Cardinals. It was in 1919, also, that Rickey assumed the management of the team.

Within three years the Rickey strategy was delivering benefits: the 1921-1923 Cardinals posted winning seasons and in the first two of those years they ended in third place. But 1924 and 1925, even though Hornsby's batting improved (.424 in 1924), were notable for the increasing acrimony between the rough-cut Hornsby and the academic Rickey. The results were destructive to the team, which finished in sixth place in 1924 and stood in last spot after 38 games in the 1925 season, when Rickey lost

**Right:** *Branch Rickey in his playing days.*

*Rogers Horsby in 1926 with John McGraw, manager of the Giants.*

his position to Hornsby. Rickey's dismissal by owner Breadon was calculated to be a promotion in disguise, resulting in Rickey's move to the position of team vice president, a post in which he could better serve the team, as he did through 1942. Rickey was elected to the Hall of Fame in 1967 – almost two years after his death on December 9, 1965, in Columbus, Missouri.

### 1925-1926 Rogers "Rajah" Hornsby

Applying the baseball knowledge that Branch Rickey, his predecessor, had taught in theory, Rogers Hornsby salvaged a fourth place in the 1925 season, after taking over 38 games into the season and with the Cardinals in last place. His .403 batting, 39 home runs and 143 RBI's accrued while managing and playing second base were no small factor in the team's rebound.

Hornsby was a tenacious competitor, both as player and manager, and he was not content with anything but exhaustive effort from his team. His will and extraordinary abilities won the highest possible returns in the "Rajah's" first full year managing, for the once-weakling Cardinals were the pennant winners for the first time in the team's history. Hornsby (born on April 27, 1896, in Winters, Texas) then went on to reach a summit he would never again achieve as a manager and beat the Yankees in seven games for the World Championship. At season's end Hornsby was, surprisingly enough, traded to the Giants.

### 1927 Robert Arthur "Bob" O'Farrell

As the second successive player-manager for the Cardinals, Bob O'Farrell, born on October 19, 1896, in Waukegan, Illinois, was able to sustain the winning pattern of the team. With three more wins than in 1926, O'Farrell's Cardinals nevertheless lost the pennant by one game. O'Farrell was traded to the Giants in 1928.

### 1928 William Boyd "Deacon" "Bill" McKechnie

The 92 wins sufficient for only second place in 1927 improved to 95 wins in 1928, Bill McKechnie's first year managing the Cardinals. (He had previously managed the Pirates.) Even better than the 95 victories was the two-game win over John McGraw's Giants at the end of the season. The once-invincible New York team, backed by big Eastern money, had twice in successive years finished behind the St. Louis team, which had only a few years earlier nearly gone into receivership because of indebtedness. The Cardinals lost the World Series, however, to the other team from New York, the Yankees of Ruth, Gehrig and Lazzeri. The World Series loss overshadowed the pennant victory, and McKechnie did not begin the 1929 season, though he would manage the Cards again later that year.

### 1929 William Harrison "Billy" Southworth

1929's Cardinal team did not have the pitching of the pennant winners the year before, and in Billy Southworth's introduction to big-league managing, his Redbirds won only 43 of his 89 games and stood in fourth place before he was relieved. Southworth, from Harvard, Nebraska (born on March 9, 1893), would get another chance with the Cardinals, but not for more than a decade.

### 1929 Charles Evard "Gabby" "Old Sarge" Street

After a disappointing performance by manager Billy Southworth through July, 1929, Gabby Street was granted the doubtful honor of setting the lineup and working the dugout as a momentary stand-in until the Cardinals could secure the services of Bill McKechnie to complete the season. Street, from Huntsville, Alabama (born on September 30, 1882) won both games he worked and performed well enough to get called back at the end of the season.

**Above:** *Billy Southworth as an outfielder for the Cardinals in 1929 – his last year in the field.*
**Left:** *Manager John McGraw (l.) of the Giants with Bill McKechnie, manager of the Cardinals, in 1928.*

**Above:** *Manager Frankie Frisch in spring training – 1936.*
**Right:** *Player-manager Frisch warming up in spring training – 1935.*

### 1929 **William Boyd "Deacon" "Bill" McKechnie**

Bill McKechnie's second time at managing the Cardinals came in the last 62 games of 1929. His team won 33 of those games, but it was unable to move up from fourth spot in the standings. McKechnie did not manage the Cardinals after that disappointment, but the next year would see him managing the Braves.

### 1930-1933 **Charles Evard "Gabby" "Old Sarge" Street**

His opening as manager of the Cardinals had produced only two wins, which merely maintained fourth place in the standings, but when he returned for his first complete season in 1930 he directed the team to the first of two consecutive pennants (the first such achievement in the team's history). Better, in 1931 the Cards defeated the Athletics in the World Series four games to three.

The productivity of six .300-or-better hitters, and of three pitchers who were just shy of 20-win seasons in 1931, vanished in 1932, however, and 1931's 101-win World Champions finished in sixth spot. Street worked in the first 91 games of 1933, but won only 46 and was let go. He would manage the Browns in 1938.

### 1933-1938 **Frank Francis "Frankie" "The Fordham Flash" Frisch**

Cardinal fans felt betrayed when team executives traded irreplaceable Rogers Hornsby to the Giants in exchange for Frankie Frisch at the end of the 1926 season. "The Fordham Flash" was not long in persuading any skeptics, though, that Branch Rickey's decision was not irrational after all. Frisch batted .300 or better for six of his first seven years playing for the Cardinals (.346 in 1930) and twice led the league in stolen bases.

Unable to extricate the team from fifth place, even though he managed them to 36 wins in the final 63 games of the 1933 season, he proceeded to lead the 1934 Cardinals to 95 wins and the pennant, before defeating Detroit in seven in the Series.

The 1934 Cardinals won one more game than they had the year before, but they finished in second place. One more second-place season, 1936, was the best that Bronx-born Frisch (born September 9, 1898) was able to achieve before the Cardinals dropped to fourth in 1937 and sixth through early 1938 – the year Frankie was fired with 17 games remaining. He would move on to manage the Pirates in 1940.

### 1938 **Miguel Angel "Mike" Gonzales**

Hired in hopes of keeping the Cardinals out of seventh place, Mike Gonzales won nine of the last 17 games to maintain sixth place. Gonzales, born on September 24, 1890, in Havana, Cuba, did not return to manage the next year, but he was destined to be called on again in 1940.

## 1939-1940 Francis Raymond "Ray" Blades

With a roster almost identical to that of the 1938 sixth-place Cardinals, Ray Blades resurrected the team to second place in 1939. A product of Branch Rickey's farm system, Blades (born in Mt Vernon, Illinois, on August 6, 1896) directed a hapless team to only 15 wins in the first 40 games of 1940 and lost his position as manager. He died on May 18, 1979, in Lincoln, Illinois.

## 1940 Miguel Angel "Mike" Gonzales

Filling in a second time in three years, Mike Gonzales lost all five games in which he managed in 1940. He did not manage again. Gonzales lived to be almost 87, dying on February 19, 1977, in Havana, Cuba.

## 1940-1945 William Harrison "Billy" Southworth

Under Billy Southworth, recalled to try to jump-start a team that had won only 15 of its first 44 games in 1940, the Cardinals played at a .633 pace for the remainder of the season, advancing from sixth to third. From 1942 through 1944 Southworth's team won 106, 105 and 105 games respectively. In 1942 they beat the Yankees four games to one to win the Series. After losing the championship to New York by the same margin the next year, the Cardinals, in an intra-city Series, beat the Browns in six games for the title.

Southworth's final year with the Cardinals netted only 95 victories and second place. He went on to manage the Braves in 1946.

## 1946-1950 Edwin Hawley "Eddie" Dyer

Eddie Dyer, born in Morgan City, Louisiana, on October 11, 1900, had had no experience in managing a major league team. Yet his debut in St. Louis was so good it stretched belief. Three hitters batted .300 or better (Musial's .365 was league best), and four of Dyer's six pitchers had ERAs of 2.88 or better (Howie Pollett's 21 wins and 2.10 ERA were league best). Dyer did not squander such an assemblage of exceptional players and won the pennant the fourth time in five seasons. The Cardinals then beat the Red Sox in the Series 4-3. Remaining pennant contenders over the next three years, Dyer's Cardinals finished second each time and came within two games of beating the Dodgers for the league title in 1949. In Dyer's last year managing the Cardinals (and in the major leagues), the team ended only three games over .500 and in fifth place. Dyer died on April 20, 1964, in Houston, Texas.

## 1951 Martin Whitford "Marty" "Slats" "The Octopus" Marion

After falling out of first division status for the first time in 14 years, the Cardinals returned to third place under Marty Marion in 1951. Marion (born in Richburg, South Carolina, on December 1, 1917), who had been a fine shortstop for the Cardinals since 1940, did not manage the Cards after 1951, moving across town, instead, to manage the hapless Browns.

**Below left:** *Southworth – 1944.*
**Below:** *Marty Marion in action.*

## 1952-1955 Edward Raymond "Eddie" "The Brat" "Muggsy" Stanky

In veteran National League second baseman Eddie Stanky's three-plus years managing the Cardinals, the team led the league in hitting for two of those three seasons and compiled the best team ERA in pitching in 1952, his first year. Regardless of exceptional individual performances though, the Cardinals were unable to finish above third place in Stanky's first two seasons. After a 72-82 record and the sixth spot in 1954 (the first sub-.500 year since 1937, "Muggsy" opened his final season with 17 victories in 36 games. As a result, Eddie (born on September 3, 1916, in Philadelphia) was forced to look for a new team. He found it 11 years later, in the form of the Chicago White Sox.

## 1955 Harry William "The Hat" Walker

In 1947 Harry Walker, a veteran outfielder from Pascagoula, Mississippi (born on October 22, 1916), had won the league batting title, hitting .363, but in 1955 only the Pirates kept the Cardinals he managed from concluding the season out of last place. He did not return to St. Louis the next year. Ten years later he would be named manager of those same Pirates.

**Above:** *Eddie Stanky was never still.*
**Below:** *Left to right: Harry Walker, Del Rice, Stan Musial, Red Shoendienst.*

**Opposite left:** *Johnny Keane.*
**Opposite right:** *Schoendienst and Musial in 1951 (top) and 1967.*

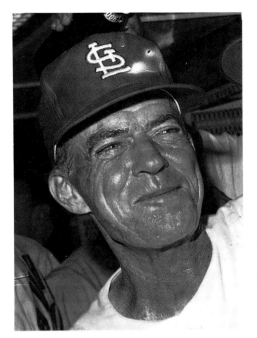

## 1956-1958 **Frederick Charles "Fred" Hutchinson**

Two and one-half years of managing in Detroit had acquainted Fred Hutchinson with the quicksands of major-league managing. And certainly the Cardinals were, in 1956, in an odd and precarious state. They were a team that had claimed nine pennants and six world titles in 20 years and that had just completed two successive seasons under .500 and had finished in seventh spot the year before.

Hutchinson needed only one year before moving the Cardinals back into contention: second place at the end of 1957. In 1958, alas, the team fell below .500 for the fourth time in five years, and Hutchinson was gone before the season closed, with the Cardinals holding fifth place. The following year, 1959, he would be managing the Cubs.

## 1958 **Stanley Camfield "Stan" "Smiling Stan" Hack**

Directing the Cardinals to three wins in the last seven games in 1958, Stan Hack, who had previously managed the Cubs, now secured a tie with the Cubs for fourth place – one game in front of the Dodgers. Hack, who died on December 15, 1979 in Sacramento, California, did not manage in the major leagues again.

## 1959-1961 **Solomon "Solly" Hemus**

Unable to forestall a continued slide in performance that had begun the year before he began managing, Solly Hemus and the Cardinals posted a seventh place finish in 1959. Hemus, born on April 17, 1923, in Phoenix,

Arizona, directed the team to 15 more wins in his second year than it had had the previous season and to a respectable third place. A veteran Cardinal shortstop for eight-plus years, Hemus could not reverse the effect of a crippling opening in 1961 (sixth position) before he closed his work with the Cardinals just before the All-Star mid-point. He did not manage in the big leagues afterward.

## 1961-1964 **John Joseph "Johnny" Keane**

For the second half of the 1961 season the Cardinal front office gambled on a name with no major league playing or managing experience – Johnny Keane, the team's seventh leader since 1950. Keane lost no time in delivering for the Cardinals, and they won 47 of their last 80 games in 1961. The next year, an unusual season, Keane's

team won 84 games, yet finished sixth. This was a season in which the first- and second-place teams won a total of 205 games, and Cincinnati, in third spot, won 98. Ninety-three wins for the Cardinals in each of the next two years thrust them into second place in 1963 and gave them the pennant the next year. In a surprise move, Johnny Keane (born in St. Louis on November 3, 1911) left the Cardinals after leading them to a World Championship over the Yankees in 1964. He went to the Yankees.

### 1965-1976 Albert Fred "Red" Schoendienst

As nearly synonymous with the St. Louis Cardinals as Mickey Mantle was with the Yankees, Hall of Famer (1989) Red Schoendienst was almost as triumphant a manager as he had been a player. Born on February 2, 1923, in Germantown, Illinois, a little town less than an hour east of St. Louis, Red began playing with the Cardinals in 1945 and, except for four-plus years playing for the Giants and Milwaukee, he stayed with the Cardinals as a second baseman through 1963.

Schoendienst ranks first in total years managing the Cardinals, and his .529 life-time winning percentage places him among the top 25 managers to direct ten years or more since 1900. His teams finished first or second in five of his 13 years, and in eight of his ten complete seasons St. Louis was over .500. Only once since Schoendienst's 101 victories in 1967 have the Cardinals won 100 or more (1985, under Whitey Herzog).

Red had earned the reputation for being precise and reliable in his work as second baseman, and many who saw him rated him the best in the league. He approached

managing with the same kind of steadiness. His 1967 team, with the heroism of titan Bob Gibson, beat the Red Sox in seven games for the World Championship. In the Series again the next year, the Cardinals lost in seven to a strong Tiger team. Fifth place at the end of 1976 cost Red his position, although he returned for a short stint in 1980.

### 1977-1978 Vernon Fred "Vern" Rapp

With no previous major league playing or managing history, Vern Rapp, born in St. Louis on May 11, 1928, lifted the Cardinals to third place in 1977. Upon winning only five of the first 15 games in his second year, however, Rapp lost his managing position. He would re-surface in 1984, managing in Cincinnati.

### 1978 John Thomas "Jack" Krol

Standing in for three games in the 1978 season, Jack Krol, a Chicagoan (born on July 5, 1936) with no previous big league playing or managing experience, won two of the three games in which he managed and advanced the Cardinals from sixth to fifth position. He would return two years later for a similar assignment.

### 1978-1980 Kenton Lloyd "Ken" Boyer

After only 18 games into the 1978 season the Cardinals named Ken Boyer, one-time third baseman and power hitter, to manage. Boyer (born in Liberty, Missouri, on May 20, 1931) was unable to improve the team's fifth position, where they were when he began working, but a better performance in 1979 resulted in third place. But only 18 wins in 51 games in 1980 terminated Boyer's

work in St. Louis by the end of May. He lived only a short time longer, dying on September 7, 1982, in St. Louis.

### 1980 John Thomas "Jack" Krol

Called upon again in 1980, as he had been in 1978, Jack Krol managed in only one game and lost. Krol has not managed in the big leagues since.

### 1980 Dorrel Norman Elvert "Whitey" "The White Rat" Herzog

Brought in from Kansas City to be the third manager of the Cardinals in 1980, Whitey Herzog (who had been an AL outfielder for eight years) directed the desperate losers in 73 games, winning only 38 but lifting the team out of last place. His accomplishments notwithstanding, Herzog did not complete the season, being relieved by Red Schoendienst in late August.

### 1980 Albert Fred "Red" Schoendienst

Completing a disappointing 1980 season, Red Schoendienst (inactive as a manager for almost four years) directed the Cardinals in the last 37 games, winning 18 and moving the team from fifth to fourth. Schoendienst has not managed since.

### 1981- Dorrel Norman Elvert "Whitey" "The White Rat" Herzog

In his second opportunity to lead the Cardinals, Whitey Herzog quickly enabled the team to regain the authority they had had a decade earlier. Second-place performances in both halves of the 1981 strike season were preparations for a pennant in 1982 and a four-to-three conquest of the Milwaukee Brewers for the World Championship.

Finishing with 101 wins in 1985, the Cardinals under Herzog led the East Division in team batting, runs scored and stolen bases (118 more than the second best in stolen bases). After beating the Dodgers in the League Championship Series, though, they lost to Dick Howser's Kansas City Royals in seven games. Again in 1987 the remarkable Herzog took a team crippled with injuries into the World Series, this time to lose to the Twins in seven. The Cardinals were impotent in 1988, and even the wiles of Herzog were insufficient to prevent a fifth-place performance.

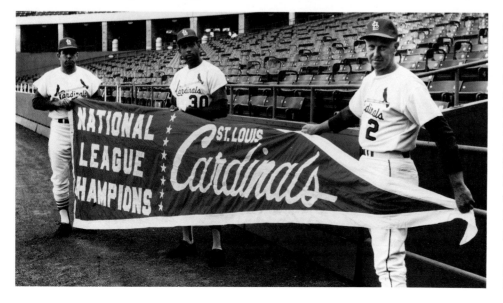

**Left:** *Schoendienst (r.) and pennant.*
**Opposite:** *Whitey Herzog (l.).*

# CUBS

## Chicago (1901-    )

### 1900-1901 Thomas Joseph "Tom" Loftus

At the turn of the new century the Chicago Cubs (who had been called the White Stockings in 1876-1893, the Colts in 1894-1897 and the Orphans in 1898) were led by their new manager, Tom Loftus. He had been brought in in 1900 after managing in Milwaukee, Cleveland and Cincinnati. Loftus, born on November 15, 1856, in St. Louis, had played only nine games (as an outfielder) in his life. He brought the Cubs to fifth place (65-75) in 1900 and sixth place (53-86) in 1901. At that point he left to manage the Senators.

### 1902-1905 Frank Gibson Selee

Selee came to Chicago from his stint as Boston Beaneaters manager and took the club to a fifth-place (68-69) finish in 1902. In 1903 it was third place (82-56), and in 1904 the Cubs ended in second place (93-60). But in 1905, with the team on the skids and in fourth place (52-38), he left the club. Selee died on July 5, 1909, in Denver, Colorado.

### 1905-1912 Frank Leroy "The Peerless Leader" Chance

Chance, born on September 9, 1877, in Fresno, California, played for the Cubs from 1898 to 1912. This Hall of Fame (1946) first baseman was one of the infielders in the celebrated "Tinker-to-Evers-to-Chance" double-play combination. He took over the team in 1905 and, with a 40-23 record, elevated the Cubs from fourth to third place (92-61).

In 1906 he brought his team in in first place with a 116-36 major league win-loss record that still stands. But the Chicago White Sox beat them in the World Series four games to two. Chance repeated his first-place finish in 1907 (107-45), and this time he won the Series four games to none, with one tie, over the Detroit Tigers. His third straight pennant came in 1908 (99-55), and this time he again won over the Tigers four games to one.

In 1909 the club slipped to second place (104-49), but they were back on top in 1910 (104-50), though they lost the Series to Phil-

adelphia four games to one. It was second place again in 1911 (92-62) and third place in 1912 (91-59). At this point Chance left Chicago to manage the New York Yankees.

### 1913 John Joseph "Johnny" "The Trojan" "The Crab" Evers

The second member of the double play combination, Evers, was born in Troy, New York, on July 21, 1883. He took over the club in 1913. This Hall of Fame (1946) second baseman managed a third-place (88-65) finish that year and then went to Boston Braves as a player. He would return to manage the Cubs in 1921.

### 1914 Henry Francis "Hank" O'Day

The Cubs' new manager was Hank O'Day who had managed the Reds in 1912. He finished the 1914 season with the Cubs in fourth place (78-76), then left the club. O'Day died in Chicago on July 2, 1935.

### 1915 Roger Philip "The Duke of Tralee" Bresnahan

Bresnahan had been the skipper of the Cardinals from 1909 to 1912. This Hall of Fame (1945) catcher could do no better than fourth place (73-80) in 1915, at which point he dropped out of the majors. He died on December 4, 1944, in Toledo, Ohio.

### 1916 Joseph Bert "Joe" Tinker

Tinker, the Hall of Fame (1946) member of

the famed double play combination, was brought back to Chicago to manage in 1916. He had managed Cincinnati in 1913 and Chicago in the short-lived Federal League from 1914 to 1915, but under him the Cubs slipped to fifth place (67-86) and he was gone. Tinker died on July 27, 1948, in Orlando, Florida.

### 1917-1920 Frederick Francis "Fred" Mitchell

Mitchell, born Frederick Francis Yapp in Cambridge, Massachusetts, on June 5, 1878, was a pitcher for the Red Sox, Phillies, Dodgers, Yankees and Braves. In 1917 he led the Cubs to another fifth-place (74-80) finish, but he won the pennant in 1918 (84-45), then lost the World Series to the

Above: *Frank Chance.*
Top: *Frank Selee.*
Opposite top left: *Roger Bresnahan.*
Opposite top center: *Hank O'Day.*
Opposite top right: *Joe Tinker.*
Opposite bottom: *Johnny Evers (center).*

Red Sox four games to two. The Cubs were third in 1919 (75-65) and fifth in 1920 (75-79). The next year Mitchell became manager of the Boston Braves.

### 1921 John Joseph "Johnny" "The Trojan" "The Crab" Evers

Evers was back for another go with the Cubs in 1921, but, with a 42-56 record and the club in seventh place, he was let go two-thirds of the way through the season. He would move on to manage the White Sox in 1924.

### 1921-1925 William Lavier "Bill" "Reindeer Bill" Killefer

Killefer, who was born on October 10, 1887, in Bloomingdale, Michigan, came in to finish the 1921 season. This catcher had played in the majors from 1909 to 1921. He was not able to do much in 1921 – he had a 22-33 record – and the Cubs ended in seventh place (64-89). Then it was fifth (80-74) in 1922, fourth (83-71) in 1923 and fifth (81-72) in 1923. Halfway through the season of 1925 (33-42), with the Cubs in seventh place, he was let go. In 1930 Killefer became the manager of the Browns.

## 1925 **Walter James Vincent "Rabbit" Maranville**

Maranville, born on November 11, 1891, in Springfield Massachusetts, was a Hall of Fame (1954) shortstop for several teams from 1912. He managed the Cubs for only part of 1925, and when they were in eighth place, at 23-30, he was fired. He went on to play with other teams until 1935 and died on January 5, 1954, in New York City.

## 1925 **George C. "Moon" Gibson**

Gibson, who had managed the Pirates from 1920 to 1925, was brought in to finish out the 1925 season. The Cubs posted a 12-14 record under him, remaining in eighth place (68-86). He was to become the Pittsburgh manager again in 1932.

## 1926-1930 **Joseph Vincent "Marse Joe" McCarthy**

The brilliant McCarthy, who began his managerial career with the Cubs, was to become one of the greatest managers of all time. In 24 years with the Cubs, Yankees and Red Sox he would never finish out of the first division. This Hall of Fame manager (1957), born on April 21, 1887, in Philadelphia, had never played in the major leagues but had been a minor league infielder. He was a perfectionist who stressed fundamentals, a stern disciplinarian who was not afraid to cut the Cubs' star pitcher, Grover Cleveland Alexander, from the club in 1926 because he wouldn't follow instructions.

In 1926 McCarthy took the Cubs from the eighth place of the previous year to fourth place (82-72). Though he improved their record in 1927 (85-68), they were still in fourth place. It was third place (91-63) in 1928, and the Cubs finally won another pennant in 1929 (90-54), but they lost the World Series to the Philadelphia Athletics four games to one. In 1930, with the club having dropped back to second place (86-64), owner Philip Wrigley fired McCarthy one week before the end of the season because he had not won the pennant. McCarthy became the Yankee manager the next year.

## 1930-1932 **Rogers "Rajah" Hornsby**

Hornsby, who had been the manager of the Braves in 1928, came in to finish out the 1930 season, winning all four of the remaining games, with the Cubs finishing second. He brought the Cubs in in third place (84-

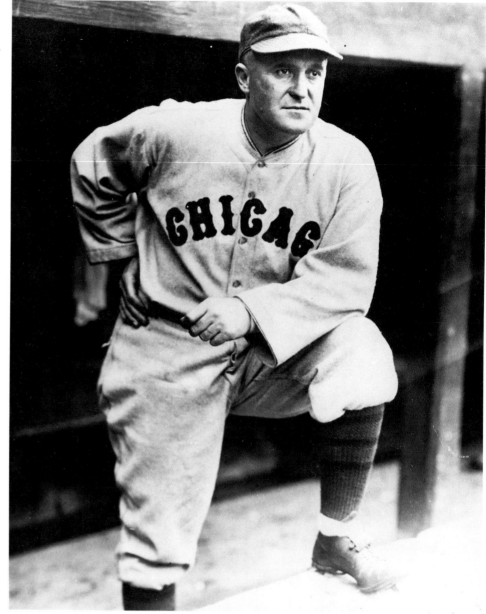

70) in 1931. In 1932, with the Cubs in second place (53-44), Hornsby was abruptly fired on August 2 after a series of vitriolic policy disputes with Club President William Veeck, Sr. The next year he was managing the Browns.

## 1932-1938 **Charles John "Charlie" "Jolly Cholly" Grimm**

Grimm, the man who came in to finish the 1932 season and who was often referred to as "the best left-handed banjo player in the National League," had been primarily a first baseman since 1916 with the Athletics, Cardinals, Pirates and the Cubs (he was to be their playing manager until 1936). Born on August 28, 1896, in St. Louis, he now recorded a 37-20 mark for Chicago, enough to make the Cubs the pennant winners, with a 90-64 season record. After the Yankees beat them four games to none in

*Hall of Famer Joe McCarthy was fired in his fifth year with the Cubs for not winning the pennant.*

the World Series, the Cub players were still so angry at previous manager Rogers Hornsby that they voted him no share in the Series money.

In 1933 the Cubs finished third (86-68), and then stayed in third place (86-65) in 1934. In 1935 they won the pennant again (100-54) but lost to Detroit in the World Series four games to two. They spent the next two years in second place – 84-64 in 1936 and 93-61 in 1937. After 81 games into the 1938 season, with the Cubs at 45-36 and in third place, Grimm was let go. He was to return, but first he turned to baseball broadcasting, and in 1941 he and Bill Veeck bought the minor league Milwaukee Brewers of the American Association and Grimm became the manager.

Cubs trounced the dispirited Pirates 10-1 to win the pennant again. Then the Yankees devoured them four games to none in the World Series.

In 1939 Hartnett brought the Cubs in fourth (84-70), and in 1940 they finished fifth (75-79) and Hartnett was on his way to play for the Giants. He died on December 20, 1972, in Park Ridge, Illinois.

**Above:** *Charlie Grimm in 1948.*
**Left:** *Grimm, McGraw and McCarthy at the 1932 World Series.*
**Below:** *Gabby Hartnett in 1938.*

### 1938-1940 **Charles Leo "Gabby" Hartnett**

Hartnett, the Hall of Fame (1955) catcher who was born on December 20, 1900, in Woonsocket, Rhode Island, had been with the Cubs since 1922. He came in as player-manager to finish the 1938 season and won the pennant himself. Literally.

Late in September the Pirates, leading the league with a 2½ half-game bulge over the Cubs, came to Chicago for a three-game series. In the opening game the sore-armed Dizzy Dean beat Pittsburgh 2-1. The next day's game was still tied in the bottom of the ninth. With darkness gathering, it seemed likely the game would be called a tie and re-played as a part of a doubleheader the next day. With two out, Hartnett took two strikes and then connected on a fastball to hit his immortal "Homer in the Gloamin'" that won the game. Now half a game up, the

**Above:** *The 1944 All-Star Game heroes – left to right: Rip Sewell, Billy Southworth, Phil Cavarretta.*
**Opposite:** *Cubs manager Frankie Frisch.*

### 1941-1944 James "Jimmy" "Ace" Wilson

Wilson had been the manager of the Phillies from 1934 to 1938, and in his first year with the Cubs he brought them in in sixth place (79-84). They stayed in sixth place (68-86) in 1942. In 1943 a fifth-place (74-79) finish was not much better, and after ten games in 1944, with the Cubs in eighth place (1-9), he was fired. Wilson died on May 31, 1947, in Bradentown, Florida.

### 1944 Roy Cleveland Johnson

Johnson, who was born February 23, 1904, in Pryor, Oklahoma, had played the outfield for several teams. He replaced Wilson in 1944 for one game, which he lost. It was the first and last game he managed in the majors. He died on September 10, 1973, in Tacoma, Washington.

### 1944-1949 Charles John "Charlie" "Jolly Cholly" Grimm

Grimm came back to finish the 1944 season and led the Cubs to a fourth-place (75-79) finish by winning 74 and losing 69. The very next year he skippered them to a pennant (98-56). This was the last of the war years, and major league talent was pretty thin. Indeed, when the Cubs faced the Tigers in the World Series, sportswriter Warren Brown of *The Chicago Tribune* wrote, "I don't think either of them can win." Actually, it was an exciting Series, with the Tigers nosing out the Cubs four games to three. Grimm led the Cubs to a third-place finish (82-71) in 1946, a sixth-place (69-85) finish in 1947 and a last-place (64-90) finish in 1948. With the Cubs in last place (19-30) after 50 games in 1949, he was let go. In 1953 he became the manager of the Boston Braves, but he was to return again to the Cubs in 1960.

### 1949-1951 Frank Francis "Frankie" "The Fordham Flash" Frisch

Frisch, with his sharp tongue and intolerance of criticism, was brought in to finish out the 1949 season. He had been the manager of the Cardinals (1933-1938) and the Pirates (1940-1946). Frisch was able only to keep the Cubs in eighth place (61-93) with his 42-62 record that year. And for the next two years all he could manage was to lift them to seventh place, going 64-89 in 1950 and being fired at 35-45 in 1951. That ended his managing career. Frisch died on March 12, 1973, in Wilmington, Delaware.

### 1951-1953 Philip Joseph "Phil" Cavarretta

Cavarretta, who was born on July 19, 1916, in Chicago, was appointed as the manager to succeed Frisch. Mainly a first baseman, he had started with the Cubs in 1934 and was to continue with them until 1953. He had won the National League Most Valuable Player Award in 1945. But his was not a brilliant managerial career, since the Cubs sank to eighth place (62-92) when they posted a 27-47 record under him that year. The next year he brought them to fifth place (77-77). In 1953 they ended in seventh (65-89), and Cavarretta was gone. He finished his career playing for the White Sox in 1954-5.

### 1954-1956 Stanley Camfield "Stan" "Smiling Stan" Hack

Hack, born on December 6, 1909, in Sacramento, California, had been a star third baseman for the Cubs from 1932 to 1947, carrying a lifetime batting average of .301. He had played on four pennant-winning teams, but he could not do much managing the Cubs. In 1954 he finished seventh (64-90), then sixth (72-81) in 1955 and last (60-94) in 1956, after which Hack was let go. He went on to manage the Cardinals in 1958.

### 1957-1959 Robert Boden "Bob" Scheffing

Born on August 11, 1913, in Overland, Missouri, Scheffing was a competent catcher for the Cubs, the Reds and the Cardinals from 1941 to 1951, with three years out for World War II service. Nineteen fifty-seven was not a good year for him, since the Cubs finished in seventh place (62-92). Then it

**Opposite:** *Grimm (l.) and Boudreau.*
**Below:** *Left to right: Bob Scheffing, Phil Wrigley, Charlie Grimm.*

was fifth place (72-82) in 1958 and fifth (74-80) again in 1959. Scheffing was dropped and went on to manage the Tigers in 1961.

### 1960 Charles John "Charlie" "Jolly Cholly" Grimm

Grimm was back with the Cubs one last time in 1960. But after a miserable 6-11 start, with the Cubs in last place, he was fired. So ended his 19 years of managing. His lifetime win-loss percentage was .546. He died on November 15, 1983, in Scottsdale, Arizona.

### 1960 Louis "Lou" Boudreau

Boudreau had been the manager of the Indians (1942-1950), the Red Sox (1952-1954) and the Kansas City Athletics (1955-1957). He took over the Cubs for most of the 1960 season and was able to take them up a peg into seventh place (60-94). But he had a lowly record of 54-83 and was released to continue as a Cubs radio broadcaster. Then the Cubs tried one of the strangest and least effective managerial systems ever seen in baseball: the owners used a rotation of head

coaches rather than appointing a manager.

### 1961 Avitus Bernard "Vedie" Himsl Harry Francis Craft Elvin Walter "El" Tappe Louis Frank "Lou" Klein

Himsl, born on April 2, 1917, in Plevna, Montana, never played in the major leagues. He was able to manage only ten wins in 32 games in 1961 and was let go at the end of the season.

Craft, born on April 19, 1915, in Ellisville, Mississippi, had played in the outfield for six years in Cincinnati and was the manager of the Kansas City Athletics from 1957 to 1959. His record in 1961 was seven wins in 16 games. He, too, was gone at the end of the season, and he went on to manage in Houston in 1962.

Tappe, born on May 21, 1927, in Quincy, Illinois, was a Cub catcher from 1954 to 1960. His record in 1961 as a co-manager was 42 wins in 96 games. He was retained as a player-co-manager for the next year.

Klein, born on October 22, 1918, in New Orleans, Louisiana, had been a utility in-

fielder for five years with the Cardinals, the Indians and the Athletics. His record as co-manager in 1961 was five wins in 12 games. He was also invited to co-manage the next year.

The Cubs finished seventh that year, with an overall 64-90 record. Nevertheless, they decided to continue their strange experiment in multiple-management.

### 1962 Elvin Walter "El" Tappe
### Louis Frank "Lou" Klein
### Charles "Charlie" Metro

Tappe was back as co-manager of the 1962 troika, but he could manage only four wins

in 20 games. He also caught in 26 games that year.

Klein was also back and led the club to a 12-18 record.

Metro, who was born Charles Moreskonich on April 18, 1919, in Nanty-Glo, Pennsylvania, had played only 171 games in the outfield over a period of three years for the Tigers and the Philadelphia Athletics from 1943 to 1945. He racked up a 43-69 record for the Cubs, left the club and subsequently became the manager of Kansas City in 1970.

Now that the league had expanded to ten teams, the Cubs were able to finish ninth (59-103) for the first time.

### 1963-1965 Robert Daniel "Bob" Kennedy

Duly chastened, the Cubs now went back to a single manager. Kennedy, who was born on August 18, 1920, in Chicago, had played in the majors for 16 years, in both outfield and infield, with the White Sox, Indians, Orioles, Tigers and Dodgers. The Cubs were still short on talent, and Kennedy was able to lead them only to seventh place (82-80) in 1963 and eighth place (76-86) in 1964. In 1965, with the club in ninth place (24-32), he was fired, but he resurfaced in 1968 to manage the Oakland Athletics for a single season.

**Right:** *Herman Franks.*
**Opposite top:** *Durocher in a rhubarb with Umpire Dave Davidson – 1969.*
**Opposite bottom:** *Durocher talks with replacement Whitey Lockman – 1972.*

### 1965 Louis Frank "Lou" Klein

Klein was back to finish the 1965 season. His record was 48-58, but he was able to bring them in in eighth place (72-90). This ended his managing career. Klein died on June 20, 1976, in Metairie, Louisiana.

### 1966-1972 Leo Ernest "The Lip" Durocher

Durocher had been a quite successful manager with the Dodgers (1939-1946 and 1948) and with the Giants (1948-1955). He came out of retirement to take over the pitiful Cubs in 1966 but was able only to manage a tenth-place (59-103) finish. Then came the turnaround. He finished third (87-74) in 1967, third (84-78) in 1968, second (92-70) in 1969, second (84-78) in 1970 and third (83-79) in 1971. In 1972, with the Cubs in fourth place (46-44), he was fired. He turned up managing Houston that same year.

### 1972-1974 Carroll Walter "Whitey" Lockman

Born in Lowell, North Carolina, on July 25, 1926, Lockman had been an outstanding outfielder-infielder for 15 years with the Giants, Cardinals and Reds. He did a fine job managing the Cubs in 1972, bringing them from fourth place to second (85-70) after Durocher had left. Lockman's record was 39-26 that year. But in 1973 the team fell to fifth place (77-84), and, still mired in fifth place (41-52) in 1974, the Cubs let Lockman go.

### 1974-1976 Rufus James "Jim" Marshall

Marshall, who was born on May 25, 1932, in Danville, Illinois, had been primarily a first baseman from 1958 to 1962 with the Orioles, Cubs, Giants and Pirates. After taking over from Lockman he led the Cubs back down to last place (66-96) by posting a 25-44 record. The next year was not much better, the club finishing in fifth place (75-87). He piloted them to a fourth place (75-87, with an identical record to the one the year before) in 1976. It was not enough, and he was gone, only to pop up managing the Athletics in 1979.

### 1977-1979 Herman Louis Franks

Franks had been the Giants' manager from 1965 to 1968 and had brought them in in second place all four years. Under him the Cubs rose to fourth place (81-81) in 1977. They finished in third place (79-83) in 1978, and were in fifth place (80-82) in 1979, when he was let go.

### 1979 John Joseph "Joey" Amalfitano

Amalfitano was brought in as manager in 1979 to finish the season. He won two and lost five, and the club stayed in fifth place (80-82). Amalfitano, who was born on January 23, 1934, in San Pedro, California, had played the infield for ten years for the Giants, the Astros and the Cubs. At the end of the 1979 season the Cubs dismissed him, but he would soon return.

### 1980 Preston Martinez Gomez

Gomez had been the manager of the Padres (1969-1972) and the Astros (1974-1975), but he didn't last long with the Cubs. After 90 games the club stood at 38-52 in last place, and he was fired.

### 1980-1981 John Joseph "Joey" Amalfitano

Amalfitano was back once again in 1980 to finish a season. He won 26 and lost 46, and the Cubs stayed in sixth place (64-98). In 1981, the year of the baseball strike, with its split season, he was finally allowed to begin a season. He brought the team in in sixth (15-37) in the first half and fifth (23-28) in the second half. He was not invited back the following year, and he would later turn up as third base coach of the Dodgers.

### 1984-1986 James Gottfried "Jimmy" Frey

Frey had been the manager in Kansas City in 1980 and 1981. He was brought to the Cubs in 1984 and performed brilliantly, leading them to the championship of the Eastern Division. This was the first time in 39 years that the Cubs had won anything. But they lost the League Championship Series to the Padres, three games to two. In 1985 the team fell to fourth place (77-84), and Frey was removed in 1986, when the team was in fifth place (23-33). He then became the Cubs' general manager.

### 1986 John Christopher Vukovich

Vukovich, born on July 31, 1947, in Sacramento, California, had been an infielder for ten years with the Phillies, Brewers and Reds, but his tenure as interim manager of the Cubs was short – he split two games.

### 1986-1987 Eugene Richard "Gene" "Stick" Michael

Michael was brought in to finish the 1986 season. This former manager of the Yankees, let go in 1982, led the club to a fifth-place (70-90) finish by winning 46 and losing 56. In 1987, after 136 games and with the Cubs in fifth place (68-68), he was fired. Michael thereafter became the chief East Coast major league scout for the Yankees.

### 1987 Frank Joseph Lucchesi

Lucchesi was brought in in 1987 to finish the last 25 games, and he went 8-17, with the Cubs ending in last place (76-85). Lucchesi had been the manager of the Phillies (1970-1972) and the Rangers (1975-1977).

**Top:** *Jim Frey smiles as he is named Manager of the Year in 1984.*

**Above:** *Mets Manager Davey Johnson with Jim Frey in 1984.*

### 1982-1983 Lee Constantine Elia

Elia, born on July 16, 1937, in Philadelphia, had played major league ball for only two years, performing at shortstop with the White Sox (1966) and Cubs (1968) in a mere 95 games. In 1982 he brought the Cubs in in fifth place (73-89), and in 1983 they were in fifth again (54-69). He was fired, but he would subsequently move on to manage the Phillies in 1987.

### 1983 Charles Francis "Charlie" "Irish" Fox

Fox, who had been the manager in San Francisco and Montreal, was brought in to finish the 1983 season. He won 17 and lost 22, the Cubs finished in fifth place (71-91), and Fox was through as manager. He became a special player consultant for the team but left the Cubs after the 1988 season to become dugout coach of the Yankees.

### 1988- Donald William "Don" Zimmer

Zimmer, who once was described by one of his Red Sox pitchers as looking "like a gerbil," came in to manage the Cubs in 1988. He formerly had been the skipper of the Padres (1972-1973), the Red Sox (1977-1980) and the Rangers (1981-1982). The Cubs were never in serious contention in 1988 (77-85), but by August, 1989 was beginning to look like a miracle year.

# DODGERS
## Brooklyn (1901-1957)

### Called **SUPERBAS** (1899-1910)

*Ned Hanlon of the Superbas.*

### 1899-1905 **Edward Hugh "Ned" Hanlon**

Hanlon had been the manager of the Brooklyn Superbas (who had earlier been called the Bridegrooms between 1890 and 1898) for a year before the turn of the century. Born in Montville, Connecticut, on August 22, 1857, he had played the outfield for 13 years in Cleveland, Detroit, Pittsburgh and Baltimore. Hanlon's Superbas had won the pennant in 1899 and repeated the feat in 1900 with an 82-54 record. The Superbas fell to third (79-57) in 1901, rose to second (75-63) in 1902, then dropped to fifth (70-66) in 1903. In 1904 they descended to sixth (56-97), and in 1905 it was eighth (48-104). Hanlon was fired, only to be picked up as the Cincinnati manager in 1906.

### 1906-1908 **Patrick Joseph "Patsy" Donovan**

Donovan came to the Superbas after managing in Pittsburgh, St Louis and Washington. Although he was able to lead the team to an improved fifth place in 1906 (66-86) and 1907 (65-83), he slipped to seventh place (53-101) in 1908 and was gone. Donovan turned up in 1910 as manager of the Red Sox.

### 1909 **Harry G. Lumley**

Lumley, who was born on September 29, 1880, in Forest City, Pennsylvania, had been an outfielder with the Superbas since 1904. As player-manager in 1909, he was able to bring his club in in sixth place (55-98), but that was not good enough. He stepped down from the manager's job and continued in the outfield in 1910. Lumley died on May 22, 1938, in Binghamton, New York.

### 1910 **William Frederick "Bill" "Bad Bill" Dahlen**

Born on January 5, 1870, in Nelliston, New York, Dahlen had played in the major leagues, mainly at shortstop, for 21 years, beginning in 1891. But his career as Brooklyn manager was not outstanding. He brought them in in sixth (64-90) in 1910.

*Robinson (r.) and Jack Coombs.*

50

## Called **DODGERS** (1911-1957)

### 1911-1913 **William Frederick "Bill" "Bad Bill" Dahlen**

It was seventh place (64-86) in 1911 for Dahlen, seventh (58-95) again in 1912 and sixth (65-84) in 1913. And that was the end of his managing career. He died in Brooklyn on December 5, 1950.

### 1914-1931 **Wilbert "Uncle Robbie" Robinson**

Robinson, who had been the manager at Baltimore in 1902, arrived in Brooklyn in 1914. This Hall of Fame (1945) catcher, born on June 2, 1863, in Bolton, Massachusetts, had played for 17 years with various teams. He eventually became a beloved figure in Brooklyn, bringing the team in fifth (75-79) in 1914, third (80-72) in 1915 and in 1916 he won the pennant (94-60). Some people then began to call the Dodgers the "Robins" in his honor, in part because of the way he was able to draw crowds into Ebbets Field with his clownish antics. But it was his skill in developing pitchers that won him the pennant. Unfortunately, the Red Sox beat the Dodgers in the World Series four games to one.

In 1917 the team took a nosedive to seventh place (70-81). Then it was two straight years in fifth place in 1918 (57-69) and 1919 (69-71). Another pennant came in 1920 (93-61), as did another World Series defeat, when the Indians beat the Dodgers five games to two. It was during this time that Robinson tried to keep his players on their toes by forming a "Bonehead Club." A player who pulled a "bonehead" play was obliged to pay a fine to the club. The first member was Robinson himself, who earned the honor when he walked up to home plate just before a game was about to begin and handed the umpire a laundry slip instead of the lineup card.

In 1921 it was fifth place (77-75), followed by sixth place (76-78) in 1922, sixth (76-78) in 1923 and, briefly out of the second division, second place (92-62) in 1924. Following that, it was six straight years in sixth place – 1925 (68-85), 1926 (71-82), 1927 (66-88), 1928 (77-76) and 1929 (70-83). Uncle Robbie did manage to finish fourth in 1930 (86-68) and 1931 (79-73), but Brooklyn fans had been too long without a decent club, and he was forced to resign in 1931. He died soon thereafter, on August 8, 1934, in Atlanta.

### 1932-1933 **Max "Scoops" Carey**

Carey, a Hall of Fame (1961) outfielder, had played for 20 years, mostly with Pittsburgh. Born Maximilian Carnarius on January 11, 1890, in Terre Haute, Indiana, he guided the Dodgers to third place (81-73) in 1932, but after they slipped to sixth (65-88) in 1933, he was let go. Carey died on May 30, 1976, in Miami.

### 1934-1936 **Charles Dillon "Casey" "The Old Perfessor" Stengel**

Stengel, who was to be elected to the Hall of Fame in 1966, was born on July 30, 1889, in Kansas City, Missouri. He was a star outfielder from 1912 to 1925 with the Dodgers, Pirates, Phillies, Giants and Braves. But he had terrible luck with the Dodgers. In 1934 he finished sixth (71-81), and in 1935 it was fifth (70-83). It was in 1935 that Stengel contributed an anecdote to the archives after his Dodgers, in a display of exquisite bumbling, ended a four-game winning streak by dropping a doubleheader to the Cubs. As the Brooklyn manager climbed into a Chicago barber chair, he muttered, "A shave please, but don't cut my throat. I may want to do it myself later." In 1936 it was seventh place (67-87), and Stengel was gone, to re-emerge as the Braves' manager in 1938.

*"Inauspicious" is the word to describe Casey Stengel's 1934 managerial debut with the Dodgers. His smile in this 1936 photo seems a little strained.*

### 1937-1938 Burleigh Arland "Old Stubblebeard" Grimes

Grimes, born on August 9, 1893, in Emerald, Wisconsin, was a spitballing Hall of Fame (1964) pitcher who played for 19 years for various National League teams. As a manager he was a flop, finishing sixth (62-91) in 1937 and seventh (68-80) in 1938. He was fired at the end of the season. When he died on December 6, 1985, in Clear Lake, Wisconsin, he was 92.

### 1939-1946 Leo Ernest "The Lip" Durocher

Durocher, born on July 27, 1905, in West Springfield, Massachusetts, had been a fiery shortstop since 1925 with the Yankees, the Reds and, most notably, the Cardinal "Gashouse Gang" of the 1930s. He was traded to the Dodgers in 1938 and became the manager in 1939. This combative baseball man seemed to have two mottos: "I come to play; I come to beat you; I come to kill you," and "Nice guys finish last."

**Above:** *Durocher and Rickey – 1943.*
**Opposite left:** *Dressen instructs.*
**Opposite right:** *Burt Shotten – 1947.*
**Below:** *Durocher (r.) in a rhubarb.*

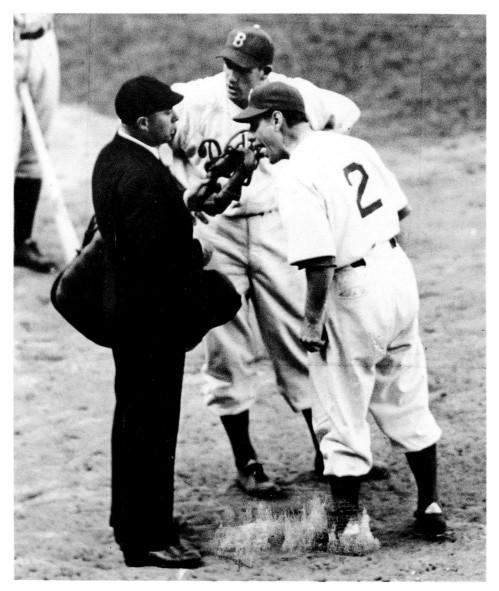

Larry MacPhail, the Dodger general manager, hired Durocher, and they were to form a powerful, volatile combination that made Brooklyn one of the most exciting and disliked clubs in the league. They battled each other as they battled for pennants, and, as a portent of things to come, MacPhail had fired and rehired Durocher at least once even before his first season as manager began.

The Lip brought the club in in third place (84-69) in 1939, and they were second (88-65) in 1940. Then came 1941. In a game against Pittsburgh on September 18 Leo's violent reaction to a call by umpire George Magurkurth caused him to be ejected from the game and fined $150. The next day, in Philadelphia, he ran into Ted Meier of the Associated Press, who questioned him about the previous day's events. Durocher responded by knocking Meier down. Bystanders separated the two, and they parted after shaking hands. Despite these antics Durocher and the Dodgers won the pennant that year, with a 100-54 record.

On the occasion of the Dodger victory celebration, which was to be held at Grand Central Terminal in New York when the team returned from their final series against the Braves, Durocher was again fired by MacPhail. On the returning train Durocher, fearing that some of the players might slip off the train to avoid the celebration, had prevented it from stopping at the 125th Street Station. But unknown to him, MacPhail had planned to board the train at 125th Street in order to join his team in its triumphal entry into Grand Central. Outraged because the train hadn't stopped, when MacPhail arrived at Grand Central he greeted his manager with "You're fired!" He rehired him the next day when he heard the whole story. But as was to become customary, the Dodgers lost to the Yankees in the World Series four games to one.

Durocher never won another pennant with the Dodgers, finishing second (104-50) in 1942, third (81-72) in 1943, seventh (63-91) in 1944, third (87-67) in 1945 and second (96-60) in 1946. By 1947 MacPhail was with the Yankees. During the spring exhibition season in Havana, Durocher climaxed a series of run-ins with baseball's top executives when he heckled MacPhail, who was apparently entertaining two well-known gamblers in a private box behind the Yankee dugout. Snapped Durocher, who had been accused of gambling on more than

### 1948-1950 **Burton Edwin "Burt" "Barney" Shotten**

Shotten was back to finish the 1948 season, and he improved the Dodgers' standing to third place by winning 47 and losing 32, with an overall 84-70 record. He won the pennant again in 1949 (93-60) and lost again to the Yankees in the World Series, four games to one. In 1950 the club went 89-65 and finished in second place. Shotten then retired. He died on July 29, 1962, in Lake Wales, Florida.

### 1951-1953 **Charles Walter "Chuck" Dressen**

Dressen had been the manager of the Reds (1934-1937) before joining the Dodgers in 1951, and he turned out to be the best manager the Dodgers had had. He led them to second place (97-60) in 1951 and then won the pennant (96-57) in 1952. But again the Yankees won the World Series, this time four games to three.

The same thing happened in 1953. Dressen won his second straight pennant but lost the World Series to the Yankees, four games to two. Still, he had won the flag in back-to-back seasons, and he formulated a demand for a three-year contract in terms of an ultimatum. The Dodgers, who preferred one-year contracts for managers, let him go. Dressen turned up again in 1955 as the Washington manager.

one occasion, "Are there two sets of rules, one for managers and one for owners?" Leo continued the fray by telling the Brooklyn *Eagle* that MacPhail had offered him the management of the Yankees. MacPhail retorted that the reverse was true, that Durocher had solicited the job from him, and MacPhail then filed a bill of particulars with Baseball Commissioner A.B. "Happy" Chandler. After a couple of hearings Chandler, who seemed to harbor a particular dislike for Leo, suspended him from baseball for one year for "conduct detrimental to baseball." Yet when the year was up The Lip was back.

### 1947 **Clyde LeRoy "Sukey" Sukeforth**

The Dodger owners were thunderstruck by Durocher's suspension and brought in Sukeforth to put his finger in the dike until they could get a regular manager. Sukeforth, born on November 30, 1901, in Washington, Maine, had been a major league catcher with the Reds and Dodgers for ten years. He managed but one game – winning it and thus achieving a lifetime managerial percentage of 1.000.

### 1947 **Burton Edwin "Burt" "Barney" Shotten**

Old-timer Shotten, who had managed the Phillies and the Reds, was called out of semi-retirement to finish the year of Durocher's suspension. He brought the team in in first place (94-60), but once again the Yankees won the World Series, this time four games to three.

### 1948 **Leo Ernest "The Lip" Durocher**

Durocher returned to the Dodgers in 1948, but only for half a season. Giant owner Horace Stoneham, who was tired of likeable but ineffectual manager Mel Ott, and Dodger General Manager Branch Rickey, who apparently had had enough of lippy Leo and his squabbles with his players, arranged one of the most startling managerial shifts in baseball history. Stoneham had gone to Rickey to ask for his approval to approach Burt Shotten to replace Ott; he found himself being offered Durocher instead. He accepted the offer, Leo agreed and The Lip took up his new duties on July 16, leaving the Dodgers in fifth place, with a 37-38 record.

**Above:** *The Dodgers win the pennant.*
**Left:** *Walter Alston (l.), Carl Erskine.*

### 1954-1957 **Walter Emmons "Smokey" Alston**

Alston, born on December 1, 1911, in Venice, Ohio, played only one game in the major leagues: as a first baseman he appeared with the Cardinals in 1936, batting 0 for 1. But he had been a successful manager of the Dodgers' Montreal club in the International League, and he was therefore brought up to manage the parent club. Alston was a platooner and a pitching juggler, and it seemed to work well, for in 1954 he led the team to a second-place (92-62) finish.

Nineteen fifty-five was a milestone year for Alston and the Dodgers. He not only won the pennant (98-55), but also gave the Dodgers their first World Series win by beating the hated Yankees four games to three. The club won the pennant again (93-61) in 1956 but lost to the Yankees in the World Series four games to three. They came in third (71-83) in 1957, and on September 24 the last game in Ebbets Field was played. The Dodgers were on their way to Los Angeles.

# DODGERS
## Los Angeles (1958-    )

## 1958-1976 **Walter Emmons "Smokey" Alston**

Alston continued as manager of the Dodgers after the move. The first year was not good, since the club finished in seventh place (71-83). But in 1959 they won another pennant (88-68) and went on to win the World Series four games to two over the White Sox. Then it was fourth (82-72) in 1960, second (89-65) in 1961 and second again (102-63) in 1962. Another pennant

(99-63) came in 1963, and then they beat the Yankees four games to none in the Series.

They fell to sixth place (80-82) in 1964 but snapped back in 1965 to win another pennant (97-65) and beat the Twins four games to three in the World Series. They won the pennant (95-67) again in 1966, but lost to the Orioles four games to none in the Series. The Dodgers took a nosedive in 1967, finishing eighth (73-89), and 1968 was little better, as they finished seventh (76-

*The team before their first game as the Los Angeles Dodgers – 1958.*

86). But they bounced back to fourth (85-77) in 1969. Then it was two straight years in second place in 1970 (87-74) and 1971 (89-73). They fell to third (85-70) in 1972 and climbed back to second (95-66) in 1973.

They won another pennant (102-60) in 1974 but then they lost to the Athletics four games to one in the World Series. After the

Series, ever the gentleman, Alston said of the Athletics, "They played the game the way it should be played." Then came two years in second place – 1975 (88-74) and 1976 (90-68). Near the end of the 1976 season, with the club in second place (90-68), Alston, after almost 23 years as Dodger manager, retired. He died on October 1, 1984, in Oxford, Ohio, one year after he had been inducted into the Hall of Fame.

## 1976- **Thomas Charles "Tommy" Lasorda**

Born on September 22, 1927, in Norristown, Pennsylvania, Lasorda had what could hardly be called an outstanding career as a player. As a left-handed pitcher, he put in three years in the major leagues. In 1954, with the Dodgers, he went 0-0 with an earned run average of 5.00. In 1954, also with the Dodgers, he went 0-0 again, and

**Above:** *Tommy Lasorda has a pleasant chat with Fred Brocklander in 1986.*
**Top:** *Walter Alston grins after the World Series championship banner is unfurled in 1965.*
**Opposite:** *Tommy Lasorda turns to talk with first baseman Steve Garvey in the dugout.*

his ERA zoomed to 13.50. Finally, with Kansas City in 1956, he was able to get into the record books by losing four games while winning none – his ERA was 6.15.

But Larsorda became a fine manager. He was loyal to his team, claiming that his blood ran "Dodger Blue" and not being afraid to have a scuffle with the "Phillie Phanatic" mascot in Philadelphia. Part of his ability to manage players came from his sense of humor. Talking about his 43-year-old pitcher, Don Sutton, he said "We've timed Sutton's fast ball at 92 miles an hour – 46 going in to [catcher] Rick Dempsey, 46 coming back." About his catcher, Mike Scioscia, and his lack of speed, he said "Mike could challenge his pregnant wife to a foot race and he'd come in third."

Lasorda came in to finish the 1976 season, taking over a second-place club and keeping it in second place (92-70) by winning two and losing two. Then, amazingly, he won two straight pennants. In 1977 the Dodgers finished first (98-64), beat the Pirates three games to one in the League Championship Series but lost to the Yankees four games to two in the World Series. In 1978 the Dodgers were 95-67 and won the League Championship Series by beating the Phillies three games to one. They lost the World Series to the Yankees four games to two.

It was third place (79-83) in 1979 and second place (92-71) in 1980. In 1981, the most complicated season in baseball history, there had been a strike, and it was decided that there would be two leaders in each of the four divisions of major league baseball – a first-half winner and a second-half winner. In the first half of the season the Dodgers came in first (36-21). In the second half they came in fourth (27-26). They faced the Astros in the Western Divisional Playoffs and beat them three games to two, after dropping the first two games. Then they faced the Expos in the League Championship Series and beat them three games to two. In the World Series they beat the Yankees four games to two.

In 1982 they were in second place (88-74) again. They came back in 1983 to win the pennant (91-71), but in the League Championship Series they lost to the Phillies three games to two. It was fourth place (79-83) in 1984, but 1985 saw them win yet

*Tommy Lasorda consoles Tommy John as he removes the pitcher from the game.*

another pennant (95-67). They then lost the League Championship Series to the Cardinals three games to one.

The Dodgers fell to fifth place (73-89) in 1986 and then to fourth place (73-89) in 1987. In the 1988 season, on August 27, Lasorda won his 1000th game as manager of the Dodgers, and his team went on to surprise the baseball world by winning the Western Division, finishing with a 94-67 record, seven games ahead of the Reds. Going into the League Championships with one of the lowest team batting averages for a

first-place finisher, the Dodgers faced the supposedly overwhelming Mets, but the Dodgers managed to win, four games to three. In the World Series, they were once more the underdogs against the all-powerful Oakland A's, but despite injuries to crucial members, the Dodgers triumphed, four games to one. Everyone conceded that Lasorda's patented combination of cheerleading inspiration and smart baseball had been the decisive factor, and he was voted both National League and Major League Manager of the Year.

# EXPOS
## Montreal (1969-    )

### 1969-1975 Gene William "Skip" Mauch

For the National League 1969 was another expansion year, witnessing the addition of the San Diego Padres and the Montreal Expos – the latter the first major league club to be located outside the United States. Gene Mauch, who had previously been the manager of the Phillies (1960-1968), was selected to be the team's first manager. The Expos, being an expansion team, had little success and started out with two straight years in last place – 1969 (52-110) and 1970 (73-89). That was followed by two years in fifth place – 1971 (71-90) and 1972 (70-86). The Expos seemed to be on their way up, with two years in fourth place – 1973 (79-83) and 1974 (79-82). But in 1975 Mauch let them slip to fifth place again (75-87) and left to become the manager of the Minnesota Twins in 1976.

### 1976 Karl Otto Kuehl

Kuehl, born on September 5, 1937, in Monterey Park, California, had had no major league experience as a player when he was appointed manager of the Expos in 1976. He was able to last only 128 games that year, and with the team in last place (43-85), he was fired.

### 1976 Charles Francis "Charlie" "Irish" Fox

Fox, who had previously been managing in San Francisco, came in as interim manager to finish the 1976 season for the Expos. He took over a team in sixth place (43-85), and kept them in sixth place (55-107) by winning only 12 while losing 22. Fox was to turn up as manager of the Cubs in 1983.

*Manager Gene Mauch finds a reason to smile in 1971.*

### 1977-1981 Richard Hirschfeld "Dick" Williams

Under Williams, who became manager in 1977, the Expos began to make their move, He had been the manager of the Red Sox (1967-1969), the Athletics (1971-1973) and the Angels (1974-1976), bringing his teams in in first place four times in nine years. Williams started out with a fifth place (75-87) in 1977, and then it was fourth place (76-86) in 1978. He brought the club in in second place in two straight years – 1979 (95-65) and 1980 (90-72). The next year, 1981, was the fateful strike-caused split season when there were to be two leaders in each of baseball's four divisions. The Expos came in in third place (30-25) in the first half of the season, and in the second half, after 26 games and with the team in second place (14-12), Williams was out. He joined the Padres as manager in 1982.

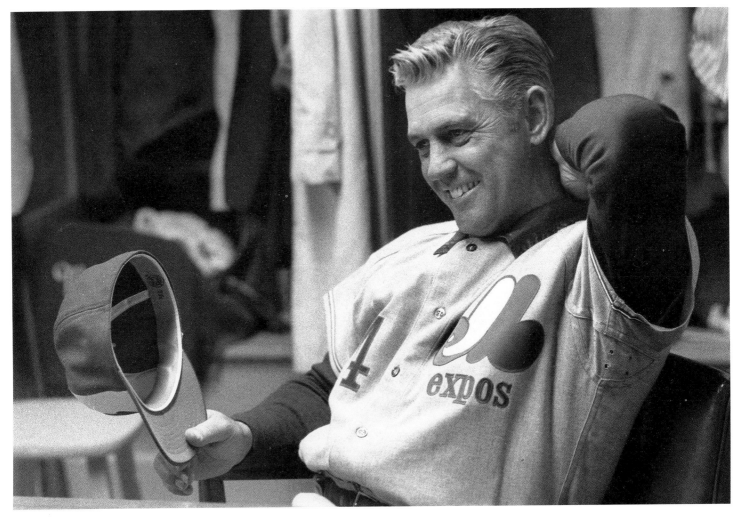

**Above:** *Manager Dick Williams had little to smile about.*
**Right:** *Manager Jim Fanning strikes a Gary Cooper pose.*
**Opposite:** *A conference on the mound – left to right: Pitcher Tim Burke, Catcher John Stefero, Manager Buck Rodgers.*

### 1981-1982 **William James "Jim" Fanning**

Fanning, born on September 14, 1927, in Chicago, was a back-up catcher for the Cubs (1954-1957) and had appeared in only 64 games in those four years. He took over the Expos in 1981, with the team in second place (14-12) in the second half of the season. Fanning then pulled off a minor miracle by winning 16 and losing 11, and the club finished in first place (30-23 overall) by one-half game in the second half of the season – the first championship of any kind for the team. In the Divisional Playoff Series they met the Phillies and beat them three games to two to take the Eastern Division pennant. But in the League Championship Series the Expos lost to the Dodgers three games to two. In 1982 the Expos fell to third place (86-76) and Fanning went back to coaching.

### 1983-1984 **William Charles "Bill" Virdon**

Virdon had been the manager of the Pirates (1972-1973), the Yankees (1974-1975) and the Astros (1975-1982) before he took over the Expos in 1983. He did manage another third-place (82-80) finish with the team, but in 1984, with the Expos in fifth place (64-67) after 131 games, he was let go.

### 1984 **William James "Jim" Fanning**

Fanning was back again as the Expos man-ager in 1984. It was strictly an interim appointment. Fanning won 14 and lost 16, and the team stayed in fifth place (78-83 overall).

### 1985- **Robert Leroy "Buck" Rodgers**

Rodgers had had reasonable success as manager of the Brewers (1980-1982) before he was hired as manager of the Expos in 1985. He was able to manage a third-place (84-77) finish in 1985, but the team fell to fourth (78-83) in 1986. In 1987 it was another third-place (91-71) standing, and in 1988, although they showed some signs of threatening, they ended up in third place (81-81) behind Pittsburgh and the Mets.

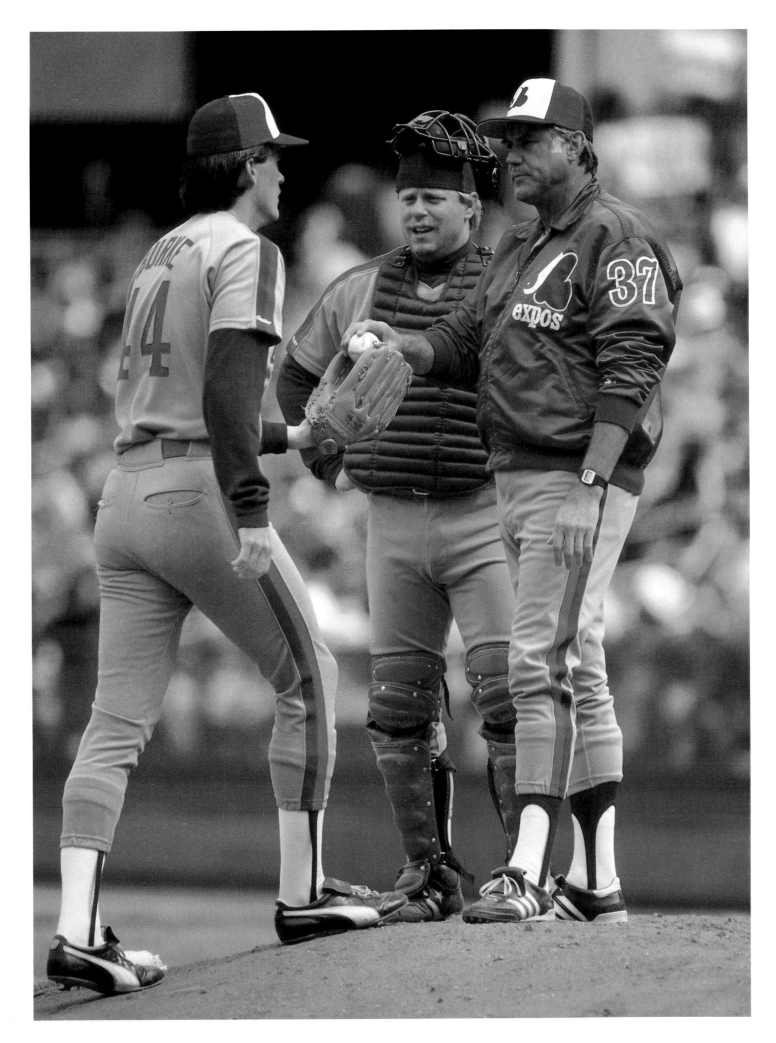

# GIANTS
## New York (1901-1957)

**1900-1901 George Stacey Davis**

Davis was the second Giants manager of the century. William "Buck" Ewing was the first. Ewing, born on October 17, 1859, in Hoaglands, Ohio, was primarily a catcher in the major leagues between 1880 and 1897. (He was elected to the Hall of Fame in 1939.) Before coming to manage the Giants he had been a manager of New York in the Player's League (1890) and Cincinnati in the National League (1895-1899). Ewing did not fare too well with the Giants, and had to leave early in the season, with the club in eighth place (21-41). He died on October 20, 1906, in Cincinnati.

Born on August 23, 1870, in Cohoes, New York, Davis was mainly a shortstop for Cleveland (1880-1892), and he continued in that position with the Giants from 1893 to 1901. He had also managed the Giants in 1895. This player-manager came in to finish the 1900 season after Ewing left but was unable to get them out of last place (60-78), since he won 39 and lost 37. In 1901 he managed a seventh-place (52-85) finish but was gone at the end of the season, moving on to play for the White Sox (1902), coming back to play for the Giants (1903), and ending his career with the White Sox (1905-1909). He died on October 17, 1940, in Philadelphia.

**1902 Horace S. Fogel**

Fogel, born on March 2, 1861, in Macungie, Pennsylvania, did not play in the major leagues, but he was the manager of the Indianapolis club in the National League in 1887. In 1902 the Giants fired him after 41 games, with the team in fourth place (18-23). It was his last managing job. He died in Philadelphia on November 15, 1928.

**1902 George Henry "Heinie" Smith**

Smith, who was born on October 24, 1871, in Pittsburgh, was promoted from his second base position to take over the club in 1902. In 32 games he could manage only a 5-27 record, the club fell to eighth place and Smith went to the Tigers as a second baseman, playing major league ball for one more season. He died on June 25, 1939, in Buffalo, New York.

*A young John McGraw.*

**1902-1932 John Joseph "Little Napoleon" McGraw**

McGraw had played mainly third base, beginning in 1891. This Hall of Famer (1937), born in Truxton, New York, on April 7, 1873, had been the manager of the Baltimore club in the National League (1899) and of the Baltimore club in the American League (1901-1902). On July 16, 1902, he was named manager of the Giants, a post he would hold for over 30 years, winning ten pennants along the way. When McGraw took over the Giants for owner John T. Brush he knew he could not escape the cellar: the Giants finished at the bottom of the league (48-88), and McGraw had a 25-38 record for the year.

McGraw was feisty and a battler. As a star player for the Orioles of the 1890s he had once succeeded in inciting a rope-toting lynch mob to lie in wait for an umpire after a game. The umpire wisely waited for the mob to disperse before he left the park.

But McGraw knew his baseball talent: for example, the legendary pitcher Christy Mathewson, who was to supply the key to the Giants' success until he retired in 1915. Even though Mathewson had won 20 games the preceding year, when McGraw took over the stewardship of the Giants he found that the outgoing managers, Fogel and Smith, had been trying to turn him into a

first baseman. McGraw, recalling the pitching weaknesses of his old Oriole clubs and anxious to create a strong pitching staff, put Mathewson back on the mound. Despite the disparities in their personalities and backgrounds, Mathewson and McGraw were to become lifelong friends and always roomed together on the road.

McGraw was also a martinet. In practice he exercised extremely close control over his men. Players did almost nothing without his guidance – the "Little Napoleon" called pitches and gave signals to his batters on every pitch. Tyrannical, brilliant and innovative, "Muggsy" (a nickname he hated) flamboyantly cursed fans, defied league presidents and was famous for his battles with umpires. But even those who hated McGraw never questioned his superiority as a manager, and many great players of the era did not consider their careers complete until they had played for him. Second baseman Larry Doyle later expressed it best: "Oh, it's great to be young and a Giant."

Although he had finished in last place in 1902, McGraw had a three-year contract and began drilling his team in the classic deadball style, adding five key men in 1903. That year he came in with an amazing second-place (84-55) finish.

In 1904 he won his first pennant (106-47), and he had created the nucleus of a franchise which was to remain the most profitable in the league and in all of major league baseball until the great Yankee teams of the 1920s.

Despite the fact that there had been a World Series the year before, the Giants refused to meet the American League pennant winners, the Boston Somersets (who were to become the Red Sox), in 1904. There had been some petty bickering between the New York Giants and the new American League. Giant owner Brush had had a long-standing feud with American League President Ban Johnson and was also angry because the American League had

**Opposite:** *Manager John McGraw (l.) and Pitcher Christy Mathewson – two future Hall of Famers – in 1916.*

# GIANTS vs YANKEES

## 1921

JOHN McGRAW

MILLER HUGGINS

## WORLDS CHAMPIONSHIP SERIES

## POLO GROUNDS

permitted a team to set up shop in New York. He and McGraw issued a statement: "There is nothing in the constitution or the playing rules of the National League which requires the victorious club to submit its championship honors to a contest with a victorious club in a minor league."

Brush and McGraw recanted after the season was over and said that if the Giants won the 1905 National League pennant they would play the American League champions. As it happened, the Giants did

*McGraw and Huggins faced each other in the 1921 World Series, which the Giants won handily – 5 games to 3 – over the Yankees.*

win the pennant in 1905. McGraw turned in a 105-48 record that year, and faced the Philadelphia Athletics in the World Series, beating them four games to one. The club fell to second place (96-56) in 1906 and went to fourth place (82-71) in 1907. Then it was second place (98-56) in 1908, third place (92-61) in 1909 and second again (91-63) in 1910.

McGraw won his third pennant in 1911 with a 99-54 record, but the Athletics had their revenge in the World Series, winning it four games to two. The Giants repeated for the pennant (103-48) in 1912, but they lost the World Series again, this time to the Red Sox, four games to three, with one tie. They took their third straight pennant (101-51) in 1913, but once again Philadelphia beat them in the World Series four games to one.

Then came some down years for McGraw. In 1914 it was second place (84-70), and it was eighth place (69-83) in 1915 (the only time that McGraw was to finish in the cellar, although he was only 3½ games behind the fourth-place Cubs). In 1916 it was fourth place (86-66). At one point during that 1916 season the disgusted McGraw stalked off the field in the middle of a Dodger game, calling his men "quitters" and yelling "I'll be no part of this."

One of the highlights of the 1917 season occurred when McGraw delivered an uppercut to the jaw of umpire Bill Byron and received a $500 fine and a 16-day suspension. When he continued the fight by attacking League President Tener and the umpires in the press he was fined another $1000. McGraw nevertheless won the 1917 pennant (98-56), only to lose to the White Sox in the World Series four games to two.

For the next three years the Giants finished in second place: 71-53 in 1918, 87-53 in 1919 and 86-68 in 1920. But this was merely a prelude to McGraw's finest hours.

In 1921 the Giants not only won the pennant (94-59) but beat the Yankees four games to two in the World Series. Another pennant came in 1922 (93-61), and again they beat the Yankees, four games to none, with one tie, in the Series. It was still another pennant in 1923 (95-58), but the Yankees won the Series four games to two. Finally, in 1924, there was a fourth pennant (93-60), yet again the Giants lost the World Series, this time to the Athletics, four games to three. But McGraw had won four straight pennants – the first time in history

that this had been done, and still the only time in the National League.

The Giants fell to second (86-66) in 1925 and then skidded to fifth (74-77) in 1926. They rose to third (92-62) in 1927 and to second (93-61) in 1928, but it was third place for the next two years – 1929 (84-67) and 1930 (87-67). McGraw led them to a second place (87-65) finish in 1931, but the next year, with the club in eighth place (17-23), he retired as manager of the Giants on June 3, 1932.

In 31 years his Giant teams had totaled ten National League pennants and 11 second places and had finished in the first division 27 times. No manager before or since has matched his impact on the game.

Strangely, only one sportswriter was on hand to report McGraw's leaving. That day, Tom Meany of the New York *World Telegram* stopped by the Giant clubhouse looking for a story. A doubleheader with the Phillies had been rained out, and the clubhouse was empty, but he found a notice on the bulletin board announcing that McGraw had resigned and had been succeeded by Bill Terry. McGraw was 59, worn out and ailing, and his departure was less of a shock than was his choice of Bill Terry to replace him, since the two men were not friends. McGraw was to die of uremia within two years, on February 25, 1934, in New Rochelle, New York.

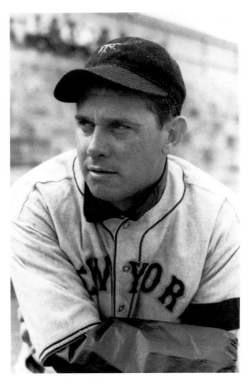

*Manager Bill Terry at spring training in 1936.*

## 1932-1941 William Harold "Bill" "Memphis Bill" Terry

Terry, who was elected to the Hall of Fame in 1954, had played first based for the Giants since 1923. Born on October 30, 1896, in Atlanta, Terry was among a growing number of players who would not put up with McGraw's authoritarian style. The two had barely spoken for years, and most observers felt that brilliant Giant third baseman Fred Lindstrom was McGraw's clear choice. (So did Lindstrom, who later asserted that he had been lied to.) Yet when faced with the task of picking a successor, McGraw rose above personal differences to pick the man he felt was best suited for the job. Terry was to be a player-manager from 1932 to 1936, when he removed himself from the lineup.

In 1932 Terry did a creditable job of managing. After inheriting the club in last place, with a 17-23 record, he was able to lead them back to a sixth-place (55-59) finish, with an overall mark of 72-82. In 1933, in Terry's first full season, the Giants moved into the league lead on June 10 and stayed the all the way, finishing 91-61, five games ahead of the second-place Pirates. They even beat the Senators in the World Series four games to one.

It was in 1934 that Terry made his biggest blunder. Asked for his evaluation of the various National League clubs, he remarked, "Brooklyn? Is it still in the league?" Terry was not given to public wisecracks, and he lived to regret that one. The Dodgers, sometimes known as the "Daffiness Boys," after a term that columnist Westbrook Pegler had coined almost a decade earlier, had fallen on hard times indeed, and Terry's quip, because it was so close to home, infuriated the fans. As fate would have it, with the Giants and the Cardinals tied for first place, the Giants' last two games of the season were against the Dodgers, whose fans carried placards bearing the hated words and booed Terry every time he made an appearance. Brooklyn won both games while the Cardinals were winning their last two games against the last-place Reds, and the Giants finished in second place (93-60). After skidding to third place (91-62) in 1935, Terry once again brought his team in in first place (92-62) in 1936. The Giants then faced the Yankees in the World Series and lost four games to two. Terry won his second consecutive pennant (95-57) in 1937 but once again lost to the Yankees in the Series four games to one. From then on it was downhill for Terry. The Giants finished third (83-67) in 1938, fifth (77-74) in 1939, sixth (72-80) in 1940 and fifth (74-79) in 1941. Terry was gone after the season ended and did not manage in the majors thereafter. He died on January 9, 1989, in Jacksonville, Florida.

### 1942-1948 Melvin Thomas "Master Melvin" Ott

Ott, who was born in Gretna, Louisiana, on March 2, 1909, and was elected to the Hall of Fame in 1951, had been an outstanding outfielder with the Giants since 1926 and had a lifetime batting average of .304. He was not as successful in his managing career. He did bring the club in third (85-67) in 1942. But the next year, 1943, it was a last-place (55-98) finish, followed by fifth places in 1944 (67-87) and 1945 (78-74). It was in 1946 that Ott became the first manager to be ejected in both games of a double-header. (The Pirates won both games, 2-1 and 5-1.) That year the club finished last

again (61-93). In 1947 they finished fourth (81-73). In 1948, after five straight years in the second division and the club in fourth place (37-38), Giant owner Horace Stoneham traded with the Dodgers and, in a surprise move, brought their manager over to head the New York club. Ott was given a job in the Giants' front office as assistant to farm director Carl Hubbell. He died on November 21, 1958, in New Orleans.

**Right:** *Mel Ott in the outfield.*
**Top:** *Left to right: Owner Horace Stoneham, Bobby Thomson, Leo Durocher, after Thomson's homer won the pennant in 1951.*

### 1948-1955 Leo Ernest "The Lip" Durocher

The manager whom Stoneham brought over from the Dodgers was Leo Durocher. In 1948 he inherited a club that was in fourth place (37-38), and was unable to do better than fifth place (78-76) by winning 41 and losing 38. The Giants stayed in fifth place (73-81) in 1949 but climbed to third (86-68) in 1950. Then Willie Mays came back from the Army, and the Giants won the pennant (98-59) in 1951, losing the World Series to the Yankees four games to two.

In 1952 it was second place (92-62), and in 1953 it was fifth place (70-84). But the club pulled itself together, and Durocher brought them in in first place (97-57) in 1954. That year the Giants beat Cleveland in the Series, four games to none. After a third-place finish (80-74) in 1955, Durocher was let go. He was to resurface as manager of the Cubs in 1966.

### 1956-1957 William Joseph "Billy" "Specs" "The Cricket" Rigney

Rigney, born on January 29, 1918, in Alameda, California, played the infield for the Giants from 1946 to 1953. He was brought in as manager in 1956 but was not able to do any better than bring them in sixth in 1956 (67-87) and 1957 (69-85).

On August 19, 1957, Horace Stoneham, the owner of the Giants, announced that the team's board of directors had voted 9-1 in favor of moving the team to San Francisco. Stoneham commented on the move: "I feel bad about the kids, but I haven't seen too many of their fathers lately." On September 29, 1957, the Giants played their last game at the Polo Grounds and then left for the West Coast.

# GIANTS
San Francisco (1958-    )

### 1958-1960 William Joseph "Billy" "Specs" "The Cricket" Rigney

Rigney took his Giants to San Francisco in 1958 and brought them in in third place (80-74). In 1959 it was again a third-place (83-71) finish. In 1960, with the club in second place (33-25) after 58 games, the Giants fired Rigney. The next year he was to turn up as the manager of the Los Angeles Angels.

### 1960 Thomas Clancy "Tom" Sheehan

Sheehan was called in to finish the 1960 season with the Giants. At 66 years, two months and 18 days, he had the distinction of being the oldest man ever to be named manager of a major league baseball team for the first time.

Born on March 31, 1890, in Sigel, Pennsylvania, he had been a right-handed pitcher for the Athletics (1915-1916), the Yankees (1921), the Reds (1924-1925) and the Pirates (1925-1926). During those six years he had gone a poor 17-39. Taking over the team in second place (33-25), he could turn in a mere 46-50. The Giants finished in fifth place (79-75), and Sheehan's brief and not very satisfying managing career was over. He died on October 29, 1982, in Chillicothe, Ohio.

### 1961-1964 Alvin Ralph "Blackie" Dark

Born on January 7, 1922, in Comanche, Oklahoma, Dark had an outstanding career as an infielder for the Braves (1946-1949), Giants (1950-1956), Cardinals (1956-1958), Cubs (1958-1959), Phillies (1960) and Milwaukee Braves (1960).

In 1961 he brought his team in in third place (85-69) and to a first-place (103-62) finish in 1962. But the Yankees beat them in the World Series four games to three. Things then went downhill, with the Giants finishing third (88-74) in 1963 and fourth (74-86) in 1964. Dark was fired and later turned up as the manager of Kansas City in 1966.

### 1965-1968 Herman Louis Franks

Franks was a decent enough back-up catcher with the Cardinals (1939), Dodgers (1940-1941), Athletics (1947-1948) and Giants (1949). Born on January 4, 1914, in Price, Utah, he took over a fourth-place Giant team and brought them in in second place (95-67) in 1965. He was to finish the season in second place every year he managed San Francisco – 1965, 1966 (93-68), 1967 (91-71) and 1968 (88-74). He left the Giants at the end of 1968 but reappeared as manager of the Cubs in 1977.

**Above left:** *Bill Rigney.*
**Above center:** *Jim Davenport.*
**Above right:** *Roger Craig.*

### 1969-1970 Clyde Edward King

Born on May 23, 1925, in Goldsboro, North Carolina, King was a right-handed pitcher with the Dodgers (1944-1945, 1947-1948, 1951-1952) and with the Reds (1953). In seven years he had amassed a tiny 32-25 record. He led the Giants to a second-place (90-72) finish in 1969, but in 1970, with the team in fifth place (19-25), he was fired. He became the Atlanta manager in 1974.

### 1970-1974 Charles Francis "Charlie" "Irish" Fox

Born on October 7, 1921, in New York City, Fox had only a short playing career in the major leagues. He caught in only three games for the New York Giants in 1942, going three for seven for a .429 batting average. When he came to San Francisco to finish the 1970 season he took over a fifth-place (19-25) club and won 67-51, for a third-place (86-76) finish. Then in 1971 he won the West Division (90-72), losing the League Championship Series to the Pirates three games to one. In 1972 it was fifth place (69-86), followed by a third-place (88-74) finish in 1973. With the Giants in fifth place

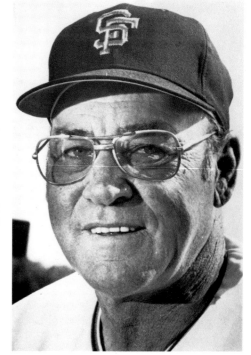

**Above left:** *Alvin Dark at the 1963 All-Star Game.*

**Above center:** *Herman Franks.*
**Below:** *Charlie Fox (l.) and Willie McCovey in the dugout in 1971.*

**Above:** *Wes Westrum in 1975.*
**Opposite:** *The first black manager, Frank Robinson (r.), with Coach Jim Davenport.*

(34-42) in 1974, Fox was out, turning up as the Montreal manager in 1976.

## 1974-1975 Wesley Noreen "Wes" Westrum

Westrum, who had been the manager of the Mets from 1965 to 1967, was brought in to finish the 1974 season. The Giants were in fifth place (34-42), and Westrum could not improve things, going 38-48 as the team ended the season in fifth (72-90). Things were a little better in 1975, when the club finished third (80-81), but Westrum was gone at the end of the season.

## 1976 William Joseph "Billy" "Specs" "The Cricket" Rigney

Former Giant manager Rigney was brought back after tenures with the Angels and Twins to manage SF in 1976. After a fourth-place finish (74-88) he was fired.

## 1977-1979 Joseph Salvatore "Joe" Altobelli

Altobelli, born on May 26, 1932, in Detroit, was brought in to manage the Giants in 1977. He had spent only three years in the majors as a first baseman and outfielder, first with Cleveland (1955, 1957) and then with Minnesota (1961). In 1977 he brought the Giants in in fourth place (75-87). They moved up a notch to third place (89-73) in

1978. In 1979, with the Giants in fourth place (61-79) after 140 games, he was let go. He became the Orioles' manager in 1983.

## 1979-1980 James David "Dave" Bristol

Bristol had spent nine years as a major league manager before he was brought to San Francisco to finish the 1979 season. He had been the skipper of the Reds (1966-1969), the Brewers (1970-1972) and the Braves (1976-1977). He took over a fourth-place (61-79) team, went 10-12 with them and ended still in fourth place (71-91). The next year, 1980, was worse: Bristol could get no higher than fifth place (75-86), and he was fired.

## 1981-1984 Frank Robinson

Robinson had been the first black manager in the major leagues – from 1975-1977 – with the Indians. In San Francisco he was not able to do much, finishing fifth (27-32) in the first half and third (29-23) in the second half of that strange split season caused by the long players' strike. He did manage to lift the team to third place (87-75) in 1982, but the Giants went downhill in 1983, finishing fifth (79-83). It was worse in 1984. With the team in sixth place (42-64), Robinson was fired. He was named manager of the Orioles in 1988.

## 1984 Daniel Leonard "Danny" "Ozark Ike" Ozark

Ozark had been the manager of the Phillies from 1973 to 1979 and was brought to San Francisco to finish the 1984 season. He took over a sixth-place club (42-64) and went 24-32 to end up still in sixth place (66-96). After that he was gone.

## 1985 James Houston "Jim" Davenport

Born in Siluria, Alabama, on August 17, 1933, Davenport was a fine infielder, most often playing third base, for San Francisco from 1958 to 1970. He became the pilot of the Giants in 1985 and lasted 144 games. With the club in sixth place (56-88), he was let go.

## 1985- Roger Lee Craig

Craig took over the reins to finish the 1985 season, won six and lost 12, and the Giants stayed in sixth place (62-100). But in 1986, he was able to lead them to a third-place (83-79) finish, and he won the pennant (90-72) in 1987; but in the League Championship Series the Giants lost to the Cardinals four games to three. In 1988, great things were predicted for the Giants, but they ended up with an 83-79 record, only good enough for fourth place in the Western Division.

# METS
New York (1962-   )

## 1962-1965 Charles Dillon "Casey" "The Old Perfessor" Stengel

In addition to the Houston club, the Mets were the other expansion club in the National League in 1962, and that old New York favorite, Casey Stengel, was brought in to manage them. He was then 72. He had been the manager of the Dodgers (1934-1936), the Braves (1938-1943) and the Yankees (1949-1960). In 1962 Stengel and the Mets may have won the hearts of many fans, but the team was certainly inept. In the middle of the season Casey was heard to say, "Can't anyone here play this game?" And at the end of the season, after the club had finished in tenth place (40-120), setting a record for number of games lost, Casey said, "I won with this club what I used to lose."

There followed another year in last place (51-111) in 1963 and still another in 1964 (53-109). The highlight of the 1964 season might well have been May 31, when the Mets and the Giants were playing a double-header. The Giants won the first game 5-3. The second went on and on for 23 innings, treating (if that is the word) the New York fans to nine hours and 52 minutes of base-ball (a modern record). Of course, the Giants finally won the game, 8-6.

In 1965, after 95 games and with the team still in tenth place (31-64), Stengel retired. His old number, 37, had been retired two times in two leagues, by both the Yankees and the Mets. Casey died on September 29, 1975, in Glendale, California, and in 1988 there was talk of his becoming the subject of a commemorative postage stamp – to be issued in 1990, when he would have been 100 years old.

## 1965-1967 Wesley Noreen "Wes" Westrum

Born on November 28, 1922, in Clear-brook, Minnesota, Westrum was a catcher for the Yankees (1947-1957) and was a Mets coach before being brought in to finish the 1965 season. He took over a tenth-place (31-64) club and kept them in tenth place (50-112) by winning 19 and losing 48. There was a slight improvement in 1966, when the

Mets finished in ninth place (66-95), but in 1967 the team was back in last place (57-94) after 151 games, and Westrum was fired. He surfaced in 1974 as the manager of the Giants.

## 1967 Francis James "Salty" Parker

Parker was born on July 8, 1913, in East St Louis, Illinois, and was a player in only 11 major league games in his life – as an in-fielder for the Tigers in 1936. As a Mets coach, he was called in to finish the last 11 games of the 1967 season with the team in last place (57-94). He won four and lost seven, and the club stayed in tenth (61-101 overall). He went back to coaching and was

**Above:** *Casey Stengel of the Mets.*
**Opposite:** *George Bamberger.*

to be a short-lived manager of the Astros in 1972.

## 1968-1971 Gilbert Raymond "Gil" Hodges

Hodges, a former Dodgers hero, had been the manager of the brand new Washington Senators (1963-1967) and had still not done too well by the time he was called to be the Mets manager in 1968. His first year fit the pattern of the Mets – ninth place (73-89). But then, in 1969, came the year of the "Miracle Mets."

**Above:** *Gil Hodges.*
**Opposite top:** *Dave Kingman (l.) and Yogi Berra at spring training in 1975.*

**Below:** *The 1969 Miracle Met team.*

Hodges was a man who knew how to get the most out of his young players – and the Mets were young, 21 of them being between 21 and 28 years old. They weren't tops at the plate, since they batted only .241 as a team, eighth in the National League, and eight other teams in the league had outscored them that year. But they had exceptional pitching. Tom Seaver's 25-7 was the best in the majors, Jerry Koosman went 17-9 and reliever Tug McGraw had nine wins and 12 saves. On August 13 the Mets were 9½ games behind the Cubs; by September 10 they had sneaked up to the lead. The Mets won 38 of their last 49 games, the Cubs collapsed and this team that had never finished above ninth place won the pennant (100-62).

Then they astonished everyone again by beating the Braves in the League Championship Series in three straight games, outscoring them 27 runs to 11, while getting 37 hits. In the World Series they beat the Orioles four games to one, and New York fans had a new favorite team.

The Mets fell to third place for two straight years, 1970 (83-79) and 1971 (83-79). At the end of the 1971 season Hodges, knowing he was critically ill, resigned. He was to die before the 1972 season began – on April 2, 1972, in West Palm Beach, Florida.

### 1972-1975 Lawrence Peter "Yogi" Berra

When Berra was fired from his job as manager of the Yankees in 1964 he had gone to the Mets as a coach, and in 1972 he was appointed their manager. Berra was able to bring them in in third place (83-73), and then, in 1973, there came another "miracle year." The Mets were in last place on August 30, but they seemed to listen to pitcher Tug McGraw's slogan, "Ya Gotta Believe!" The team won 20 of their last 28 games and won the Eastern Division (82-79) with a won-lost record of .509, the lowest of any winner in major league history. They had been outscored by every team they played except one, and their team batting average of .246 was ninth in the league.

In the League Championship Series the Mets beat the Reds three games to two. The World Series went seven games, but the miracle was over, for the A's beat the Mets four games to three.

In 1974 the Mets fell to fifth place (71-91), and after 109 games in 1975, with the team in third place (56-53), Berra was let go. He was to become the Yankee manager for the second time in 1984.

### 1975 Roy David McMillan

McMillan, who had managed the Brewers for two games in 1972, was brought in to finish the last 53 games for the Mets in 1975. He inherited them in third place (56-53) and kept them there by winning 26 and losing 27 (82-80 overall). Then he was relieved of his duties.

### 1976-1977 Joseph Filmore "Joe" "Cobra Joe" Frazier

Born on October 6, 1922, in Liberty, North Carolina, Frazier had been an outfielder for the Indians (1947), the Cardinals (1954-1956), the Reds (1956) and the Orioles (1956). He was able to bring the Mets in in third place (86-76) in 1976, but after 45 games in 1977 the club was in last place (15-30), and he was fired.

**Right:** *Manager Joe Torre.*

**1977-1981 Joseph Paul "Joe" Torre**
Torre, born on July 18, 1940, in Brooklyn, was a superstar catcher-first baseman-third baseman for the Braves (1960-1968), the Cardinals (1969-1974) and the Mets (1975-1977). He had been the National League's Most Valuable Player in 1971, and became the player-manager of the Mets in 1977, when he took them over in last place (15-30). Torre was unable to improve on that sixth-place standing, as he won 49 while losing 68, to end up 64-98 overall. At the end of the season he gave up his playing career to concentrate on being the manager. Then came two straight sixth-place finishes – 1978 (66-96) and 1979 (63-99). Those were followed by a fifth-place finish (67-95) in 1980, and, in the strike-interrupted 1981 season, he led the team to fifth place (17-34) in the first half and fourth (24-28) in the second half. Torre was fired and then became the manager of the Braves in 1982.

**1982-1983 George Irvin "Bambi" Bamberger**
Bamberger had been the manager of the Brewers (1978-1980) and had never come in lower than third. But when he was appointed manager of the Mets in 1982 he could do no better than last place (65-97). In 1983 it was again last place (16-30) after 46 games, and he was fired. He found himself back as manager of the Brewers in 1985.

**1983 Frank Oliver "The Capital Punisher" "Hondo" Howard**
Howard had been the manager of the Padres (1981) before being brought in to finish the season for the Mets. He kept them in sixth place (68-94 overall), winning 52 and losing 64, and was fired.

**1984- David Allen "Davey" Johnson**
Born on January 30, 1943, in Orlando, Florida, Johnson was primarily a second baseman with the Orioles (1965-1972), the Braves (1973-1975), the Phillies (1977-1978) and the Cubs (1978) before being appointed manager of the Mets in 1984. Immediately there was an upturn in the fortunes of the team. He led them to a second-place (90-72) finish in 1984. Then, in 1985, it was second place (98-64) again, helped along by the rookie pitcher Dwight Gooden who, at the age of 20, was the youngest pitcher ever to win 20 games.

In 1986 the Mets had moved into first place on April 23 and ended the season an astonishing 21½ games ahead of the second-place Phillies. The Mets won the League Championship Series four games to two, piling up 22 runs to the Astros' 17. In the World Series they faced the Red Sox and lost the first two games before winning the whole thing four games to three.

In 1987 there was a little letdown as the club finished in second place (92-70). But in 1988 they were picked for going all the way, and although they slowed down on a few stretches, they went out in front of their division and never were in serious danger.

**Above:** *Davey Johnson.*
**Left:** *Davey Johnson (waving) in the 1968 victory parade.*
**Opposite:** *Frank Howard.*

In the end they took the Eastern Division with a 100-60 record, finishing 15 games ahead of the Pirates. Heavily favored in the League Championship Series, Johnson was clearly outmanaged by the underdog Dodgers manager, Tommy Lasorda, and Los Angeles won the Series four games to three. Johnson's contract with the Mets, however, was renewed.

# PADRES
San Diego (1969-    )

## 1969-1972 Preston Martinez Gomez

In addition to the Expos, the Padres were also created as an expansion team in 1969, and Gomez was hired as their first manager. Born Pedro Gomez Martinez on April 20, 1923, in Central Preston, Cuba, Gomez had appeared in only eight games as a shortstop-second baseman for the Senators in 1944. He was a shrewd manager, however, and his knowledge of Spanish was a great help in dealing with the many Latin-American players on the Padres team. As was to be expected, this expansion team did not do well and finished in last place for three straight years – 1969 (52-110), 1970 (63-99) and 1971 (61-100). In 1972, with the team in fourth place (4-7) after 11 games, Gomez was fired. He was to become the manager of the Astros in 1974.

## 1972-1973 Donald William "Don" Zimmer

Born on January 17, 1931, in Cincinnati, Zimmer played third base, shortstop and second base (he also caught and played the outfield for a few games) for the Dodgers (1954-1959), the Cubs (1960-1961), the Giants (1962), the Reds (1962), the Dodgers again (1963) and the Senators (1963-1965). He took over the fourth-place (4-7) Padres in 1972, but they proceeded to fall to last place (58-95 overall) by losing 88 and winning 54. It was another sixth place (60-102) finish in 1973, and Zimmer was gone. He would turn up as the manager of the Red Sox in 1976.

## 1974-1977 John Francis McNamara

McNamara had been the manager of the Oakland Athletics (1969-1970), bringing them in second both years, before he came to San Diego to manage the Padres in 1974. But it was the same old story, with the team finishing last (60-102) that year. This was followed by a fourth-place (71-91) standing in 1975. They were to fall to fifth (73-89) in 1976, and, with the team in fifth place (20-28) after 48 games in 1977, McNamara was fired. He went to greener pastures, becoming the manager of the Cincinnati Reds in 1979.

## 1977 Robert Ralph "Bob" Skinner

Skinner had had a brief tenure as the Phillies' manager in 1968 and 1969. He was sent in as interim manager of the Padres for one game – which he won – in 1977. Then it was back to coaching.

## 1977 Alvin Ralph "Blackie" Dark

Dark, who had managed the Giants (1961-1964), the Athletics (1966-1967), the Indians (1968-1971) and the A's (1974-1975), was brought in to finish the 1977 season with the Padres. He inherited a team in fifth place (21-28) but was able to win only 48 while losing 65, and the team finished in fifth (69-93 overall). Dark was let go at the end of the season.

## 1978-1979 Roger Lee Craig

Craig, who was born on February 17, 1931, in Durham, North Carolina, was a right-handed pitcher with the Dodgers (1955-1961), the Giants (1962-1963), the Cardinals (1964), the Reds (1965) and the Phillies (1966) before taking the helm of the Padres in 1978. He managed a fourth-place (84-78) finish in 1978, but in 1979 the team fell to fifth (68-93), and Craig was fired. He resurfaced as the manager of the San Francisco Giants in 1985.

**Above:** *Roger Craig (l.) and Ray Kroc.*
**Opposite:** *Frank Howard in the dugout.*

## 1980 Gerald Francis "Jerry" Coleman

Born on September 14, 1924, in San Jose, California, Coleman was primarily a second baseman for the Yankees (1949-1957) before coming to the Padres as manager. He was able to carry on the tradition by bringing the team in in sixth place (73-89) and was duly fired.

## 1981 Frank Oliver "The Capital Punisher" "Hondo" Howard

Howard, who was born on August 8, 1936, in Columbus, Ohio, was a slugging outfielder (382 home runs) for the Dodgers (1958-1964), the Senators (1965-1971), the Rangers (1972) and the Tigers (1972-1973). He came in to manage the Padres in the strike-torn 1981 season and was able to lead them to last place in both the first half (23-33) and second half (18-36). He was fired but turned up as manager of the Mets in 1983.

## 1982-1985 Richard Hirschfeld "Dick" Williams

Williams had been the manager of the Red

Sox (1967-1969), the A's (1971-1973), the Angels (1974-1976) and the Expos (1977-1981) before being hired as manager of the Padres. He immediately improved things, with two consecutive fourth-place finishes – in 1982 (81-81) and 1983 (81-81). Then came a minor miracle in 1984, when the Padres won the Western Division Championship by going 92-70. Not only that, they also beat the Cubs three games to two in the League Championship Series, after dropping the first two games. In the World Series they fell to the Tigers four games to one. Williams could manage only a third-place (83-79) finish in 1985, and left to become manager of the Mariners in 1986.

### 1986 Stephen "Steve" Boros

Boros came to the Padres after managing the A's (1983-1984) and was only able to bring them in in fourth place (74-88) before he was let go.

**Right:** *Manager Dick Williams.*
**Opposite:** *Larry Bowa before a game.*

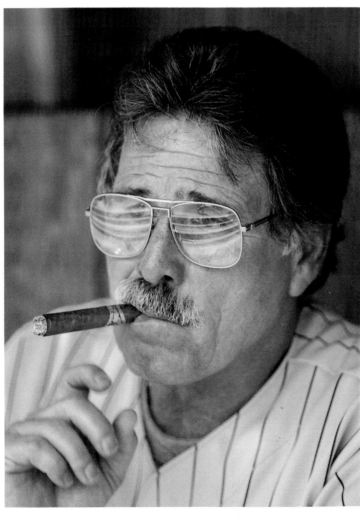

### 1987-1988 Lawrence Robert "Larry" Bowa

Bowa, born on December 6, 1945, in Sacramento, California, was an outstanding shortstop for the Phillies (1970-1981), the Cubs (1982-1985) and the Giants (1985). As manager of the Padres he let the team slip to sixth place (65-97) in 1987. In 1988, after 36 games, they were in fifth (16-30), and Bowa was fired, mostly because of altercations with club president Chub Feeney.

### 1988- John Aloysius "Jack" McKeon

Bowa was replaced by McKeon with the team in fifth place (16-30). McKeon was the vice president of baseball operations for the Padres, but he had been the manager of the Royals (1973-1975) and the A's (1977-1978). At one point, it looked as though McKeon might overtake the Dodgers in the Western Division, but in the end their 83-78 record gained them only third place.

**Left:** *Jack McKeon relaxes. Though he had had previous managerial experience, he was a Padres VP when he was summoned to manage again in the 1988 season.*

# PHILLIES
## Philadelphia (1901-   )

**1898-1902 William Joseph "Bill" Shettsline**

Philadelphia had had a ball club in the National League in 1876, but that was its last year there. Then, in 1883, the Worcester, Massachusetts, team moved to Philadelphia to stay. In 1898 Bill Shettsline, who was born on October 25, 1863, in Philadelphia, took over the club. At the turn of the century Shettsline, who had never played in the major leagues, brought the club in in a third-place finish (75-63). He guided them into second (83-57) in 1901, but they fell to seventh (56-81) in 1902, and that was the end of Shettsline's managing career. He died on February 22, 1933, in Philadelphia.

**1903 Charles Louis "Chief" Zimmer**

Born on November 23, 1860, in Marietta, Ohio, Zimmer began as a catcher in 1884 with the old Detroit club in the National League. He then went to the American Association, where he played with New York (1886) and Cleveland (1887-1888). Back in the National League, he caught for Cleveland (1889-1899) and Pittsburgh (1900-1902). Joining the Phillies in 1903 as player-manager, he was able to do no better than to lead them to another seventh-place (49-86) finish, and was fired. Zimmer died in Cleveland on August 22, 1949.

**1904-1906 Hugh Duffy**

Duffy, who was elected to the Hall of Fame in 1945, was born on November 26, 1866, in Cranston, Rhode Island. He was a star outfielder with a lifetime .328 batting average for the Cubs (1888-1889), the Chicago club in the Player's League (1890), the Red Sox (1891), the Braves (1893-1900) and Milwaukee of the American League (1901), where he was the player-manager. He came to the Phillies in 1904 as a player-manager and led them to an eighth place (52-100) record. Somehow this great catcher was able to lead them into the first division with a fourth-place (83-69) finish in 1905 and another fourth-place (71-82) finish in 1906. After that season he was gone, only to resurface as the manager of the White Sox in 1910.

*Patrick Joseph "Pat" Moran.*

**1907-1909 William Jeremiah "Billy" Murray**

Murray, born on April 13, 1864, in Peabody, Massachusetts, never played in the major leagues. But he was able to raise the Phillies to third place (83-64) in 1907. Then it was downhill, with a fourth-place (83-71) finish in 1908 and a fifth-place (74-79) finish in 1909, after which Murray was fired. He died on March 25, 1937, in Youngstown, Ohio.

**1910-1914 Charles Sebastian "Red" Dooin**

The promotion of this capable catcher to player-manager of the Phillies was something of an experiment. He was only 31 and had been the Phils' regular backstop since 1902. Dooin was able to bring the club up to fourth place (78-75) in 1910. It was another fourth place (79-73) in 1911. The Phillies slipped to fifth (73-79) in 1912, but they zoomed to second place in 1913, with a 88-63 record. Dooin finished his career with Philadelphia in 1914, bringing them in in sixth place (74-80). The 35-year-old Dooin, who had been born on June 12, 1879, in Cincinnati, then went on to catch for the Reds (1915) and the Giants (1915-1916). He died in Rochester, New York, on May 14, 1952.

**1915-1918 Patrick Joseph "Pat" Moran**

Moran was another of the many catchers who went on to become managers. Born on February 7, 1876, in Fitchburg, Massachusetts, he had caught for the Braves (1901-1905), the Cubs (1906-1919) and the Phillies (1910-1914). Moran was able to do what no other man had been able to do. In his first year as a manager and the Phillies' 33rd year of existence, he won a pennant (90-62) for them. Unfortunately, the Red Sox beat them four games to one in the World Series. Still, Moran followed up with two straight years in second place – 1916 (91-62) and 1917 (87-65). The team finished in sixth place (55-68) in 1918, and Moran was off to become the Reds' manager in 1919.

**1919 John Wesley "Jack" "Colby Jack" Coombs**

Born on November 18, 1882, in LeGrand, Iowa, Coombs, a right-handed pitcher, was a very successful player with the Athletics from 1906 to 1914. Indeed, he led the league, with 31 wins in 1910 and with 28 victories in 1911. From 1915 to 1918 he was with the Dodgers. Coombs lasted only 62 games managing the Phillies in 1919, going 18 and 44 and leading the team to last place. After he was fired he returned to pitching with the Tigers in 1920. He died on April 15, 1957, in Palestine, Texas.

**1919-1920 Clifford Carlton "Gavvy" "Cactus" Cravath**

Cravath, who was born on March 23, 1881, in Escondido, California, played the outfield for the Red Sox (1908), the White Sox (1909) and the Senators (1909). He came to the Phillies in 1912 and was selected player-manager to finish the 1919 season. He could not improve the eighth-place position of the club, going 29-46 to give the team a 47-90 record. After bringing the Phillies in in eighth place (62-91) once again in 1920, he was fired. Cravath died on May 23, 1963, in Laguna Beach, California.

**Opposite:** *Art Fletcher and the mayor of Philadelphia – 1925.*

place (57-96) and was subsequently fired. He died on May 21, 1936, in Rochester, New York.

## 1923-1926 Arthur "Art" Fletcher

Born on January 5, 1885, in Collinsville, Illinois, Fletcher, a good shortstop, began his major league career with the Giants in 1909, playing with them until 1920. He was traded to the Phillies in 1920 and was an active player until 1922. Fletcher took over as manager of the Phillies in 1923, and the club once again finished in last place (50-104). It was in seventh place (55-96) in 1924, sixth place (68-85) in 1925 and eighth place (58-93) in 1926, and Fletcher was on his way out. He reappeared as manager of the Yankees in 1929.

## 1927 John Phalen "Stuffy" McInnis

McInnis, born on September 19, 1890, in Gloucester, Massachusetts, came in to manage the Phillies in 1927. Primarily a first baseman, he had had a distinguished career with the Athletics (1909-1917), the Red Sox (1918-1921), the Indians (1922), the Braves (1923-1924) and the Pirates (1925-1926), carrying a .308 lifetime batting average. But it was yet another eighth-place (51-103) finish for the Phillies, and McInnis was fired. He died on February 16, 1960, in Ipswich, Massachusetts.

## 1928-1933 Burton Edwin "Burt" "Barney' Shotten

When Shotten was appointed manager of the Phillies in 1928 he was already a veteran. Born on October 18, 1884, in Brownhelm, Ohio, he had started his playing career in 1909 with the Browns. As an outfielder, he stayed in St. Louis until 1917, then went to the Senators (1918) and the Cardinals (1920-1923). In his first year as manager of the Phillies things were completely normal, the club coming in in last place (43-109). It was a little better in 1929, with the club in fifth place (71-82), and then it was back to the cellar in 1930 (52-102). In 1931 Shotten managed a sixth-place (66-88) finish, and in 1932 he registered his only winning record with the club, when they came in fourth (78-76). But it was back to seventh (60-92) in 1933, and Shotten was gone. He showed up the next year as manager of the Reds.

## 1934-1938 James "Jimmie" "Ace" Wilson

Once again the Phillies turned to a catcher

## 1921 William Edward "Wild Bill" Donovan

Donovan had been the Yankee manager from 1915 to 1917 and was brought in to manage the Phillies in 1921. He didn't last long – only through 102 games, with the team in last place with a 31-71 record. Donovan died two years later on December 9, 1923, in Forsyth, New York.

## 1921-1922 Irvin Key "Kaiser" Wilhelm

Wilhelm, born on January 26, 1874, in Wooster, Ohio, was a right-handed pitcher who began his major league career with the Pirates in 1903. He was traded to the Braves in 1904 and played two years there. He went to the Dodgers (1908-1910) and then on to Baltimore in the Federal League (1914-1915). He was brought in to finish the 1921 season as manager of the Phillies, and even pitched in four games for them. Wilhelm could manage but a 20-32 record that year, and the club stayed in last place, with a 51-103 mark. The only highlight in 1921 was that the Phillies were one of the two teams to play in the first game ever broadcast on radio. Station KDKA of Pittsburgh sent announcer Harold Arlen to Philadelphia to cover the contest between the Phillies and the Pirates. The Phillies lost 8-5. In 1922 Wilhelm brought the club in in seventh to be their manager. Wilson, born on July 23, 1900, in Philadelphia, had started his career with the Phillies (1923-1928), then moved to the Cardinals (1929-1933). He was brought back as a player-manager by the Phillies in 1934 and had two straight years finishing in seventh place – 1934 (56-93) and 1935 (64-89). Then, in 1936, it was back to the usual last place (54-100). After a seventh-place (61-92) finish in 1937, he was again back in last place (45-103) in 1938 after 148 games, when he was let go. By 1939 he was back catching for Cincinnati. He would become the Cubs' manager in 1941.

## 1938 John Bernard "Hans" "Honus" Lobert

Lobert was brought in to manage the last two games of the season for the Phillies. He lost both of them, and the club finished in last place (45-105). Lobert was born on October 18, 1881, in Wilmington, Delaware, and had been primarily a first baseman for the Pirates (1903), Cubs (1905), Reds (1906-1910), Phillies (1911-1914) and Giants (1915-1917). He would come back again to manage the Phillies in 1942.

## 1939-1941 James Thompson "Doc" Prothro

Prothro, born on July 16, 1893, in Memphis, Tennessee, had a relatively short career as a major league third baseman. He broke in with the Senators in 1920 and then played for Washington in 1923 and 1924. In 1925 he was with the Red Sox and ended with the Reds in 1926. Although he played in a mere 180 games in his five-year career, he carried a lifetime batting average of .318. But he was a typical Phillies manager, leading them to three straight years in the cellar – 1939 (45-106), 1940 (50-103), and 1941 (43-111). Prothro died on October 14, 1971, in Memphis.

## 1942 John Bernard "Hans" "Honus" Lobert

Lobert was brought back for another go at managing the Phillies in 1942. But he didn't improve over his previous outing, bringing the club in once again in eighth place (42-109), and he was fired at the end of the season. Lobert died on September 14, 1968, in Philadelphia.

**Opposite:** *Manager Burt Shotten of the Phillies.*

## Called BLUE JAYS (1943-1944)

### 1943 Stanley Raymond "Bucky" Harris

Since the club had been mired in last place for so many years, the management thought that a change of luck might be in order. So they changed the name of the team to the Blue Jays and brought in Bucky Harris to manage. Harris had had some degree of success in his many years as a manager with the Senators (1924-1928), the Tigers (1929-1933), the Red Sox (1934) and the Senators again (1935-1942). But in Philadelphia he was just another Phillies manager, and, with the team in fifth place (40-53) after 93 games, he was let go. He reappeared as the manager of the Yankees in 1947.

### 1943-1944 Frederick Landis "Freddie" "Fat Freddie" Fitzsimmons

Born on July 26, 1901, in Mishawaka, Indiana, Fitzsimmons, a right-handed pitcher, had a long career in the big leagues, winning 217 games with the Giants (1925-1937), where his won-lost percentage of .731 in 1930 led the league, and with the Dodgers (1937-1943). He was called in to finish the 1943 season but led Philadelphia from fifth to seventh place (64-90) by winning 24 and losing 37. In 1944 things were worse, and the team ended in last place (61-92).

**Below:** *Bucky Harris when he was with the Senators.*

## Called **PHILLIES** (1945-    )

### 1945 **Frederick Landis "Freddie" "Fat Freddie" Fitzsimmons**

Fitzsimmons continued his losing ways in 1945, and, with the team in last place (17-50) after 67 games, he was fired. He went on to become the baseball coach at Northwestern University. He died on November 18, 1979, in Yucca Valley, California.

### 1945-1948 **William Benjamin "Ben" Chapman**

Chapman, born on December 25, 1908, in Nashville, Tennessee, came in to finish the 1945 season as Phillies manager and kept the team in eighth place (46-108) with a 29-58 record. He had been primarily an outfielder who sported a .302 lifetime batting average with a variety of clubs – the Yankees (1930-1936), Senators (1936-1937), Red Sox (1937-1938), Indians (1939-1940), Senators again (1941), White Sox (1941) and Dodgers (1944-1945). In 1946 he played, as player-manager of the Phillies, in a single game – his last – and brought the team up to a fifth-place (69-85) finish. But in 1947 he slipped to seventh (62-92), and, with the team in seventh place again in 1948 after 79 games and a 37-42 record, he was fired. That ended his managing career in the majors.

### 1948 **Allen Lindsey "Dusty" Cooke**

Born on June 23, 1907, in Swepsonville, North Carolina, Cooke had played the outfield for the Yankees (1930-1932), the Red Sox (1933-1936) and the Reds (1938). He was brought to Philadelphia to hold the fort in 1948, and he did a creditable job for a mere 11 games, winning six and losing five.

### 1948-1952 **Edwin Milby "Eddie" Sawyer**

Sawyer was born on September 10, 1920, in New Orleans, Louisiana, and never played in the major leagues. Brought in at the end of the 1948 season by the Phillies to pick up the pieces, he won 23 and lost 41, and the club finished the season in sixth place (66-88). Things improved in 1949, when the Phillies finished third (81-73). Then, in 1950, the Phils became the "Whiz Kids," named for their spirited play and their youth – their average age was only 26. They won the pennant (91-63) on the last day of

*Freddie Fitzsimmons when he pitched for the Giants.*

the season – only their second pennant in history – but lost the World Series to the Yankees four games to none. In 1951 it was back to fifth place (73-81), and in 1952, after 63 games, Sawyer was let go with the team in sixth place (28-35). He would return to the Phillies in 1958.

### 1952-1954 **Stephen Francis "Steve" O'Neill**

O'Neill was brought in to finish the 1952 season. Previously he had been a fairly successful manager with the Indians (1935-1937), the Tigers (1943-1948) and the Red Sox (1950-1951). In 1952 he won 59 and lost 32, raising the Phillies from sixth to fourth place (87-67). In 1953 it was third place (83-71), and in 1954, after 77 games and the team at 40-37, O'Neill was gone. He died on January 26, 1962, in Cleveland.

### 1954 **Terry Bluford Moore**

Moore, who was born on May 27, 1912, in Vernon, Alabama, had a fine 11-year career playing the outfield for the Cardinals (1935-1942, 1946-1948), losing three years in service during World War II. He was brought in by the Phillies to finish the 1954 season, and the club went 35-42 for him, finishing in fourth place (75-79).

### 1955-1958 **Edward Mayo Smith**

Mayo Smith was born on January 17, 1915, in New London, Missouri, and played only 73 games in the major leagues – he was an outfielder for the Athletics in 1945. In 1954 he led the Phillies to a fourth-place (77-77) finish, but they fell to fifth (71-83) in 1956 and were fifth (77-77) again in 1957. In 1958, after 83 games, with the club nosediving into seventh place (39-44), Smith was fired. He later surfaced as manager of the Tigers in 1967.

### 1958-1960 **Edwin Milby "Eddie" Sawyer**

Sawyer was brought back again to manage the Phillies in 1958. He took a team that was in seventh place, won 30, lost 41 and guided them to an eighth-place (69-85) finish. It was eighth place (64-90) again in 1959. In 1960 Sawyer was fired after managing only a single game, which he lost. He did not manage in the majors thereafter.

### 1960 **Andrew Howard "Andy" Cohen**

Cohen was born on October 25, 1904, in Baltimore, and had been primarily a shortstop for the Giants from 1926 to 1929. He was permitted to manage the Phillies for just one game, which he won.

### 1960-1968 **Gene William "Skip" Mauch**

After two games had been played in the 1960 season, Gene Mauch was brought in to be the third Phillies manager that year. Born on November 18, 1925, in Salina, Kansas, Mauch had been a run-of-the-mill second baseman for the Dodgers (1944) and, after time out for the service, the Pirates (1947). Then he played for the Dodgers again (1944), the Cubs (1948-1949), the Braves (1950-1951), the Cardinals (1952) and the Red Sox (1956-1957). Once again, the Phillies came in in last place (59-95), and Mauch himself had a 58-94 record. Another eighth-place finish (47-107) followed in 1961. The highlight of that season was that the Phillies started off the season with a major league record of 23 straight losses. The only bright spot in that string was a win over the Minnesota Twins in an exhibition game.

In 1962 the club climbed up to a seventh-place (81-80) finish, and then it was fourth (85-75) in 1963. Things continued on an upswing in 1964, with the Phillies finishing second (92-70). But then it was sixth place

### 1969 George Edward "Mercury" "Stud" "Foghorn" Myatt

Myatt returned as manager in 1969 to pick up the pieces. He took over a fifth-place team (44-64) and kept it in fifth place by winning 19 and losing 35. The club finished the year at 63-99, and Myatt was gone.

### 1970-1972 Frank Joseph Lucchesi

Lucchesi was born on April 14, 1926, in San Francisco, and never played in the big leagues. He was unable to improve the fortunes of the Phillies, managing them to a fifth-place (73-88) finish in 1970 and a sixth-place (67-95) finish in 1971. In 1972, with the team in sixth place (26-50) after 76 games, he was fired. Lucchesi was to return to managing with the Rangers in 1975.

(85-76) in 1965. In 1966 they were fourth (87-75), and in 1967 they were fifth (82-80). In 1968, with the club in fourth place (26-27) after 53 games, Mauch was fired. He would later appear as manager of the Expos in 1969.

### 1968 George Edward "Mercury" "Stud" "Foghorn" Myatt

Myatt was born on June 14, 1914, in Denver, Colorado, and had played shortstop for the Giants (1938-1939) and the Senators (1943-1947). His appointment as manager in Philadelphia was a stopgap measure, and he led the team for only two games, winning both of them. Still, he had taken over the club when it was in fourth place (76-86) and left it in fifth place (77-86). He was to return to the Phillies in 1969.

### 1968-1969 Robert Ralph "Bob" Skinner

Skinner was born on October 31, 1931, in La Jolla, California, and played the outfield for the Pirates (1954, 1956-1963), the Reds (1963-1964) and the Cardinals (1964-1966). He took over the fifth-place (77-86) Phillies club and led them to another eighth-place (76-86) finish in 1968 by winning 48 and losing 59. In 1969, with the Phillies in fifth place (44-64) after 108 games, Skinner was let go. He later went to San Diego as manager in 1977.

**Right:** *Manager Gene Mauch.*

## 1972 Paul Francis "The Pope" Owens

Owens, born on February 7, 1924, in Salamanca, New York, was another major league manager who had not played in the big leagues. He came in to finish the 1972 season, with the Phillies in sixth place (59-97), and he kept them there by winning 33 and losing 47 for an overall 59-97 record. Owens would return as the Philadelphia manager in 1983.

## 1973-1979 Daniel Leonard "Danny" "Ozark Ike" Ozark

Ozark was born on November 24, 1923, in Buffalo, New York, and had never played major league ball when he was appointed manager of the Phillies in 1973. It was at about this time in history when James Michener, the famous novelist and lifelong Phillies fan, said to an acquaintance, "Young man, when you root for the Phillies, you acquire a sense of tragedy." Ozark brought them to a last-place finish (71-91) that year. Things looked better in 1974, with a third-place (80-82) finish, and in 1975 they fought their way to second place (86-76).

Ozark pulled off a minor miracle in 1976 when he brought them in first in their division (101-61) – only the third first place record in 93 years. But in the League Championship Series they lost to the Reds three games to none. The miracle continued in 1977, with another divisional first-place finish (101-61) and a record identical to the previous year's. This time they lost the League Championship Series to the Dodgers three games to one. There was a third straight first-place finish (90-72) in 1978, but the Phillies lost the League Championship Series to the Dodgers again by the same score of three games to one. The "miracle" was over, and in 1979, after 132 games, with the Phillies in fifth place (65-67), Ozark was let go. He would return to baseball as the manager of the Giants in 1984.

## 1979-1981 George Dallas Green

Dallas Green was born on August 4, 1934, in Newport, Delaware, and was a right-handed pitcher with a limited career (20-22) for the Phillies (1960-1964), the Senators (1965), the Giants (1966) and the Phillies again (1967). After managing the Phils from fifth place to fourth (84-78) by posting a 19-11 record in 1979, he came in first in their

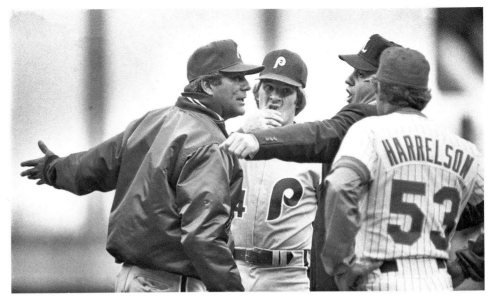

division (91-71) in 1980. This time they won the League Championship Series by beating the Astros three games to two. Not only were they now in the World Series for the third time, but also they won it for the first time, beating the Royals four games to two.

Then came that awful 1981 season in which the game was interrupted by the players' strike. The Phillies won the first half championship (34-21) and came in third (25-27) in the second half of the season. In the Divisional Playoff Series the Phillies lost to the Expos three games to two, and Green was off to become general manager of the Cubs.

## 1982-1983 Patrick "Pat" "Ike" Corrales

Corrales had been the manager of the Rangers (1979-1980) before he came to Philadelphia to take over the Phillies in 1982. He didn't do badly, bringing them in in second place (89-73). But in 1983, after 85 games and with the club in first place (43-42), he left to become manager of the Indians.

## 1983-1984 Paul Francis "The Pope" Owens

Owens, who had last managed the Phillies in 1972, was brought back to finish the 1983 season. He inherited them in first place (43-42) and kept them there, with a 47-30 mark, to end the season at 90-72. They then beat the Dodgers four games to three in the League Championship Series and followed that up by losing to the Orioles in the World Series four games to one. Owens was able to manage only a .500 record (81-81) in 1984, and then he was gone.

**Above:** *Pat Corrales in a rhubarb.*
**Opposite top:** *Gene Mauch argues.*
**Opposite bottom left:** *Dallas Green (r.) and Pete Rose celebrate.*
**Opposite bottom right:** *Pat Corrales.*

## 1985-1987 John Fredrick Felske

Felske, born in Chicago on May 30, 1942, had been a catcher, playing a modest 54 games for the Cubs (1968) and the Brewers (1972-1973). In 1985 he brought the Phillies in in fifth place (75-87). The next year it was second place (86-75). But when the team slipped to fifth place (29-32) after 61 games in 1987, he was fired.

## 1987-1988 Lee Constantine Elia

Elia had been the manager of the Cubs (1982-1983) and was brought in to finish the 1987 season as manager of the Phillies. He took over with the club in fifth place (80-82) and was able to raise them to fourth place with his 51-50 record (80-82 overall). In 1988, on September 23, with the Phillies in last place (60-92) after 152 games – 34½ games out of first place – Elia was fired. He was to go to the Yankees as third base coach in 1989.

## 1988 John Christopher Vukovich

Vukovich, a Phillies' coach who had been the manager of the Cubs for two games in 1986, was brought in to be interim manager of the sixth-place (60-92) club. There was no place lower for the Phillies to go, and they finished the season 65-96. Vukovich was replaced as manager for the 1989 season by Nick Leyva, who had been a minor league manager and third base coach for the Cardinals.

# PIRATES
## Pittsburgh (1901-    )

### 1900-1915 Fred Clifford "Cap" Clarke

In his 16 years as manager of the Pirates, Fred Clarke's teams did not finish in the second division until his last two seasons. After ending in second place at the end of Clarke's first year, the Pirates went on to win the pennant the next three seasons and, with the exceptions of fourth-place closings in 1904 and 1913, remained either contenders or winners from 1904-1913. During nine of his 16 years at Pittsburgh Clarke's teams won 90 or more games. Only Earl Weaver, Al Lopez, Joe McCarthy and John McGraw retired with better winning percentages after 15 or more seasons.

Only 24 years old when he began managing a major league team (the Louisville Colonels), Clarke became Pittsburgh's player/manager three years later (1900) when Louisville joined the team further up the Ohio River to form the Pittsburgh Pirates. Clarke, who had been born on October 3, 1872, in Winterset, Iowa, along with Honus Wagner, became the nucleus of a fearsome team. "Cap" Clarke's playing-cum-managing   responsibilities were not uncommon, especially during baseball's early years, but his appearance in 110 games in 1911, his twelfth year managing at Pittsburgh, suggests how important the playing side of the equation was. The Bucs won 85 games that year and finished third; Clarke, in 392 at-bats, hit .324, with a slugging percentage of .492.

An undeniable reason for Clarke's exceptional work in Pittsburgh was the mutual respect he and owner Barney Dreyfuss held for one another. Nevertheless, the manager never relinquished his independence. Once, after a loss brought on at least in part by ragged playing, Dreyfuss forced his way into the team's quarters after the game and demanded an explanation for such inept performance. Clarke, just as angry as his boss, commanded him to leave. Dreyfuss was aghast, but he yielded when Clarke insisted that any criticism of the team must come in a personal meeting with the manager, not with the whole team as audience.

Clarke managed in two World Series. His (and baseball's) first was in 1903, when the Pirates lost to the Boston Somersets (Red Sox) five games to three. The Second was a 1909 contest with the Tigers, which Pittsburgh won in seven games. Although Clarke did not win another pennant after the 1909 World Championship, the Pirates finished among the top three teams for the next three years. Not until his fifteenth year with Pittsburgh did Fred Clarke have a losing season. His 1914 team ended next to last and then moved up to fifth in 1915 – the closing year for Clarke in Pittsburgh and in the major leagues as a manager. He lived to be almost 88 years old, dying on August 14, 1960 – 15 years after becoming a member of the Hall of Fame.

### 1916-1917 James Joseph "Nixey" Callahan

"Nixey" Callahan, who had managed the White Sox, came to Pittsburgh with a reputation for intolerance of player mistakes. After a disappointing sixth-place finish in his first year and eighth spot in the standings after 60 games in the 1917 season, he suddenly and mysteriously disappeared. He showed up days later in Philadelphia amid stories that he had left the Pirates in an alcoholic stupor. Whatever the truth, he never managed again. He died on October 4, 1934, at the age of 60.

### 1917 Honus John Peter "The Flying Dutchman" Wagner

With characteristic selflessness Honus Wagner, the fine Pirate shortstop, agreed to direct the Pirates while the team's secretary tried to quash rumors about what manager Jimmy Callahan had been doing when he disappeared in Philadelphia. Wagner (born on February 24, 1874, in Carnegie, Pennsylvania), gave up managing after winning only one of five games. One of the five original inductees into the Hall of Fame (1936), Wagner lived until December 6, 1955. He died where he was born, in Carnegie.

### 1917-1919 Hugo Francis Bezdek

A 240-pound Czechoslovakian who grew up in Chicago and who had wrestled and played football in college but had never played baseball in the major leagues, Hugo Bezdek (born on April 1, 1883, in Prague) directed the Pirates in 91 games to close the 1917 season in last place – the position they had occupied when he stepped in to relieve Honus Wagner. In 1918, a year the Bucs were among the league leaders in the number of men they contributed to fight in World War I, Bezdek led them to a first-division slot (fourth). Bezdek's last year was a fourth-place season again, and the manager subsequently resigned his position to coach football, his first interest, at Penn State. There he developed some of the strongest teams in the school's history. Bezdek died on September 19, 1952, in Atlantic City.

### 1920-1922 George "Moon" Gibson

Pittsburgh fans in 1920 watched the Pirates perform much as they had the year before, but there was a new manager – George Gibson. "Moon" Gibson, a Canadian, had been born July 22, 1880, in London, Ontario,

**Opposite:** *Fred Clarke.*
**Above:** *Clarke (in suit) with his players.*

and had played catcher for the Pirates for 12 years (1905-1916). He was recognized as a smart baseball man, but Gibson's second year was the kind of season that fans recount, albeit gloomily, to their grandchildren. After threatening to run away from the second-place New York Giants through most of August, the Pirates had to defend their position in a five-game series in the Polo Grounds. John McGraw's New Yorkers won all five games and a month later completed the season with 94 wins to the Bucs' 90.

Owner Barney Dreyfuss was not pleased by the team's collapse and was even less amused by the shenanigans of some of the players. A man with little tolerance for foolishness, Dreyfuss admonished Gibson to be more unforgiving in enforcing rules and decorum. The next season (Gibby's last) started off little different from the demoralizing close of 1921, and Gibson resigned after 52 games, with the team in fourth place. "Moon" Gibson would return to Pittsburgh, but not until the next decade.

## 1922-1926 **William Boyd "Bill" "Deacon" McKechnie**

Born on August 7, 1886, in Wilkinsburg, Pennsylvania, McKechnie had played third base for various teams for 11 years. In 1925, his fourth season as manager at Pittsburgh, after three third-place performances, "Deacon" McKechnie (Bill had been serving as an elder in his church in Wilkinsburgh, Pennsylvania, when he became manager) directed one of the most potent teams in Pirate history – the best since the early years of Fred Clarke – and won the pennant nine games in front of John McGraw's Giants. Fred Clarke, in fact, interrupted his retirement on his ranch in Kansas to coach for McKechnie.

In a famous seven-game World Series with the Senators (the Bucky Harris team that had stung McGraw's Giants the year before) the Corsairs trailed in the final game through the seventh inning before winning 9-7 to become World Champions. Expecting the Pirates to be marauders again in 1926, fans and prognosticators were ecstatic

during a spectacular surge from seventh to first place in the course of 18 days in June, but they reeled when the team lost all but one game in a critical six-game series with the Cardinals late in August, and the Bucs eventually fell to a familiar third position when the season ended. It was McKechnie's last season in Pittsburgh. He would next manage the Cardinals in 1928.

## 1927-1929 **Owen Joseph "Donie" Bush**

Seasoned as a manager in Indianapolis and Washington, Donie Bush led a turmoil-riven 1927 team to their second pennant in three years. Among the noisiest complainers was Kiki Cuyler, whom Bush eventually had to pull out of the line-up for the remainder of the season after Cuyler waltzed into second base on a double play hit. Also playing in the outfield in 1927 were the Waner brothers, Paul and Lloyd ("Big

**Above:** *Hall of Famer Honus Wagner – probably the best shortstop of all time.*
**Opposite:** *Bill Hinchman (l.), a Pirate coach, with his manager, Moon Gibson.*

July 23 in 1929, the Pirates won only 13 of 29 games in August and fell out of contention – a reversal that brought on a meeting with Dreyfuss and Bush's dismissal. Donie was gracious about his demise and applauded the team's play, offering no alibis. His next managerial post was with the Chicago White Sox in 1930.

### 1929-1931 Jewel Willoughby Ens

After playing second base for the Pirates and having coached under Donie Bush, Jewel Ens was familiar with the problems the Pirates faced when he became manager with 35 games remaining in 1929. Forty-year-old Ens (born in St Louis on August 24, 1889), recognized for his intelligence and baseball judgment, led the Bucs to 21 wins in those 35 games, but the team nonetheless finished in second place, ten games behind the Giants. After two disheartening fifth-place seasons Jewel Ens lost his position as manager of the Pirates and abandoned managing in the major leagues. He lived to be 60, dying on January 17, 1950, in Syracuse, New York.

### 1932-1934 George "Moon" Gibson

Ten years after George Gibson first managed in Pittsburgh, owner Barney Dreyfuss died of pneumonia, but not before making clear his plan to retrieve Gibson to manage again. This time the story was more flattering to Gibson than it had been in his first appearance in Pittsburgh, for the Pirates quickly moved to second place in the first year of Gibson's return and stayed in second the next season. Fourth place by June of "Moon's" third year was not satisfactory for new team president Bill Benswanger (Dreyfuss's son-in-law), and he fired Gibson. George Gibson lived almost 33 more years, dying on January 25, 1967, at his birthplace, London, Ontario.

### 1934-1939 Harold Joseph "Pie" Traynor

A favorite of Pirates' president Bill Benswanger, Pie Traynor accepted the position of manager when the team was in fourth place in June, 1934. Winning only 47 of the remaining 99 games, the team dropped one more spot, to fifth, by season's end. Traynor had performed excellently as a third baseman for 15 years before trying to double as a manager, but he was by now slowing down and played only sparingly in 1934 and stopped entirely in 1937.

Poison" and "Little Poison"). Paul won the league batting title (.380) and Lloyd hit .355, but the Pirates still lost to the Yankees in a World Series sweep, for that was the historic year when Ruth hit 60 home runs, and Gehrig, right behind him in the line-up, hit 47 homers and batted .373.

Leading the league in team batting in 1928, with .309, the Pirates nonetheless finished in fourth spot (although only eight games out of first). In first place through

Pie, a New Englander (born on November 11, 1899, in Framingham, Massachusetts), whose tag came about as a result of his appetite for the traditional Yankee dessert, kept the Pirates in the first division in his first four full seasons, but the team was never better than second, at best three games behind the Cubs in the win column in 1938. The season's closing in 1938 was especially demoralizing: leading the Cubs by one and one-half games at the end of September, the Pirates entered Chicago needing to win only one game of a three-game series to take the pennant. They lost all three. Traynor's final year managing, 1939, was a sixth-place season, the team's poorest finish since 1917. Traynor remained with the Pirates as a scout after 1939's dismal conclusion. Elected to the Hall of Fame in 1948, Pie died in Pittsburgh on March 16, 1972.

## 1940-1946 Frank Francis "Frankie" "The Fordham Flash" Frisch

Under the tutelage of the Giants' John McGraw, Frankie Frisch had learned many lessons that he brought with him to Pittsburgh in 1940. Above all, Frisch had learned to value the importance of authority – an attitude that had earlier cost "The Fordham Flash" loyalties among the members of the Gashouse Gang in St. Louis, where he had been fired as manager after a sixth-place finish in 1938.

After a year of broadcasting baseball in Boston the Hall of Famer (1947) came to Pittsburgh to revitalize a team that had so disappointed owners and fans the year before. In his first year the Pirates regained first-division status (fourth), where they remained in 1941. Frisch, however, won more attention for baiting umpires than for winning games in Pittsburgh; and the Pirates sagged to fifth place in 1942.

Frisch's best season with the Bucs came in his fifth year, 1944, when the team posted their best winning percentage in 18 years, .588, and Pittsburgh fans greeted the Pirates with the kind of applause usually given only to winners, despite their second-place finish, 14½ games behind the Cardinals.

Frisch was the Pirates' manager in Forbes Field's first game under lights on June 4, 1940; and he became the last manager to work under the directorship of the Dreyfuss family, which sold the team in August, 1946. Frisch ended his employ-

ment in Pittsburgh that same year, with three games remaining and the Pirates leading the Giants by two games to stay out of last place. He became the Cubs' manager in 1949.

## 1946 Virgil Lawrence "Spud" Davis

A member of Frankie Frisch's coaching staff and a former catcher, Spud Davis closed the 1946 season by managing the last three games after the Dreyfuss family sold the Pirates and Frisch lost his job. Davis, born on December 20, 1904, in Birmingham, Alabama, won one game and continued as a scout for the Pirates after 1946. He died on August 14, 1984, also in Birmingham.

## 1947 William Jennings Bryan "Billy" "Bryan" Herman

Secured from the Boston Braves by the new owners of the Pirates, former second baseman Billy Herman came to Pittsburgh with the promise of being a superlative leader. In the deal that brought Herman, however, the Pirates' new President, Frank McKinney, had to give up too many first-rank players. Consequently, Hall of Famer (1975) Herman (born in New Albany, Indiana, on July 7, 1909) did not finish his first year managing, but yielded his position

**Opposite:** *Bill McKechnie and his 12-year-old son, Bill, Jr. – 1925.*
**Below:** *Manager Donie Bush.*

92

with one game remaining and the team in peril of ending in last place. He resurfaced managing the Red Sox in 1964.

## 1947 **William Edwin "Bill" Burwell**

A coach during the season, former pitcher Bill Burwell, born on March 27, 1895, in Jarbalo, Kansas, stood in for the last game of the season when manager Billy Herman gave up after losing three of four games to the Phillies in a series in September. The Pirates were in danger of finishing in last place, but they beat Cincinnati in Burwell's game and tied for seventh. This was Burwell's only appearance as a manager. He died on June 11, 1973, in Ormond Beach, Florida.

**Above:** *Pie Traynor in his playing days.*

## 1948-1952 **William Adam "Billy" Meyer**

Billy Meyer had caught in the majors and had managed in the minor leagues, including a team in the Yankee system, and he knew the necessity of constructing a strong club by beginning with the patient tutoring of young players. The Pirates had spent generously in acquiring and keeping glamorous players, but the results had too often been teams without depth and unable to remain competitive throughout an entire season.

After the 1947 tie for last place the consortium of Pirates executives at last decided to begin developing a team instead of trying to buy one. At least they could count on the loyalty of the fans. Even though the team's poor performance had been a cause for des-

**Above:** *Frankie Frisch being thumbed out of a game in 1941.*

pair, fan attendance in 1947 had totalled almost 1,300,000.

The new approach resulted in a remarkably quick recovery, for the Pirates won 21 more games in Meyer's first year than they had in 1947 and advanced to fourth spot (only two games behind second-place St. Louis). Four years later, however, the Tennessee native (Knoxville, born on January 14, 1892) led the team to only 42 wins, the weakest showing since 1917. That ended Meyer's managing career. He died on March 31, 1957, in Knoxville.

## 1953-1955 **Fred Girard "Pudge" Haney**

Fred Haney came over from managing in St. Louis in 1953 to lead the Pirates to eight more wins than the total of the preceding year, but they were still a distant 15 games behind the seventh-place Cubs. Without

the home run threat of Ralph Kiner, who had won the league crown with 37 the year before, and with no one batting better than .294, the Bucs had no offensive potency; and the best pitching ERA was barely under 4.00 from a hurler who won only three of nine games.

After two more last-place years Haney was let go. He would continue his managing career in Milwaukee, starting in 1956.

## 1956-1957 **Robert Randall "Bobby" Bragan**

Faced with the assignment of nursing a team which had not yet coalesced but was potentially strong, former shortstop Bobby Bragan was a kind of manager well suited to carry on the patient incubation of the new

**Above:** *Bobby Bragan (l.) in 1956.*
**Right:** *Danny Murtaugh (l.) and pitcher Harvey Haddix.*

stock that had been introduced since the disastrous late 1940s. His roster in 1956 included names that would soon become distinguished: Roy Face, Vern Law, Dick Groat, Bob Friend and, most sensational, Roberto Clemente. Bragan was willing to nurse Clemente, for example, by abiding his quarrelsome moodiness and not insisting that he play when he didn't feel like it.

The 39-year-old Bragan, who had been born in Birmingham, Alabama, on October 30, 1917, was prepared to try any configuration of his line-up to improve the team, but he finally had to concede that the 1956 Pirates were likely to finish in last place, regardless of his innovations. They did finish last his first year, and they were also last when Bragan got the word from general manager Joe Brown in August of his second year that his work was unsatisfactory after 36 wins in 104 games. He would move on to manage for Cleveland in 1958.

## 1957-1964 Daniel Edward "Danny" Murtaugh

It was no miracle that the Pirates performed as though they were two distinct teams in the 1957 and 1958 seasons. The names on the roster were almost the same both years (with the exception of the arrival of Ted Kluzewski), but the change in performance was evidence that the patience and calculated work that the owners and managers had applied for the past decade were beginning to pay dividends. When former second baseman Danny Murtaugh began his work in Pittsburgh in August, 1957, he was unable to advance the team's position in the standings (tied for last place with the Cubs), but the Pirates won 26 of the 51 games in which he managed.

A year later, in 1958, the winning pattern continued, and the team finished with 22 more victories and second spot. Pitching became a problem in 1959, and for the first time since 1955 no hitter batted .300 or better – a mediocre performance, but still strong enough to hold a first-division ranking (fourth).

In the third full season for the 43-year-old Pennsylvanian (born on October 8, 1917, in Chester), however, the Bucs silenced critics and elated fans with both a

pennant and a 4-3-game conquest of the Yankees of Maris and Mantle in the 1960 World Series. No one was prepared for the precipitous fall to sixth place the very next year, nor for the disappointment of finishing in fourth position in the standings from 1962 through 1964, when Murtaugh lost his chance (at least for the time being) to reverse the Pirates' weak performance. He would, however, soon be back.

## 1965-1967 Harry William "The Hat" Walker

Relieving Danny Murtaugh, who had not produced a winner since 1960, Harry Walker came over from managing in St. Louis and realized instant results by taking a team that had finished one game under .500 the year before to 90 wins and third place in the 1965 standings. The following year was even more satisfying, with 92 victories – but still third place (1½ games behind San Francisco and only three out of the pennant slot occupied by Los Angeles).

1967 was a sensational season for Roberto Clemente, whose .357 won the league batting title, but Harry Walker's .500 record after the first 84 games earned him only a shortened year in Pittsburgh, and he was replaced shortly after mid-season. The next year he was managing in Houston.

## 1967 Daniel Edward "Danny" Murtaugh

Idle for two and one half years (at least as a major league manager), Danny Murtaugh returned for the second half of the 1967 season to direct a Pirates team that was in the same spot (sixth) they had held when he yielded his position at the end of 1964. He was unable to improve the team's performance, however, and they remained in sixth place. Murtaugh was forced to leave Pittsburgh for a second time in three years, but again not permanently.

## 1968-1969 Lawrence William "Larry" Shepard

Dismayed by the sixth-place humiliation of 1967, the office in Pittsburgh elected in 1968 to risk their aspirations on a name untested in either major league managing or playing. Larry Shepard, who had been born in Lakewood, Ohio, on April 3, 1919, did not improve the team's record or standing during his first year, but, in an exhilarating reversal, the Pirates in Shepard's second year finished in third place. Clemente and

Above: *Manager Chuck Tanner.*
Left: *Jim Leyland (in jacket) has a conference on the mound.*
Opposite top: *Harry "The Hat" Walker.*
Opposite bottom: *Manager Bill Virdon.*

four other hitters batted .301 or better. Shepard did not complete the season, however, but was released with only five games remaining. It was his last major league managerial assignment.

### 1969 **Alexander Peter "Alex" Grammas**

In his entrance to the ranks of major league managing, Alex Grammas could hardly have been more successful. The erstwhile short-stop, who had played ten years for National League teams (1954-1963), led the Pirates to four wins in the five he directed and closed the 1969 season in third spot, four games behind the Cubs. But Grammas

(born in Birmingham, Alabama, on April 3, 1926) did not return to the Pirates the following year. He would resurface in Milwaukee in 1976.

### 1970-1971 **Daniel Edward "Danny" Murtaugh**

In 1970 Danny Murtaugh came back to Pittsburgh a third time, and again to a team that had been gathering strength the year before. The 1970 Pirates won the East Division, only to lose to Cincinnati in a three-game sweep in the League Championship Series. The next year, though, the Bucs won 97 games in the regular season before defeating San Francisco 3-1 in the Cham-

pionship Series and then dispatching the Orioles in seven for the World Championship. On that triumphal note Murtaugh stepped down. But yet again he would return.

### 1972-1973 **William "Bill" Virdon**

Not merely maintaining hold on first place, but improving their winning margin over the nearest rival by five games, the Pirates under Bill Virdon, in his first year managing in the major leagues, continued to set a high standard for the East Division of the league. Yet theirs was not as lofty as the mark set by the Big Red machine in 1972. The Pirates won 96 games to Cincinnati's

*Chuck Tanner explains something to umpire Lee Weyer – 1982.*

99 during the season and lost the pennant in a five-game Championship Series.

Former outfielder Virdon (born in Hazel Park, Michigan, on June 9, 1931) returned the next year, but the Pirates were not the same without Roberto Clemente, tragically killed in a plane crash on December 31, 1972; and despite 44 home runs by Willie Stargell they were unable to win their division a fourth successive year. When Virdon lost his job, with only 26 games remaining in 1973, Pittsburgh was in second spot in a season that ended with only five games separating the top five teams in the East Division. Virdon's performance was considered good enough to bring him to the Yankees the following year.

### 1973-1976 Daniel Edward "Danny" Murtaugh

With the Pirates in second place and with only 26 games remaining in 1973, Danny Murtaugh assumed the Pirates' manager's post for a fourth time. But instead of moving up from the second-place finish of the year before, the Pirates dropped one place and finished third. In Murtaugh's next two years, however, Pittsburgh fans rejoiced in first-place teams – but only in the East Division: both years the Pirates lost in the League Championship playoffs. In Danny Murtaugh's last opportunity to manage a championship Pirates team, the Bucs closed the 1976 season in second, two months before his death on December 2, 1976, in his home town of Chester, Pennsylvania.

### 1977-1985 Charles William "Chuck" Tanner

Nine years managing the Pirates entitled Chuck Tanner, who had earlier managed the A's, to be ranked third for longevity as the team's field strategist (behind Fred Clarke and Danny Murtaugh). Half of Tanner's tenure with the Pirates resulted in first-division teams, and in seven of his first eight years (the strike year of 1981 being the only exception) the Pirates had winning seasons.

Tanner's 1977 team won 96 games but finished second to the Phillies, the cross-state rivals whom Pirates fans had once scorned. Two years later, however, Pittsburgh was jubilant again as Tanner and the Pirates finished two games in front of surging Montreal and faced Cincinnati, the best team in the National League in the 1970s, for a five-game divisional playoff series. The Bucs skunked the Reds as a prelude to a World Series title won in seven games against Earl Weaver's Orioles, winner of 102 regular-season games. The supremacy of the 1979 Pirates turned out to be their last for a decade. In 1980 they finished third, and five years later they had fallen to last place in their division. It was at that point, 1985, that Chuck Tanner left Pittsburgh and the Pirates, turning up the following year as manager of the Braves.

### 1986-1988 James "Jim" Leyland

Needing only one season of running in place before reviving a team that was sleep-walking, Jim Leyland, a Buckeye born on December 15, 1944, in Toledo, Ohio, in his first major league managing assignment, improved the Pirates' winning record by 16 games in his second year (1987) and advanced them two places in the standings to tie for fourth place. Leyland's 1988 Pirates became the only East Division team to present a sustained threat to the Mets, who had moved to the front position and never did relinquish first spot, despite a tenacious pursuit by Pittsburgh. In mid-July the Pirates closed to within a single game before losing four of five games in a series in New York. The spread between the 100 wins of the Mets and the 88 of the Pirates was convincing, but the fans in Pittsburgh saw a glimpse of former combative Pirates teams as the Bucs ended the season in second place, their best year since 1983, and good enough to secure another chance for Jim Leyland in Pittsburgh.

# REDS
## Cincinnati (1901-    )

### 1901-1902 John Alexander "Bid" McPhee

The Cincinnati Red Stockings were America's first fully professional baseball team, beginning their schedule in 1869. In their first year of play the Red Stockings won all of their 66 games. The sparkplug of the team and America's first baseball star was George Wright, who batted .518 and hit 59 home runs in the 66 games, all for a modest salary of $1400 for the season.

McPhee was actually the second twentieth-century Reds manager, since Bob Allen was called to be the manager of the Reds in 1900. Born on July 10, 1867, in Marion, Ohio, Allen had been a fine shortstop for the Phillies (1890-1894) and the Braves (1897). As the player-manager of the Reds he was able only to bring them in in seventh (62-77), and that was the end of his managing career in the majors. Allen died on May 4, 1943, in Little Rock, Arkansas.

McPhee, born on November 1, 1859, in Massena, New York, had had an 18-year career in the major leagues as a second baseman before becoming the Reds' manager in 1901. He had played with the Reds (1882-1889) when they were in the American Association and again in 1891-1899 after they joined the National League. In 1901 he led them to eighth place (52-87), and in 1902, after 64 games and the club holding a 27-37 record, he was let go. McPhee died on January 3, 1943, in San Diego.

### 1902 Frank Carter Bancroft

Bancroft was brought in to relieve McPhee in the middle of the 1902 season. He was born on May 9, 1846, in Lancaster, Massachusetts, and had never played in the major leagues. He did have, however, several years' experience as a manager with Worcester (1880), Detroit (1881-1882), Cleveland (1883) and Providence (1884-1885) – all in the National League – as well as with Philadelphia (1887) in the American Association and Indianapolis of the National League. Bancroft inherited a team in seventh place (27-37) and had them in fifth place (37-44) before being replaced. He died on March 31, 1927, in Cincinnati.

*Manager Joe Kelley.*

### 1902-1905 Joseph James "Joe" Kelley

Born on December 9, 1871, in Cambridge, Massachusetts, Kelley had been an outstanding outfielder for many years and would be elected to the Hall of Fame in 1971. His major league playing career began with the Braves in 1891, and he went on to play with the Pirates (1891-1892), the Orioles (1892-1898), the Brooklyn Superbas (1899-1901) and, for 60 games, the Orioles again (1902). He was brought to Cincinnati to become player-manager in 1902. He took over the fifth-place (37-44) team and brought them in in fourth place (70-70) by winning 33 and losing 26. It was fourth place (74-65) again in 1903, and then he guided them into third place (88-65) in 1904. In 1905 the Reds fell back to fifth (79-74), and Kelley returned to playing the out-

field for the Reds in 1906. In 1908 he became the manager of the Braves.

### 1906-1907 Edward Hugh "Ned" Hanlon

Hanlon had been the manager of Pittsburgh of the National League (1889), Pittsburgh of the Players League (1891) and Pittsburgh of the National League (1891). He went on to manage the Orioles (1892-1898) and the Brooklyn Superbas (1899-1905) before coming to Cincinnati in 1906. His career with the Reds lasted two years, and he came in sixth in both 1906 (64-87) and 1907 (66-87) before he was dismissed. Hanlon died on April 14, 1937, in Baltimore.

### 1908 John Henry Ganzel

Born on April 7, 1874, in Kalamazoo, Michigan, Ganzel had been a first baseman for the Pirates (1898), the Cubs (1900), the Giants (1901), the New York Highlanders (1903-1904) and the Reds (1907-1908). As the Reds' player-manager in 1908 he brought them in in fifth place (73-81), after which he was fired. He later managed the Brooklyn club in the Federal League. He died on January 14, 1959, in Orlando, Florida.

### 1909-1911 Clark Calvin "The Old Fox" Griffith

Griffith had been the manager of the White Sox (1901-1902) and the New York Highlanders (1903-1908). He was brought in to manage the Reds in 1909 and led them to an unaccustomed fourth-place (75-79) finish. Then things went downhill. It was fifth (75-79) in 1910 and sixth (70-83) in 1911. The following year Griffith was managing the Senators.

### 1912 Henry Francis "Hank" O'Day

O'Day became the Cincinnati manager in 1912. He was born on July 8, 1862, in Chicago, and he had become a not-too-successful right-handed pitcher (71-112) with Toledo (1884) and Pittsburgh (1885) of the American Association. Then he played for Washington (1886-1889) and New York of the National League and ended up with

New York of the Players League (1890). His record with the Reds was 75-78, good enough for a fourth-place finish. That was the end of his tenure with the Reds, but he would manage the Cubs two years later.

### 1913 Joseph Bert "Joe" Tinker

Born on July 27, 1880, in Muscotah, Kansas, this Hall of Fame (1946) shortstop was a part of the famous "Tinker-to-Evers-to-Chance" double-play combination for the Cubs. He had been a fixture with the Cubs from 1902 to 1912, but when the Reds called him in to be player-manager in 1913 he was ready to go. He was able to achieve only a seventh-place (64-89) finish, and he went off the next year to be the player-manager of the Chicago club in the Federal League (1914-1915). In 1916 he was back with the Cubs as manager.

### 1914-1916 Charles Lincoln "Buck" Herzog

Herzog, a major league utility infielder for 13 years, had had a fine career with the Giants (1908-1909), the Braves (1910-1911), the Giants again (1911-1913), the Reds (1914-1916), the Giants once again (1916-1917), the Braves again (1918-1919) and the Cubs (1919-1920). It was during his tenure with the Reds that he became a player-manager. He had a terrible record: eighth (60-94) in 1914 and seventh (71-83) in 1915. With the

club in last place again (34-49) after 83 games in 1916, he was let go but, as noted above, continued playing. Herzog died on September 4, 1953, in Baltimore.

### 1916 Ivey Brown "Ivy" Wingo

Wingo was born on July 8, 1890, in Gainesville, Georgia, and was to have a long career as a catcher in the major leagues. He began with the Cardinals (1911-1914) and then played for the Reds from 1915 to 1929. It was during the 1916 season in Cincinnati that he had his lone chance to be a big league manager. Taking over the club in last place (34-49), he led them for just two games, which they split. Then it was back behind the plate for several more years. Wingo died on March 1, 1941, in Norcross, Georgia.

**Above:** *Manager Clark Griffith.*
**Far left:** *Manager Buck Herzog.*
**Opposite:** *A Sparky Anderson rhubarb.*

### 1916-1918 Christopher "Christy" "Big Six" "Matty" Mathewson

Mathewson was born on August 12, 1878, in Factoryville, Pennsylvania. One of the most overpowering pitchers in major league history, Mathewson (Hall of Fame, 1936) won 373 and lost 188, striking out 2502 along the way. Except for one game that he pitched with the Reds in 1916, his entire career was spent with the Giants (1900-1916). He took over the Reds with the team in eighth place (35-50) and brought them in in seventh place (60-93 overall) in 1916 by winning 25 and losing 43. In 1917 it was fourth place (78-76), and, with the team in

fourth place (61-57) after 118 games in 1918, Mathewson was let go. He died on October 7, 1925, in Saranac Lake, New York.

### 1918 Henry Knight "Heinie" Groh

Primarily a third baseman, Groh, who was born on September 18, 1889, in Rochester, New York, played for 16 years in the majors – with the Giants (1912-1913), the Reds (1913-1921), the Giants again (1922-1926) and the Pirates (1927). It was while he was with the Reds that he became a stopgap player-manager to finish the 1918 season. Groh inherited a fourth-place (61-57) team and, by winning seven and losing three, was able to bring them up to third place, with a 68-60 overall mark. Groh died on August 22, 1968, in Cincinnati.

### 1919-1923 Patrick Joseph "Pat" Moran

Moran had been the manager of the Phillies from 1915 to 1918, and he was brought in to manage the Reds in 1919. He started off splendidly, bringing the team in in first place (96-44) – the first National League pennant in the team's history. (That season was also notable for being the one in which the last triple-header was played – between the Reds and the Pirates). The Reds met the White Sox in the World Series and beat them five games to three. But it was a tainted victory, for this was the year of the "Black Sox Scandal" and its game-fixing charges against the Chicago team.

Moran brought the Reds in in third place (82-71) in 1920 and in sixth place (70-83) in 1921. Then came two straight second-place finishes in 1922 (86-68) and 1923 (91-63). During spring training in Orlando, Florida, in 1924, Moran literally died in harness. Seemingly suffering a stroke in the dugout, he turned to his new coach, former Cub manager Johnny Evers, and said, "Hello, John. Take me out of here." Those were his last words. The date was March 7, 1924.

### 1924-1929 John Charles "Jack" Hendricks

Hendricks had had very little major league experience. He had been an outfielder in only 42 games with the Giants, Cubs and Senators in 1902 and 1903, and he was managing the Cardinals in 1918 when he was brought in to take over from Moran. He finished in fourth place (83-70) in 1924 and took the Reds to third place (80-73) in

**Above:** *Heinie Groh in his playing days.*
**Top:** *Manager Christy Mathewson.*
**Top right:** *Manager Pat Moran.*
**Bottom right:** *Manager Jack Hendricks.*

1925. Nineteen twenty-six was his best year: Cincinnati finished second, with an 87-67 record. Then it was all downhill – fifth (75-78) in 1927, fifth (78-74) again in 1928 and seventh (66-88) in 1929. After that Hendricks was let go. He died on May 13, 1943, in Chicago.

### 1930-1932 Daniel Philip "Dan" "Dapper Dan" Howley

Howley had been the manager of the St. Louis Browns from 1927 to 1929 and had had some degree of success with that terrible ball club. Accordingly, he was brought in to manage the Reds in 1930. He was capable only of maintaining their seventh-place position of the year before with his 59-95 record. He then went on to lead the club to two straight last-place finishes in 1931 (58-96) and 1932 (60-94), after which he was fired. Howley died on March 10, 1944, in East Weymouth, Massachusetts.

### 1933 Owen Joseph "Donie" Bush

Bush was brought in to turn the Reds around in 1933. He had been a successful manager of the Senators (1923), the Pirates (1927-1929), and the White Sox (1930-1931), but he couldn't do it in Cincinnati. He brought the club in in their third straight eighth-place (58-94) finish and was fired. He died on March 28, 1972, in Indianapolis, Indiana, at the age of 85.

### 1934 Robert Arthur "Bob" O'Farrell

O'Farrell had been able to manage the 1927 Cardinals into second place, so he was brought to Cincinnati to stem the tide of last-place finishes. But after 84 games the club was still in last place (26-58), and O'Farrell was gone. He did not manage in the majors thereafter.

### 1934 Burton Edwin "Burt" "Barney" Shotten

Shotten, who had been the Phillies' manager from 1928 to 1933, was brought in as a stopgap skipper in 1934. He appeared in but one game, which he won. He was to become the Dodger manager in 1947.

### 1934-1937 Charles Walter "Chuck" Dressen

Born on September 20, 1898, in Decatur, Illinois, Dressen had been a third baseman for the Reds (1925-1931) and the Giants (1933) and carried a lifetime batting average

of .272. Called in to finish the disastrous 1934 season, Dressen took over with the team in last place, with a 27-58 record, and was unable to improve matters. He won 25 and lost 41, and the club remained in eighth place, with a 52-99 overall record.

He improved things in 1935, when the Reds finished in sixth place (68-85), and in 1936 the Reds moved up to fifth place (74-80). But in 1937, with the team in eighth place (51-78) after 129 games, he was fired. It took many years, but Dressen turned up once again as a manager – this time of the Dodgers in 1951.

*Owner Powell Crosley, Jr. (l.) with Manager Bill McKechnie.*

### 1937 Roderick John "Bobby" 'Rhody' Wallace

Wallace had not managed in the majors since 1912, when he left the Browns, but he was brought in to finish the 1937 season with the Reds. He couldn't get them out of eighth place, winning five and losing 20, and the team finished with a 56-98 overall record, at which point Wallace left. He did not manage again and died on November 3, 1960, in Torrance, California.

because he never had a club where he could be one." In this Series, however, Vander Meer pitched only three innings, the hurling honors going mainly to Bucky Walters and, especially, to Paul Derringer.

The only thing to mar the euphoria of that 1940 season for the Reds was the death of Willard Hershberger, a reserve catcher. Depressed because he thought he had not given his all, this 29-year-old killed himself on August 2 by cutting his throat in a Boston hotel room while the Reds were on the road. The Cincinnati club voted Hershberger's widowed mother a full World Series share of nearly $6000.

The Reds fell to third (88-66) in 1941 and fourth (76-76) in 1942. In 1943 it was second place (87-67).

## Called REDLEGS (1944-1945)

### 1944-1945 William Boyd "Bill" "Deacon" McKechnie

McKechnie brought the Redlegs in in third place (89-65) in 1944 and in seventh place (61-93) in 1945.

## Called REDS (1946-    )

### 1946 William Boyd "Bill" "Deacon" McKechnie

Nineteen forty-six was McKechnie's last year at the helm of the Reds, and he could manage only a sixth-place (67-87) finish. So ended his 25-year career in the majors. He died on October 29, 1965, in Bradenton, Florida.

### 1947-1948 John Henry "Johnny" Neun

Neun had been the manager of the Giants in 1946 and had brought them in in third. In 1947, however, he could do no better with the Reds than fifth place (73-81). In 1948, after 100 games and with the club in seventh place (44-56), he was let go. He did not manage in the majors thereafter.

### 1948-1949 William Henry "Bucky" Walters

Walters was brought in to finish the 1948 season as the Reds' manager. Born on April 19, 1909, in Philadelphia, he had been in the major leagues since 1931. At first he was primarily a third baseman with the Braves (1931-1932) and the Red Sox (1933-1934).

### 1938-1942 William Boyd "Bill" "Deacon" McKechnie

McKechnie had been the manager of the Newark club in the Federal League (1915), of the Pirates (1922-1926), of the Cardinals (1928-1929) and of the Braves (1930-1937). He took over the rag-tag Reds in 1938 and promptly brought them in in fourth place (82-68). Even better, in 1939 McKechnie led them to the pennant, with a 97-57 record. But they collapsed in the World Series, losing to the Yankees in four straight games.

In 1940 McKechnie led the Reds to another pennant (100-53), and this time they won the World Series, beating the Tigers four games to three. It was the second championship for baseball's oldest professional team, but the first one had been tainted by the Black Sox Scandal of 1919. McKechnie had become the only manager to win the World Series with two different National League teams – the 1925 Pirates and the 1940 Reds. Johnny Vander Meer, the Reds' pitcher of back-to-back no-hitter fame, later said of his manager, "Bill was an outstanding defensive manager. He wasn't much of an offensive manager

Then he was traded to the Phillies in 1934. His problem, if it was a problem, was that sometimes he had so much on the ball when he threw to first base that the first baseman had trouble handling it. In 1935, because of his throwing arm, he was persuaded to convert to pitching by the Phillies' manager, Jimmy Wilson, a former catcher. Walters would subsequently pitch for the Phillies until 1938 and for the Reds between 1939 and 1948, winning a total of 198 games.

He took over as player-manager of the Reds in 1948, when they were in seventh place (44-56), and he was able only to maintain that position, with a 20-33 mark (64-89 overall). Nor was he able to get them out of seventh place in 1949, and, after 151 games (61-90), he was let go. Walters ended his baseball career in 1950 as a pitcher with the Braves.

### 1949-1952 **James Luther "Luke" Sewell**

Sewell was brought in to finish the 1949 season with the Reds. He had been the manager of the Browns from 1941 to 1946 and had won their only pennant for them. He inherited a club in seventh place, with three games to go. He won one and lost two, and the Reds finished the season in seventh place (62-92). Sewell brought the team to two straight sixth-place finishes in 1950 (66-87) and 1951 (68-86). But with the club in seventh place (39-59) after 98 games in 1952, he was fired and did not manage in the major leagues again.

### 1952 **Earle Francis Brucker, Sr.**

Born on May 6, 1901, in Albany, New York, Brucker was a catcher for the Athletics (1937-1940, 1943). He was brought in to manage the Reds for a mere five games in 1952, and went three for five, but the club was still in seventh place. He did no more managing in the majors. He died on May 8, 1981, in San Diego.

### 1952-1953 **Rogers "Rajah" Hornsby**

Hornsby had just been fired from his job as manager of the seventh-place St. Louis Browns in 1952 when he was hired by the Reds. He inherited another seventh-place (42-61) team in Cincinnati and, by going 27-24, was able to bring them in in sixth (69-85 overall). In 1953 he was unable to improve their position, and, after 146 games and with the team in sixth place (64-82), he was fired. It was his last managing job.

Hornsby died on January 5, 1963, in Chicago.

### 1953 **Colonel Buster Mills**

Buster Mills was born on September 16, 1908, in Ranger, Texas, and was a journeyman outfielder with the Cardinals (1934), the Dodgers (1935), the Red Sox (1937), the Browns (1938), the Yankees (1940) and the Indians (1942, 1946). When he took over the Reds in 1953 they were in sixth place (68-86), and Mills split the last eight games of the season. The Reds stayed in sixth place (68-86 overall), and Mills departed, never to manage again.

### 1954-1958 **George Robert "Birdie" Tebbetts**

Born on November 10, 1912, in Burlington, Vermont, Tebbetts was a fine catcher in the major leagues for 14 years with the Tigers (1936-1942, 1946-1947), the Red Sox (1947-1950) and the Indians (1951-1952). He

**Above:** *Manager Pete Rose.*
**Opposite:** *Manager John McNamara.*

turned the Reds around, relatively speaking, starting by finishing fifth for two straight years – 1954 (74-80) and 1955 (75-79). Then he contrived to finish in the first division for two straight years – third (91-63) in 1956 and fourth (80-74) in 1957. In 1958, with the club in seventh place (52-61), he was let go, only to turn up as manager of the Milwaukee Braves in 1961.

### 1958 **James Joseph "Jimmy" Dykes**

Dykes, who had managed for years with the White Sox (1934-1946), the Athletics (1951-1953) and the Orioles (1954), was brought in to finish the 1958 season for the Reds. He inherited a seventh-place (52-61) club and won 24 and lost 17, bringing them in in fourth place, with a 76-78 record. Dykes went on to become the manager of the Detroit Tigers in 1959.

## 1959 Edward Mayo Smith

Mayo Smith had been the manager of the Phillies (1955-1958) and was brought in to begin the Reds' 1959 season. After 80 games the club was in seventh place (35-45), and he was let go. He surfaced again in 1967 as manager of the Tigers.

## 1959-1964 Frederick Charles "Fred" Hutchinson

Hutchinson had been the manager of the Tigers (1952-1954) and the Cardinals (1956-1958) before he was called to Cincinnati to manage. He took over a seventh-place (34-48) club and, by winning 39 and losing 35, was able to bring them in in a tie with the Cubs for fifth place (74-80 overall). It was sixth place (67-87) in 1960, but then Hutchinson led the Reds to the league championship (93-61) in 1961. Unfortunately, they lost the Series to the Yankees four games to one. In 1962 the Reds finished third (98-64) and then fell to fifth (86-76) in 1963. In 1964, after 109 games and with the Reds in third place (60-49), Hutchinson, knowing he had terminal cancer, retired. He died on November 12, 1964, in Bradenton, Florida.

## 1964-1965 Richard Allan "Dick" Sisler

Sisler, born on November 2, 1920, in St. Louis, was an outstanding first baseman-outfielder with the Cardinals (1946-1947), the Phillies (1948-1951), the Reds (1952) and the Cardinals again (1952-1953). He inherited a third-place (60-49) Reds team and, by winning 32 and losing 21, he was able to bring them in in second place (92-70 overall). But it was fourth place (89-73) in 1965, and Sisler was gone.

## 1966 Donald Henry "Don" "Jeep" Heffner

Born on February 8, 1911, in Rouzerville, Pennsylvania, Heffner had been mainly a second baseman for the Yankees, Browns, Athletics and Tigers. After 83 games the club was in last place (37-46), and Heffner was let go. He died in Pasadena, California, in August, 1989.

## 1966-1969 James David "Dave" Bristol

Bristol, born on June 23, 1933, in Macon, Georgia, had had no major league experience when he took over with the Reds in last place (37-46) in 1966. By winning nine games and losing 38 he was able to

move them up to a seventh-place (76-84 overall) record. Then came two straight years in fourth place – 1967 (87-75) and 1968 (83-79). In 1969 he raised them to third place (89-73), but he resigned at the end of the season to take over the reins with the Braves.

## 1970-1978 George Lee "Sparky" Anderson

Anderson, born on February 22, 1934, in Bridgewater, South Dakota, played second base for the Phillies for just one year, 1959, batting .218. When he was appointed manager of the Reds he became the youngest manager in the major leagues. Nineteen seventy was the year that the new Riverfront Stadium was dedicated, and Anderson celebrated the event by bringing in the Reds in first place (102-60) in his first managerial year. Cincinnati's Big Red Machine polished off the Pirates three games to none in the League Championship Series but lost the World Series to the Orioles four games to one.

In 1971 the Reds finished fourth (79-83), but they came in first in their division (95-59) in 1972 and knocked off the Pirates in the League Championship Series three games to two. They lost the World Series again that year, this time to Oakland, four games to three.

It was another first-place (99-63) finish in 1973, but this time they lost the League Championship Series to the Mets three games to two – a series marked by riotous disturbances at Shea Stadium. In New York the Mets fans threw so many objects at Pete Rose in left field that Anderson refused to continue playing until manager Yogi Berra and some of the Mets players went out and calmed down their fans.

It was a second-place (98-64) finish in 1974. Then came the monumental year of 1975.

Anderson called the 1975 Reds the best bunch he ever had. That was the year he became known as "Captain Hook," because his starting pitchers completed only 22 of 164 games. They set a record by going 45 straight games without a pitcher having finished what he started. Anderson would later say, "That's one record I'm not too proud of." On May 16 Joe Morgan was hurt in Montreal during an Expos 4-2 victory. He had been spiked, and the wound required 14 stitches in his shin. The next day he offered to play despite the injury, and

Anderson told his men, "If Joe can play, we all can play." It shook up the team, and they were off to the pennant.

They not only finished the season in first place (108-54), they had nailed down first place in their division by September 17 – the earliest in the history of the National League. The Reds once again knocked off the Pirates in the League Championship Series – this time three games to none – and then edged out the Red Sox in the World Series four games to three.

Anderson was always a team man and never bragged about his own accomplishments. Indeed, he once said, "My biggest job as manager is that I don't trip the players going down the runway." After winning the 1975 World Series he said, "It was our 115th victory, and we took the seventh game with the qualities that got us into the Series – speed, power, defense, relief pitching and the best spirit I ever saw."

The Reds came in first in their division again in 1976 and blew out the Phillies three games to none in the League Championship Series. Then they went on to give the Yankees an unaccustomed whitewash in the World Series, four games to none. Then came two straight second-place years – 1977 (88-74) and 1978 (92-69). And for that Anderson was fired. He briefly tried his hand at reporting baseball on television but returned to active participation in the game in 1979 by assuming the managership of the Tigers in midseason.

### 1979-1982 John Francis McNamara

McNamara had been a not-too-successful manager for the Athletics (1969-1970) and the Padres (1974-1977) before he was brought in to manage the Reds in 1979. In his very first year, he brought them in in first place in their division (90-71). But they were beaten by the Pirates in three straight games in the League Championship Series. It was third place (89-73) in 1980 for McNamara.

Then came that strike-split 1981 season in which there were first-half winners and second-half winners in all four divisions of major league baseball. It was decreed that the four teams leading their divisions when the strike began would face the division leaders from the second half of the season. But there was a flaw in the plan – a team might still have the best record for the season but still not have led in either half. In the National League Western Division the

Reds had the best total record, 66 wins and 42 losses, but they came in second (35-21 and 31-21) in both halves of the season.

In 1982, after 92 games and with the Reds in sixth place (34-58), McNamara was fired. He was to turn up the next year as manager of the Angels.

### 1982-1983 Russell Eugene "Russ" Nixon

Born on February 19, 1935, in Cleveland, Nixon was a fine catcher with the Indians (1957-1960), the Red Sox (1960-1965), the Twins (1966-1967) and the Red Sox again (1968). He took over the Reds when the team was in sixth place (34-58), and he was not able to improve their position, since he won only 27 while losing 43. The team ended up still in last place (61-101 overall). In 1983 the team stayed in sixth place (74-88), and Nixon was fired. He went on to manage the Braves in 1988.

### 1984 Vernon Fred "Vern" Rapp

Rapp had been the manager of the Cardinals (1977-1978) before being called to Cincinnati to manage the Reds. After 120 games and with the team in fifth place (51-69) he was fired.

### 1984- Peter Edward "Pete" "Charlie Hustle" Rose

Rose was genuinely a home-town hero. Born in Cincinnati on April 14, 1941, he had been an outfielder, first baseman, second baseman and third baseman for the Reds (1963-1978) and for the Phillies (1979-1984). He was called back to become player-manager of the Reds to finish out the 1984 season. As a player, Rose had been phenomenal. He had set the major league career base-hit record, with 4256 hits, and the career record for singles, with 3215. He inherited a fifth-place (51-69) team and could not improve their standing, winning 19 and losing 23 (70-92 overall). But in the succeeding years he led the Reds to second-place finishes – 1985 (89-72), 1986 (86-76) and 1987 (84-78). In 1988 some regarded the Reds as pennant contenders, but the best they could do with their 87-74 record was to remain in second place in the Western Division. On August 24, 1989, disaster struck when Rose was banned from baseball for gambling. Former Reds infielder and now coach Tommy Helms (born on May 5, 1941, in Charlotte, NC) took over, with the Reds at 61-66.

Above: *Sparky Anderson.*
Top: *Dick Sisler in his playing days.*
Opposite top: *Chuck Dressen.*
Opposite center: *Bucky Walters.*
Opposite bottom: *Rogers Hornsby.*

**Below left:** *Connie Mack.*
**Below center:** *Manager Bucky Harris of the Senators.*
**Below right:** *Manager Jeff Torborg of the Indians.*

The American League

**1961-1964 William Joseph "Billy" "Specs" "The Cricket" Rigney**
The American League added two expansion teams in 1961 – the Los Angeles and the Washington Senators. The Angels were owned by former movie singing cowboy Gene Autry and by tycoon Bob Reynolds, and they selected Rigney to be their first manager. Rigney had previously been a reasonably successful manager with the Giants (1956-1960), but, as might be expected with an expansion club, he was only able to bring them in in eighth place in 1961. In 1962 the Angels were the most surprising club in baseball, nipping at the heels of the Yankees through most of the season before finishing third (86-76). In 1963 they fell to ninth place (70-91) and in 1964 climbed to fifth place (82-80). Ending in the first division twice in their first four years in the league was quite an achievement. (The American League had not yet divided itself into Eastern and Western Divisions, and there were ten teams in the league.) At the end of the year the owners decided to move to Anaheim, California and to re-christen the team the California Angels.

# ANGELS
California (1965-    )

**1965-1969 William Joseph "Billy" "Specs" "The Cricket" Rigney**
Rigney remained as manager of the Angels through their move from Los Angeles to Anaheim, just as he had remained as manager of the Giants through their move from New York to San Francisco after the 1957 season. In 1965 he guided the Angels to a seventh-place (75-87) finish and then started a slow climb upwards. It was sixth place (80-82) in 1966 and fifth place (84-77) in 1967. They nosedived to eighth place (67-95) in 1968, and in 1969, the year that the league was divided into Eastern and Western Divisions, after 39 games and with the team in last place (11-28), Rigney was fired. In 1970 he became the manager of the Twins.

**1969-1971 Harold Ross "Lefty" Phillips**
Phillips, born on May 16, 1919, in Los Angeles, had had no major league playing experience when he took over the sixth-place (11-28) Angels in 1969. But he was able to win 60 while losing 63, and that was enough to raise the team to third place (71-91 overall). Phillips kept them in third place in 1970, but with a much better record (86-76). It was fourth place (76-86) in 1971, but then Phillips had to retire. He died eight months later on June 10, 1972, in Fullerton, California.

**1972 Delbert W. "Del" Rice**
Rice was born on October 27, 1922, in Portsmouth, Ohio, and had been a catcher for 17 years with the Cardinals (1945-1955), the Braves (1955-1959), the Cubs (1960), the

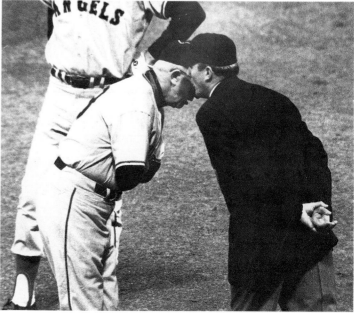

Cardinals again (1960), the Orioles (1960) and the Angels (1961). He lasted only one year as Angels manager in 1972, bringing in the team in fifth place (75-80). Rice died on January 26, 1983, in Buena Park, California.

### 1973-1974 Bobby Brooks "Winks" Winkles

Winkles, born on March 11, 1932, in Swifton, Arkansas, had had no major league playing experience, but he had spent several years as a college baseball coach before coming to the Angels in 1973. A cerebral manager, he was able to bring them up to a fourth-place (79-83) finish in his first year, but in 1974 the team found itself in last place (32-46) after 78 games, and Winkles was fired. He was to become manager of the A's in 1977.

**Above:** *Dave Garcia (r.) with Coach Frank Robinson.*
**Left:** *Manager Dick Williams.*
**Opposite left:** *Bill Rigney is warned.*
**Opposite right:** *Rigney makes up.*

### 1974-1976 Richard Hirschfeld "Dick" Williams

Williams, who had been a very successful manager with the Red Sox (1967-1969) and the A's (1971-1973), finishing in first place four of those six years. He came to manage the Angels in 1974, when the team was in sixth place (32-46). He was unable to do any more than win 36, while losing 48, and the club stayed in last place (68-94 overall). In 1975 the Angels stayed in sixth place (72-89), and in 1976, with the team in fourth place (39-57) after 96 games, he was gone. Williams went on to manage the Expos in 1977.

### 1976-1977 Norman Burt "Norm" Sherry

Sherry, born on July 16, 1931, in New York City, had been a catcher in the majors for five years – with the Dodgers (1959-1962) and the Mets (1963). He didn't last long as manager of the Angels. Sherry finished the 1976 season by winning 37 and losing 29, but that was not enough to lift the team out of fourth place (76-86 overall). In 1977, after 81 games and with the club in fifth place (39-42), Sherry was let go.

### 1977-1978 David "Dave" Garcia

Born on September 15, 1920, in East St. Louis, Illinois, Garcia had had no major league playing experience before becoming manager of the Angels. He inherited a team in fifth place (39-42), and, by winning 35 and losing 46, he kept them in fifth place (74-88 overall). In 1978 he had won 25, while losing 20, and had the team in third place after 45 games when he was let go. Garcia was to manage the Indians beginning in 1979.

### 1978-1981 James Louis "Jim" Fregosi

Fregosi, born on April 4, 1942, in San Francisco, had been a shortstop in the major leagues for 18 years with the Angels (1961-1971), the Mets (1972-1973), the Rangers (1973-1977) and the Pirates (1977-1978). After appearing in 20 games behind the plate for the Pirates in 1978 he was called back by his old team to take over the helm. The Angels were in third place (25-20) when he arrived, and he was able to raise them to second place (87-75) by winning 62 and losing 55.

The Angel mini-miracle occurred in 1979. The club had been finishing an average of 23½ games down for the previous 18 seasons, but that year Fregosi brought them in in first (88-74). The Angels lost to the Orioles in the League Championship Series, however, three games to one. It was sixth place (65-95) in 1980, and, after 47 games in 1981 and with the team in fourth place (22-25), Fregosi was let go. He turned up as manager of the White Sox in 1986.

### 1981-1982 Gene William "Skip" Mauch

The year 1981 was the strike-torn year in which the season was split in two. Mauch, who had been the manager of the Phillies (1960-1968), the Expos (1969-1975) and the Twins (1976-1980), was brought in to manage with the Angels in fourth place (22-25) in the first half-season. He won nine and lost four, but that was not enough to raise the club in the standings, and they finished fourth (31-29 overall). In the second half of the season they finished in seventh (20-30). In 1982 came a complete turnaround, and Mauch led them to first place (93-69). The Angels had struggled all year with the Royals, but they won the division by three games. In the League Championship Series they won the first two games against the Brewers, but then they lost the next three. Mauch left managing for a while, then came back to the Angels in 1985.

## 1983-1984 John Francis McNamara

McNamara was brought in to manage in 1983. He had previously been the manager of the A's (1969-1970), the Padres (1974-1977) and the Reds (1979-1982). He brought the Angels in in fifth (70-92) in 1983 and then led them to a second-place (81-81) finish in 1984. But after that he moved on to become the manager of the Red Sox in 1985.

## 1985-1987 Gene William "Skip" Mauch

Mauch was back in 1985 and was able to guide the Angels to another second-place (90-72) finish, but they were only one game out. Then, in 1986, he brought them in in first (92-70). They finished five games ahead of the Rangers but went on to lose the League Championship Series 4-3 to the Red Sox. In 1987 the Angels fell to a sixth-place (75-87) finish, and Mauch was forced to resign because of illness ten days before the 1988 opener.

## 1988 Octavio Victor Rivas "Cookie" Rojas

Born on March 6, 1939, in Havana, Cuba, Rojas had been primarily a second baseman for the Reds (1962), the Phillies (1963-1969), the Cardinals (1970) and the Royals (1970-1977). He took over the Angels just ten days before the 1988 season began and was able to lead them to fourth place (75-79) after 159 games – but during that time they had had a slump in which they had lost ten of 12 games and were 23½ games out of first place. Rojas was fired on September 23.

## 1988 Lawrence George "Moose" Stubing

Stubing, an Angels coach who had pinch hit five times for the Angels in 1967, was brought in as interim manager of the fourth place (75-79) club and managed to lose the last eight games as the Angels finished fourth (75-87).

## 1989- Douglas Lee "Doug" "Rojo" "The Red Rooster" Rader

Rader, who had managed the Texas Rangers (1983-85) and the Chicago White Sox (1986), had been serving as a coach for the Angels when he was asked to take over as manager starting in 1989.

**Right:** *Manager Cookie Rojas.*
**Opposite top:** *Manager Gene Mauch.*
**Opposite bottom:** *Manager Jim Fregosi.*

# ATHLETICS
## Philadelphia (1901-1954)

**1901-1950 Cornelius Alexander "Connie" "The Tall Tactician" "Mack" McGilicuddy**

All the statistics in baseball history pale when placed alongside the one most likely to stand forever. In 1930 Cornelius Alexander McGilicuddy was 68 years old, but the Philadelphia Athletics, the team he had owned and managed for 30 years, won 102 games in the regular season and then defeated the Cardinals, four games to two, to win the World Championship – the team's second consecutive world title and the fourth of five Connie Mack would eventually claim before retiring. Ten years later "The Tall Tactician" was still a decade away from relinquishing command. (By comparison, Casey Stengel stepped down at the age of 76, after 25 years of directing major league teams, and John McGraw yielded his post with the Giants at 59, after 33 years of big league managing.)

By the time Connie Mack did give over to a personally-chosen successor, he had triumphantly persevered through 53 years of managing in the major leagues (his first three years at Pittsburgh – 1894-1896). He stands third in total number of World Series games managed, fourth in games won and fourth in World Series winning percentage in baseball history. His Philadelphia teams won nine pennants and finished in the first division 22 times. Furthermore, in his first 30 years at the helm of the A's he finished in either first or second position 14 times.

Connie Mack defined standards not only for longevity and durability in managing, he was influential, as well, in elevating baseball from a pastime of idlers and brawlers to a dignified and cherished national institution. Mack was the incarnation of the New World doctrine that preached the values of ambition, tireless work and studied management of time and resources. In his own account of his ascent to the pinnacle of achievement he proclaimed that his entrepreneurship and its rewards should stand as monuments to the American promise of success. Horatio Alger himself could have chosen no better model for his rugged, in-

*Manager Connie Mack.*

dividualistic heroes than Connie Mack.

A child of post-Civil War Yankee industrialism, Mack was born and grew up in a mill town in central Massachusetts – East Brookfield, one of scores of small Massachusetts settlements that had become home to multitudes of Irish immigrants during the nineteenth century. His father was fighting with the Massachusetts 51st Infantry and President Lincoln was less than two weeks from announcing the Emancipation Proclamation when Cornelius was born on December 22, 1862. He reminisced fondly about the formative influences that his parents and family had had on his boyhood, but he also emphasized that the town itself nurtured attitudes which he credited as a fundamental to his achievements. Nor did he hesitate to assert that the moral fiber and character of many of the nation's best young athletes were the direct products of the wholesome environment of the American small town.

In his own case, work, unvarnished and relentless, was just as much a part of being a boy as was respecting one's elders; and grammar and high school (for those privileged enough to finish) were not only a means to literacy and guarantors of self-betterment, but were often, as well, staging

for many promising male athletes who went on to schools like Holy Cross, Amherst, Williams and Yale to become sprinters, halfbacks, athletic directors and even baseball players. The young Mack was, in fact, one of three major league catchers to come out of the little enclave of towns called the Brookfields (Brookfield, East Brookfield, North Brookfield and West Brookfield), where boys became proficient at playing a rudimentary ball game called "four'o cat" in warehouse yards or on the town common.

Mack recalled how he would spend his summers when, as a nine-year-old, he worked as an errand boy in a cotton mill for 33 cents a days. Employees had an hour for lunch, and Mack and his friends would use all but ten or fifteen minutes of the time tossing a homemade ball made of rags wrapped up in a hand-stitched cover to someone waving a piece of one-by-two. Put-outs were made by hitting the batter with the ball before he could reach base.

At the age of 21, in 1884, Connie left a job making shoes at a local factory, explaining to his mother that he could better serve her and his four brothers by getting a higher-paying job someplace away from home. Despite his mother's protestations, Mack insisted that his opportunities lay in professional baseball. He promised her that he would not fall prey to the evils of drinking, carousing and gambling, which had become indigenous to baseball, and when he retired, 66 years later he was still utterly true to that promise.

Mack somehow applied the simple Horatio Alger virtues and made them work in a glitzy, high-risk business. After managing the Pirates for three years, followed by a year as part-owner/manager of a Milwaukee team in the Western League, he had a chance to put together a second team in Philadelphia under the banner of a new league. Acting on a suggestion by league founder Ban Johnson that he approach industrialist Benjamin F Shibe to secure capital, Mack was persuasive, and Shibe, with the help of his friend Charles Somers from Cleveland, joined the 38-year-old Cor-

himself to become too preoccupied with profit and loss.

Mack blamed the A's' astonishing collapse on the threatened usurpation of the American League's position by the new Federal League and on World War I recruitment of his best players, but other teams in the league faced the same threats and survived (indeed some flourished). Nor was he successful in disguising the fact that he regarded yielding to what he considered unreasonable salary demands from players unthinkable. The owner-manager who had achieved a reputation for unimpeachable baseball judgment and business savvy in 1910 had become an owner recognized and sometimes scorned for parsimony.

There was recovery, however, and it came in a sustained performance almost as

**Left:** *Mack (r.) with his ace pitchers.*
**Below:** *Mack and his score card.*

nelius in financing the Philadelphia Athletics as one of eight teams in a new American League.

Mack had little time to put together a team, but he knew enough people in the game, and was a shrewd enough horse-trader, to quickly assemble a strong roster – strong enough to win the pennant in his second year (1902) and to contend for the World Champion title in 1905 (only the third World Series to be played). The Athletics lost to the New York Giants in that Series (four games to one), but after falling to second place from 1907-1909, Connie Mack's Athletics began to set new standards for baseball. Save for one year (1912) – the season of the Red Sox' Tris Speaker, Harry Hooper and Duffy Lewis (the best outfield in baseball up to that time, according to Mack) – the A's dominated baseball from 1910-1914.

Even the most talent-laden teams in baseball history have had lean periods, and some have fallen from dominant positions to intervals of weakness within just a few seasons. But the reversal that occurred with the Athletics after 1914, coming off four World Series appearances in five years, has been rarely equalled in baseball history. From 1915 to 1922 Connie Mack's Athletics finished in last place and in fact did not re-enter first division ranking until 1925, when they ended the season in second spot, six games behind the Senators. The reason is not a mystery: Connie Mack had allowed

dazzling as that of the 1910-1914 teams. The Athletics met the Yankees head on in 1929 and 1931 (the Yankees of Gehrig, Ruth, Lazzeri and Dickey) and beat them almost effortlessly (16 games in 1929 and 13 in 1931) each time. They won a total of 107 games in 1931 before losing to St. Louis in the Series in seven games. Again, however, as if to recapitulate his questionable judgment after the 1914 season, Mack proceeded to dismantle a team which he claimed could not stand prosperity, and four years later the Athletics once more occupied the cellar, where they remained for ten of Connie Mack's last 16 seasons as owner/manager. It was a sad end to an awesome career. He finished his 53 years managing in 1950 with a .484 lifetime won-lost average. By that time he had been in the Hall of Fame for 13 years. This grand old man of baseball died in Philadelphia on February 8, 1956.

## 1951-1953 James Joseph "Jimmy" Dykes

No stranger to baseball's most durable manager, Jimmy Dykes had played every infield position for Connie Mack during the course of his 1918-1932 residence in Philadelphia. When Mack personally chose him to be his successor in managing a desperately weakened Athletics team, no one was surprised, since Dykes had already accumulated extensive managerial judgment as a result of 12 years directing the White Sox.

Dykes had readily admitted to leniency as a disciplinarian during his years working as both manager and player for the Chicago White Sox, but he insisted, nonetheless, that he would not blink at some infractions. The Athletics did not lack discipline as much as talent, however, when Dykes received the call to relieve Connie Mack. They had occupied the bottom spot seven

**Above:** *Manager Jimmy Dykes with two of his outfielders, Dave Philley (l.) and Gus Zernial (r.).*

of the past 12 seasons and had finished no better than fourth. Jimmy Dykes improved the winning record by 18 games in his first year (sixth place) and improved to fourth his second year (1952) before falling to seventh his final season. The following year, 1954, he was managing the Baltimore Orioles.

## 1954 Edwin David "Eddie" Joost

Another former infielder who played for Connie Mack (1947-1950), Eddie Joost, born in San Francisco on June 5, 1916, had no more success than did his predecessor, Jimmy Dykes. The A's dropped one more slot to eighth, and that was the end of Joost's managing career in the majors.

# ATHLETICS
## Kansas City (1955-1967)

### 1955-1957 Louis "Lou" Boudreau

Successful as player-manager in Cleveland, but far less so in Boston with the Red Sox, Lou Boudreau accepted the risks of rehabilitating a dispirited Athletics franchise the year they abandoned Philadelphia and went west to Kansas City. Even though Boudreau had some good hitters in his opening year, the pitching was abominable and the change of venue was no help. The result was a sixth-place finish. Boudreau's second season with the A's, 1956, was one of the poorest in their history, and in August of 1957 (his final year) he left after winning only 36 of 104 games. During the 1957 calamity Boudreau and his successor called on the services of 20 pitchers, none of whom pitched enough innings to qualify for ERA ranking in championship contention. Boudreau would manage in the majors one more time, for the Cubs in 1960.

### 1957-1959 Harry Francis Craft

But for the dismal performances of the Washington Senators, the Athletics would have claimed last place in the standings during the two-plus years former outfielder Harry Craft was manager. To his credit, he won 23 of the 50 games in which he worked to complete the 1957 season – enough to prevent the humiliation of a second last-place finish in two years.

Craft, born in Ellisville, Mississippi, on April 19, 1915, directed a team which continued to provide respectable hitting, but its pitching remained the poorest in the major leagues. Roger Maris played under Craft in 1958 (99 games) and in 1959, when he hit 16 home runs. Two years later he reached his record 61 with the Yankees. Craft moved on to manage the Cubs in 1961.

### 1960 Robert Irving "Bob" Elliott

A fifteen-year third baseman with four National League teams (1939-1953), Bob Elliott became the second manager of the Athletics who had not played for Connie Mack at one time. Elliott, born in San Francisco on November 26, 1916, managed only one year in Kansas City and finished in last place. He lived only six years after his sea-

*Manager Harry Craft.*

son directing the Athletics, dying on May 4, 1966, in San Diego.

### 1961 Joseph Lowell "Flash" Gordon

In an expansion year for the American League that marked the entry of the Minnesota Twins and the Los Angeles Angels, Joe Gordon, who had been managing in Detroit, was still unable to improve upon the standing (eighth place) of a mediocre team with no one batting better than .296 and only one pitcher delivering an ERA better than 4.00. Gordon left after 70 games.

### 1961-1962 Henry Albert "Hank" Bauer

Playing alongside Mickey Mantle during most of his 12 years with Casey Stengel's Yankees, Hank Bauer was the fourth all-time highest in the American League in total World Series games played (46) and fifth highest in total hits (46) for League Series competition. Nevertheless, his steady work as an outfielder and hitter had no effect on the inept performance of the Athletics when he joined them as a player in 1960. Nor did it help them when he managed the last 92 games in 1961 and then led

them through the 1962 season.

Bauer, born in East St. Louis, on July 31, 1922, was unable to perform magic with a team of limited talent, and the Athletics finished in a tie with Washington for last spot in 1961 and second to last the next year. Bauer moved on to manage in Baltimore.

### 1963-1964 Edmund Walter "Ed" "Steady Eddie" Lopat

Still unable to regain even a glimpse of the stature attained by the once-dominating team assembled by Connie Mack a full 30 years earlier, the Athletics front office looked to the Yankees a second time in hopes of finding a workhorse from a winning team who could become a winning manager. Lopat, born Edmund Walter Lopatynski in New York City on June 21, 1918, had pitched four winning World Series games under Casey Stengel and had lost only one. His managing experience with the Athletics, however, was as disappointing as that of his predecessor, Hank Bauer. After finishing eighth of ten teams in his first season, he left managing permanently during his second year, with only 52 games (17 wins) played.

### 1964-1965 Fred Melvin "Mel" McGaha

With the A's in tenth (last) place when he accepted the position of manager after the dismissal of Ed Lopat, Mel McGaha (born in Bastrop, Louisiana, on September 26, 1926) was unable to transform a team that had become accustomed to second-division status. McGaha, who had directed Cleveland to a sixth place season in 1962, could not field a single hitter who was batting higher than the .280s, and the only lustre in his pitching stable was a contingent of relievers who combined for 26 saves (almost half the total wins for the year). The starting pitcher rotation averaged an ERA of almost 4.80. McGaha ended the season where he started – in last spot, and he won only five of the first 21 games in 1965 before the Kansas City Athletics' executives appointed a new manager. He never managed in the majors again.

Above: *Eddie Lopat receives an award during his playing days.*
Above left: *Manager Hank Bauer.*
Left: *Owner Charles Finley (l.) with Manager Alvin Dark.*
Opposite: *Luke Appling as a player.*

## 1966-1967 **Alvin Ralph "Blackie" Dark**

No stranger to managing and winning, Alvin Dark came to Kansas City after directing the San Francisco Giants to a pennant in 1962. Dark worked with an Athletics team that still presented a weak offense (a total of 68 home runs for the entire roster, including the bench, with the best hitter batting .286); but the pitching improved, with only half the starting rotation finishing with ERA's over .3.00 (the first time in the history of the Kansas City franchise).

Dark's team won 74 games, the most since Jimmy Dykes' 1952 season in Philadelphia (79 wins), and finished in seventh spot. In August of his second season (1967), however, Dark left Kansas City after losing 69 of the 121 games he directed, with the A's in last place. Yet when Dark left, the team was fielding its most talented and promising roster since Connie Mack's teams of 1929-31. Perhaps one reason that the team didn't do better was that owner Charley Finley had managed to rouse the ire of almost everyone on the team, including Alvin Dark. Dark turned up the following year managing in Cleveland.

## 1965 **Haywood Cooper Sullivan**

Sullivan, who was born in Donalsonville, Georgia, on December 15, 1930, had played for the A's between 1961 and 1963, making 252 appearances, mostly as a catcher. Thus he knew the problems of the Athletics from the inside; but his understanding of the team's weaknesses didn't help their performance, and they won about the same ratio of games under Sullivan (54 of 136) as they had under the direction of the preceding six managers. Sullivan neither played nor managed in the major leagues thereafter.

**1967 Lucius Benjamin "Old Aches and Pains" Appling**

Agreeing to nurse the Athletics for the last 40 games of the 1967 season (the last month and a half that the team would play in Kansas City) as a favor to owner Charley Finley, Luke Appling, who entered the Hall of Fame in 1964, won only ten games of the 40 he orchestrated during his entire managerial experience. Born on April 2, 1909, in High Point, North Carolina, the White Sox' 20-year veteran shortstop had already coached for Finley, but now he incurred the owner's rage by unwisely calling a team meeting secretly, despite Finley's order that he not interfere in the war between the young team and its owner. Appling was fired and never managed again.

# ATHLETICS
## Oakland (1968-)

**1968 Robert Daniel "Bob" Kennedy**
The Chicago Cubs' pilot from 1963 through the first 58 games of 1965, Bob Kennedy now moved the Athletics, a team that had finished in last place in Kansas City in 1967, to the "top" – the top, that is, of the second division (sixth) – in the first season the team played as Charley Finley's Oakland Athletics. Sixth spot was not good enough, and Kennedy left Oakland after only one year, even though it was the first time the A's had concluded a season over .500 (.506) since Jimmy Dykes' 1952 season in Philadelphia. This marked the end of Kennedy's managing career.

**1969 Henry Albert "Hank" Bauer**
Hank Bauer, who had managed the Kansas City Athletics in 1969, returned to lead the Athletics in their second year at Oakland. Winning 30 games and losing 69 through the first week in September was an un-satisfactory performance, however, and owner Charley Finley fired Bauer (the fourth manager to work for Finley in less than three years). Bauer did not manage in the majors thereafter.

**1969-1970 John Francis McNamara**
The best season for the Athletics in 20 years was 1969, when they finished in second place in the West Division. The new manager who was brought in to finish the season was John McNamara, who had never played in the majors and was just beginning what was to be a considerable managerial career. Born in Sacramento on June 4, 1932, McNamara led the team in only the final 13 games of the 1969 season. Since he won eight, the A's did not slip in the standing from second spot. McNamara stayed on throughout 1970 and maintained second spot, but the A's were still nine games out and only two games closer to first place, occupied by the Twins, for the second consecutive year. McNamara directed a 1970 team resplendent with power hitters (four with 20 or more home runs), but not one member of the usual starting line-up hit over .290, and the highest RBI count was 74. McNamara left at the end of 1970 with an 89 and 73 record. In 1974 he began a four-year stint as manager of the San Diego Padres.

**1971-1973 Richard Hirshfield "Dick" Williams**
In a sensational three-year flourish of superiority, the Athletics, under the steady guidance of former Red Sox manager Dick Williams, proceeded to win not only their division by margins of 16, six and six games respectively in each of Williams's years, but

**Top:** *Manager Billy Martin.*
**Opposite:** *Manager Tony LaRussa.*

120

*Manager Dick Williams had much to smile about during his three seasons.*

two World Series as well. The A's, regarded only a few years before as pretenders in designer uniforms and white shoes, had unexpectedly become the bullies of the league.

Williams did not have a chance to fall from first place as manager in Oakland – he was gone after his third year (1973) and his second consecutive World Championship banner. He was immediately snapped up by the Angels.

### 1974-1975 **Alvin Ralph "Blackie" Dark**

After managing the A's and then spending four years in Cleveland, Alvin Dark returned to the Athletics and directed them to their fourth and fifth consecutive pennants and their third World Series conquest. In spite of this impressive performance Dark was gone at the beginning of the 1976 season. A year later he was managing the Padres in San Diego.

### 1976 **Charles William "Chuck" Tanner**

The Athletics' home run count in 1976 was almost 40 fewer than it had been in 1975 (Reggie Jackson had moved to the Angels), and the front line of pitchers was less sturdy (no 20-game winners for the first time in six years). Not surprisingly, the team was not the juggernaut it had come to be through-

out the first half of the 1970s. Despite these problems, former White Sox manager Chuck Tanner completed a strong season – 87 wins – but one strong enough only for second place behind (of all teams) Kansas City. Tanner was not with the A's in 1977, but he was with the Pirates.

### 1977 **John Aloysius "Jack" McKeon**

Two of the Athletics' most formidable pitchers (one of them Vida Blue) tied for the most losses in the league in the 1977 season (19). All the big power hitters had gone somewhere else, and the best team in the American League in the first half of the 1970s came unraveled, finishing dead last. Jack McKeon came to the Athletics from the Kansas City Royals, where he had tallied two second-place finishes in three years (1973 and 1975). McKeon lasted 53 games, winning 26, before being replaced. He would, however, return to the A's.

### 1977-1978 **Bobby Brooks "Winks" Winkles**

Former Angels manager Bobby Winkles won only 37 of the last 108 games in which he managed in 1977, and the team remained in last place in the West Division – where it had been when he took charge and where it had finished the year before. Winkles continued in his post the next year (1978) for the first 38 games and won 23, good enough to move the team one notch up to sixth. Winkles, however, lost his job in May and did not manage in the majors thereafter.

### 1978 **John Aloysius "Jack" McKeon**

Accepting the invitation to come back after an abrupt dismissal the year before, Jack McKeon worked in all but the first 39 games of 1978, the second of three transition years for the Athletics. The team moved out of the cellar to sixth position, only two games behind the White Sox, but McKeon was not invited back and did not manage in the majors again.

### 1979 **Rufus James "Jim" Marshall**

Jim Marshall was the last manager to fall victim to the predatory environment which had come to permeate the Athletics during three glamourless years when they weren't contenders. Marshall had managed the Cubs before coming to Oakland at the age of 49. The Athletics won 54 games and lost 108. Jim Marshall did not manage in the major leagues after working in Oakland.

### 1980-1982 **Alfred Manuel "Billy" Martin**

In a rare three-consecutive-season tenure with the Oakland Athletics, former Yankee manager Billy Martin tantalized fans with a sensational vault into second place in his first season (1980) and with a divisional play-off win over Kansas City at the end of the strike year (1981) – all of this as staging for a precipitous collapse to fifth place in 1982, his last year at Oakland.

Martin had acquired a reputation even before coming to the Athletics for hasty and often brash behavior, followed by not always convincing attempts at rationality. Nevertheless, Martin's impassioned approach to managing riveted fans not only in Oakland, but wherever writers could make him the center of a sensational story.

### 1983-1984 **Stephen "Steve" Boros**

With Steve Boros came a new attitude toward and among the Athletics – no longer associated with personalities and individual idiosyncracies. Boros, born in Flint, Michigan, on September 3, 1936, went to Oakland for his first managing job. A stranger to A's fans and with no reputation to defend or nurture (he had played infield for Detroit, the Cubs and the Reds intermittently from 1957-1965), he had nothing to gain in Oakland but recognition for a good job. His performance was respectable – the team moved up one notch to fourth place during his first year and held the same position in 1984, when he left after 44 games.

### 1984-1986 **Jackie Spencer Moore**

Fourth place was where the Athletics stood when Jackie Moore accepted his first managing job as pilot of the Athletics barely two months into the 1985 season. Moore, born in Jay, Florida, on February 19, 1939, directed the A's for the remaining 118 games of 1984, and the team did not change position, finishing in fourth place. Having played as catcher in 21 games for Detroit in 1965, Moore came to Oakland much as his immediate predecessor had – without any managing history he might have to live up to or explain away.

Moore's first full year was about the same as his first four months and ended with another fourth place in the standings. As a result of losing 44 of the first 73 games in 1986, however, Jackie Moore's managing experience in Oakland ended in June of his third year, with his team in sixth place.

### 1986 Jeffrey Lynn "Jeff" Newman

To stand in while someone more permanent could be found to come to Oakland, Jeff Newman, one-time catcher for the Athletics (1976-82) who had played most recently as back-up catcher for the Red Sox, worked as interim manager. Newman (born September 11, 1948, in Ft. Worth, Texas) directed in only ten games, winning two.

### 1986-1988 Anthony "Tony" LaRussa

An indication of the kind of results that former White Sox manager Tony LaRussa would bring about in Oakland was the team's rapid advance from seventh to third place as a result of the 79 games in which he managed in 1986. The Athletics ended an even .500 in 1987 before posting in 1988 one of the best records of the 1980s in the major leagues (104 wins – tied with Detroit's 1984 total for best in the league through 1988).

LaRussa's Athletics caught the Red Sox in a slump and demolished them in the first sweep in the 1988 American League Championship Series (4-0). Entering the World Series as overwhelming favorites against the Dodgers, the A's explosive hitting suddenly became puny against brilliant Los Angeles pitching; and the mighty Athletics lost the Series in five games. Tony LaRussa, however, was named League Manager of the Year.

# BLUE JAYS
## Toronto (1977-   )

### 1977-1979 Roy Thomas Hartsfield

The American League expanded once again by adding two teams in 1977 – the Seattle Mariners and the Toronto Blue Jays. The Blue Jays thus became the second major league baseball team outside the United States. Ray Hartsfield was appointed the team's first manager. Born on October 25, 1925, in Chattahoochee, Georgia, Hartsfield had had only three years of major league playing experience as a second baseman for the Braves (1950-1952). As was to be expected from an expansion team, the Blue Jays were terrible. Hartsfield led them to three straight last-place finishes – in 1977 (54-107), 1978 (59-102) and 1979 (53-109) – before he was fired.

### 1980-1981 Robert James "Bobby" Mattick

Born on December 5, 1915, in Sioux City, Iowa, Mattick had been a shortstop with the Cubs (1938-1940) and the Reds (1941-1942). In 1980 he carried on the Jays' tradition by leading them to a seventh-place (67-95) finish. Then, in the strike-split 1981 season, he outdid himself by bringing them in in seventh place twice – in the first half-season 16-42, and the second half-season 21-27. Then he was let go.

### 1982-1985 Robert Joe "Bobby" Cox

Cox had been manager of the Braves (1978-1981) before taking over the Blue Jays. In 1982, for the first time in the team's history, he led them out of last place to sixth (78-84). It was fourth (89-73) in 1983 and second (89-73) in 1984. Then, in 1985, Cox brought them in in first place (99-62) – two games ahead of the Yankees. But they lost to the Royals in the League Championship Series, and Cox was gone.

### 1986-1989 James Francis "Jimmy" Williams

Williams, born on October 4, 1943, in Santa Maria, California, had had only 14 games of major league experience as a shortstop-second baseman for the Cardinals (1966-1967) before he took over the reins of the Blue Jays. In 1986 he brought them in in fourth place (86-76), and in 1987 it was a second-place (96-66) finish. In 1988 Williams could lead his team to no better than fourth place (87-75) again. In 1989, after winning 12 and losing 24, Williams was let go.

*Manager Jimmy Williams didn't last out the 1989 season.*

### 1989- Clarence Edwin "Cito" Gaston

Williams' replacement was the Jays' batting coach, Cito Gaston. Born on March 17, 1944, in San Antonion, Gaston had played the outfield for the Braves (1967), Padres (1969-1974), Braves again (1975-1978) and Pirates (1978). At the time he took over, the Jays were in sixth position in the AL East and had lost 15 of their last 18 games.

# BREWERS
## Milwaukee (1970-    )

**Above:** *Manager Harvey Kuenn.*
**Right:** *Manager Tom Trebelhorn.*

### 1970-1972 James David "Dave" Bristol

When the one-year-old Seattle Pilots franchise was moved to Milwaukee after the 1969 season the team was re-christened the Brewers, partly because brewing is the best-known industry in Milwaukee and partly out of deference to the city's old minor league baseball team, the Brewers of the American Association. Dave Bristol, who was appointed manager of the new team, had previously been the manager of the Reds (1966-1969). He was able to bring the team in in fifth place (65-97) in 1970, but it was sixth place (69-92) in 1971. In 1972, with the team in sixth place (10-20) again after 30 games, he was fired. Bristol would reappear as manager of the Braves in 1976.

### 1972 Roy David McMillan

McMillan, born on July 17, 1930, in Bonham, Texas, was a coach when he was brought in as interim manager for two games – which he split. He had been an excellent shortstop with the Reds (1951-1960), the Braves (1961-1964) and the Giants (1964-1966) and would reappear as manager of the Giants in 1975.

### 1972-1975 Delmar Wesley "Del" Crandall

Crandall was born on March 5, 1930, in Ontario, California, and had been a catcher with the Braves (1949-1950, 1953-1963), the Giants (1964), the Pirates (1965) and the Indians (1966). Crandall took over the Brewers in 1972, when they were in sixth place (11-21), but by winning only 54, while losing 70, he was unable to get them out of last place (65-91 overall). Then it was two straight years in fifth place – 1973 (74-88) and 1974 (76-86). In 1975, with the team still in fifth place (67-94) after 161 games, Crandall was fired. He became the Mariners' manager in 1983.

in only ten games in those three years (he was credited with one save), winning none and losing none, and had an astronomical 9.42 earned run average. In 1978 Bamberger was able to take the Brewers to the unaccustomed height of third place (93-69), and then to second place (95-66) in 1979. In 1980 he decided to take some time off from managing, but he was to return during the season.

## 1980 Robert Leroy "Buck" Rodgers

Rodgers was born on August 16, 1938, in Delaware, Ohio, and had been a catcher with the Angels from 1961 to 1969. He took over the managership of the Brewers in 1980, but, after 47 games and with the team in second place (26-21), he took sick leave. He was to return later in the season.

## 1980 George Irvin "Bambi" Bamberger

Bamberger was back to take over the second-place (26-26) Brewers, and he managed them for 92 games, winning 47 and losing 45 and causing them to drop to fourth place (73-66). When Rodgers was ready to come back, and Bamberger bowed out again, only to return as manager of the Mets in 1982.

## 1975 Harvey Edward Kuenn

Kuenn, born on December 4, 1930, in West Allis, Wisconsin, had been a star outfielder and shortstop (he also played third base and first base) for the Tigers (1952-1959), the Indians (1960), the Giants (1961-1965), the Cubs (1965-1966) and the Phillies (1966). He was a Milwaukee coach and was brought in to manage the last game of the 1975 season – which he won. But the team ended up still in fifth place (68-94). Kuenn was to return as manager of the Brewers in 1982.

## 1976-1977 Alexander Peter "Alex" Grammas

Grammas had been the manager of the Pirates in 1969 and was brought in to manage the Brewers in 1976. He was to lead them to two sixth-place finishes in 1976 (66-95) and 1977 (67-95) before he was fired.

## 1978-1980 George Irvin "Bambi" Bamberger

Born on August 1, 1925, on Staten Island, New York, Bamberger had been a right-handed pitcher for the Giants (1951-1952) and the Orioles (1959). But he had appeared

**Above:** *Manager George Bamberger returns to the team in 1980.*
**Opposite top:** *Manager Harvey Kuenn holds a news conference in 1982.*
**Opposite bottom:** *Manager Buck Rodgers in 1982.*

## 1980-1982 **Robert Leroy "Buck" Rodgers**

Rodgers took over the fourth place (73-66) Brewers once again in 1950 and, by winning 13 and losing ten, was able to boost them up to third place (86-76 overall). That was the year that the team hit a phenomenal 203 home runs. Then came the strike-torn 1981 season in which each league had winners of the first half and second half of the season. In the first half of the season the Brewers came in third (31-25), but it was first place (31-22) in the second half – 1½ games ahead of the Red Sox – and that was only because the Brewers won 11 of their last 17 games. In the Divisional Playoffs the Yankees won the first two games, the Brewers won the next two and the Yankees won the final

game. In 1982, after 47 games and with the team in fifth place (23-24), Rodgers was gone. He was to show up in 1985 as the manager of the Twins.

## 1982-1983 **Harvey Edward Kuenn**

Kuenn was back once more in 1982 as the Brewers' manager, taking over a fifth-place (23-24) club and, by winning 72 and losing 43, he had them in first place (95-67) at the end of the season. He was named American League Manager of the Year. With four games to go in the regular season, the Brewers had had a three-game lead over the Orioles, but they had to face them in the final four games. The Orioles won the first three games, the teams were tied and it turned out to be a one-game season. The Brewers won the final game 10-2. The Brewers then met the Cardinals in the World Series and lost four games to three. (In the seven games the two teams had scored 72 runs – 33 for the Brewers and 40 for the Cardinals.) In 1983 Kuenn led the team to a fifth-place (87-75) and was let go. He died on February 28, 1988, in Peoria, Arizona.

## 1984 **Rene Lachemann**

Lachemann had been the manager of the Mariners (1981-1983), and was brought in to manage the Brewers in 1984. He brought them in in last place (67-94) and was fired. He was later a coach for the A's.

## 1985-1986 **George Irvin "Bambi" Bamberger**

Bamberger, after managing the Mets for two years (1982-1983), was back for yet another term as Brewers manager in 1985. But he could manage only a sixth place (71-90) finish that year, and in 1986, after 152 games, the team was still in sixth place (71-81) and Bamberger was gone.

## 1986- **Thomas "Tom" Trebelhorn**

Trebelhorn, born on January 27, 1948, in Portland, Oregon, had had no major league playing experience when he was brought in to finish the 1986 season. With nine games to go, he won six and lost three, but the team stayed in sixth place (77-84 overall). In 1987 he brought them up to third place (91-71), and in 1988 it was third place (87-75) again.

# BROWNS

## St. Louis (1902-1954)

**Above:** *Jimmy McAleer in 1909.*
**Opposite:** *Bamberger changes pitchers.*

## 1902-1909 James Robert "Jimmy" McAleer

McAleer was born on July 10, 1864, in Youngstown, Ohio, and had been a good outfielder for many years before coming to the Browns. He had played for Cleveland of the National League (1889), Cleveland of the Players League (1890), and again for Cleveland of the National League (1891-98). In 1901 he became the player-manager of the Indians, and in 1902 he moved in as Browns manager (he was to put himself in the lineup twice in 1902 and twice in 1907).

In 1902 McAleer brought the Browns in in second place (78-58), the best finish they were to have in many years. Then came two straight sixth-place finishes, in 1903 (65-74) and 1904 (65-87). There was no place to go but down in 1905, and they finished in eighth place (54-99). In 1906 they climbed to fifth (76-73), but it was back to sixth place (69-83) in 1907. The Browns made the first division in 1908, finishing fourth (83-69), but then it was back to seventh again in 1909 (61-89). McAleer was out, and the next year he appeared as manager of the Washington Senators.

## 1910 John Joseph "Jack" "Peach Pie" O'Connor

Born on March 3, 1869, in St. Louis, O'Connor had been a catcher-outfielder-first baseman-shortstop-second baseman-third baseman for many years with Cincinnati of the American Association (1887-1888), Columbus of the American Association (1889-1891), the Indians (1892-1898), the Cardinals (1899), the Pirates (1899-1902) and the New York Highlanders (1904, 1906-1907). He came to the Browns as manager in 1910 and brought them in in last place (47-107). That was the year that Nap Lajoie of the Indians and Ty Cobb of the Tigers were engaged in a tight battle for the batting title. Cobb eventually won the title, but O'Connor was accused of having his pitchers take it easy on Lajoie so that he could win the batting honors, and O'Connor was kicked out of the league by Ban Johnson, the president of the American League. O'Connor died on November 14, 1937, in St. Louis.

## 1911-1912 Roderick John "Bobby" "Rhody" Wallace

Wallace, who was born on November 4, 1873, in Pittsburgh, was to become a Hall of Fame (1953) player – at shortstop, third base, second base, first base and in the outfield (he even pitched in 57 games) for Cleveland in the National League (1894-

*A picture of John O'Connor taken in 1899.*

1898) and the Cardinals (1899-1901). He joined the Browns as a player in 1902. Wallace took over the player-manager role with the Browns in 1911, but was able to do no better than eighth place (45-107). It was eighth place again after 39 games (12-27) in 1912, and Wallace was relieved of his managerial duties, but he was kept on to play in the field until 1916. In 1937 he was appointed manager of the Reds.

## 1912-1913 George Thomas "Firebrand" Stovall

Stovall had been the manager of the Indians in 1911 and had managed to bring them in in third. He joined the Browns as manager in 1911 when the team was in eighth place (12-27). By winning 41 and losing 74 he was able to steer them to seventh place (53-101 overall). But in 1913, with the team still in seventh place (50-84) after 134 games, he was let go, only to show up in 1914 as the manager of the Kansas City Club of the Federal League, where he brought them in sixth (67-84) in 1914 and fourth (81-72) in 1915. Stovall died on November 5, 1951, in Burlington, Iowa.

## 1913 James Philip "Jimmy" "Pepper" Austin

Austin was born on December 8, 1879, in Swansea, Wales, and had played third base for the New York Highlanders (1909-1910) before he was traded to the Browns in 1911. As a stopgap maneuver, he was put in to be the player-manager of the seventh-place team in 1913. He managed for a mere eight games, winning two and losing six, and the Browns fell to eighth place. He, too, was fired, but continued playing in the field.

## 1913-1915 Wesley Branch "The Mahatma" Rickey

With the Browns in last place (52-90), Rickey was appointed manager in 1913. There were only 11 games left in the season. He won five and lost six, but the Browns stayed in last place. Rickey, born on December 20, 1881, in Lucasville, Ohio, had been a catcher with the Browns (1905-1906) and with the New York Highlanders

*A young Branch Rickey.*

*Manager George Sisler.*

(1907). In 1914 he was able to raise the club to fifth place (71-82), and he even appeared as a catcher in two games. But in 1915 it was back to sixth place (63-91), and Rickey was gone. He would resurface in 1919 as manager of the Cardinals.

### 1916-1918 Fielder Allison Jones

Jones had been the manager of the White Sox (1904-1908) and St. Louis in the Federal League (1914-1915) before he took over the Browns in 1916. That year he was able to guide them to a fifth-place (79-75) finish, but it was seventh place (57-97) in 1917. In 1918, with the club in fifth place (23-24), he was let go. Jones died on March 13, 1934, in Portland, Oregon.

### 1918 James Philip "Jimmy" "Pepper" Austin

Austin was again brought in to put his finger in the dike. He managed for 14 games, winning six and losing eight, while the team fell from fifth to sixth (29-32). Austin went back to playing third base and shortstop.

### 1918-1920 James Timothy "Jimmy" "Sunset Jimmy" Burke

Burke had been the manager of the Cardinals in 1905. He inherited the sixth-place Browns in 1918 and was able to raise them to fifth place by winning 29 and losing 32 (58-64 overall). In 1919 it was another fifth-

place (67-72) finish, and in 1920 the club ended in fourth place – back in the first division (76-77) – but Burke was let go. He died on March 26, 1942, in St. Louis.

### 1921-1923 Leo Alexander "Lee" Fohl

Fohl had been a moderately successful manager with the Indians (1915-1919) before coming to the Browns. He performed a minor miracle (for the Browns, that is) by bringing the team in in third place (81-73) in 1921. He then compounded the miracle in 1922 by finishing second (93-61). But the team fell to third place (51-49) after 100 games in 1923, and Fohl was ousted. He was to turn up the next year as the manager of the Red Sox.

### 1923 James Philip "Jimmy" "Pepper" Austin

With 52 games to go in the 1923 season, Austin was once again brought in as a stop-gap manager. He inherited a third-place club and fell with them to fifth place by winning 23 and losing 29, giving them a 74-78 overall record. He left the club but returned to coach and also play third base for three games – one in 1925, one in 1926 and one in 1929. Austin died on March 6, 1965, in Laguna Beach, California.

### 1924-1926 George Harold "Gorgeous George" Sisler

Sisler, born on March 24, 1893, in Man-

chester, Ohio, was elected to the Hall of Fame as a player in 1939. Mainly a first baseman, he played for the Browns from 1915 to 1922 and was brought back in 1924 to become the player-manager of the team. He did bring them in in fourth place (74-78) in 1924, and he even made it to third place (82-71) in 1925. But in 1926 it was back to seventh place (62-92), and Sisler returned to being a full-time first baseman for the Browns in 1927. He was traded to the Senators (1928), then went to the Braves (1928-1930). Sisler, the father of two major league stars, Dick and Dave, died on March 26, 1973, in Richmond Heights, Missouri.

### 1927-1929 Daniel Philip "Dan" "Dapper Dan" Howley

Howley was born on October 16, 1885, in Weymouth, Massachusetts, and had been a catcher who had played only 26 games in the major leagues – with the Phillies in 1913. He was able to do no more than finish in seventh place (59-94) in 1927, but in 1928 he brought the team in in third (82-72). The Browns fell to fourth place (79-73) in 1929, and Howley went to manage the Reds in 1930.

### 1930-1933 William Lavier "Bill" "Reindeer Bill" Killefer

Killefer had been a mediocre manager with the Cubs (1921-1925), and things didn't get much better when he took over the reins of the Browns in 1930. In 1930 he brought them in in sixth place (64-90), and in 1931 it was fifth (63-91). Then it was back to sixth place (63-91) in 1932, and, after 93 games in 1933 and with the club in the cellar (34-59), Killefer was fired. He died on July 2, 1960, in Elsmere, Delaware.

### 1933 Allen Sutton Sothoron

Once again the Browns brought in a stop-gap manager Sothoron, born on April 29, 1893, in Bradford, Ohio, had been a big league right-handed pitcher for 11 years with the Browns (1914-1921), the Red Sox (1921), the Indians (1921-1922) and the Cardinals (1924-1926). With the Browns in eighth place (34-59), he managed for only four games – winning one and losing three – and the club was still in the cellar. That ended his managing career. Sothoron died on June 17, 1939, in St. Louis.

**Opposite:** *Manager Bill Killefer (l.) with Walter Johnson.*

**1933-1937 Rogers "Rajah" Hornsby**
Hornsby was called in to finish the 1933 season, with the Browns in last place (35-62). He had been the manager of the Cardinals (1925-1926), the Braves (1928) and the Cubs (1930-1932). He was able to win only 20, while losing 34, in 1933, and the Browns ended last (55-96 overall). In 1934 the Browns finished in sixth place (67-85), and it was seventh place (65-87) in 1935 and 1936 (57-95). In 1936, with the Browns in eighth place (25-50), Hornsby was fired, only to return to the Browns in 1952.

**Left:** *Player-manager Rogers Hornsby in 1936.*
**Right:** *Manager Gabby Street (l.) coaches Vito Tamulis – 1938.*

**1937 James LeRoy "Jim" "Sunny Jim" Bottomley**
With 79 games to go and the Browns in last place, Bottomley was brought in to finish the season. This Hall of Fame (1974) first baseman, born on April 23, 1900, in Oglesby, Illinois, had played for the Cardinals (1922-1932), the Reds (1933-1935) and the Browns (1936-1937) and carried a .310 lifetime batting average. He was able to win only 21, while losing 58, and the club ended up in last place (46-108 overall), at which point Bottomley was out. He died on December 11, 1959, in St. Louis.

**Left:** *Manager Luke Sewell.*

was back to sixth (72-80) in 1943, and then came the miracle.

In 1944, for the first time (and the last time) in their history, the Browns won the pennant, clinching it by one game in the final contest of the season after a knock-down-drag-out fight with the Tigers for the flag. In the World Series – called "The Trolley Series" because both St. Louis teams were in it – the Browns lost to the Cardinals four games to two. Sewell led the Browns to third place in 1945 – that war year when most of the healthy ball players were in service. Indeed, one of walking wounded on the St. Louis team that year was an outfielder named Pete Gray, who had but one arm, yet still managed to bat .218. In 1946, with the Browns in seventh place (53-71) after 124 games, Sewell was gone – to resurface in 1949 as the manager of the Reds.

### 1946 James Wren "Zack" Taylor

Taylor, born on July 27, 1898, in Yulee, Florida, had been a catcher in the major leagues for 16 years, with the Dodgers (1920-1925), the Braves (1926-1927), the Giants (1927), the Braves again (1928-1929), the Cubs (1929-1933), the Yankees (1934) and the Dodgers again (1935). He was brought in to finish the last 30 games as Browns manager and won 13, while losing 17. The Browns stayed in seventh place (66-88 overall). He was let go but would return to the club in 1948.

### 1947 Herold Dominic "Muddy" Ruel

Ruel was born on February 20, 1896, in St. Louis, and had been a catcher for the Browns (1915), the Yankees (1917-1920), the Red Sox (1921-1922), the Senators (1923-1930), the Red Sox again (1931), the Tigers (1931-1932), the Browns again (1933) and the White Sox (1934). Like so many other Browns managers, he brought the team in in last place (59-95) in 1947 and was let go. Ruel died on November 13, 1963, in Palo Alto, California.

### 1948-1951 James Wren "Zack" Taylor

Taylor was back in 1948 to pick up the pieces and, in a way, he did – at least the club came in sixth (59-94). Then came two consecutive seventh-place finishes – 1949 (53-101) and 1950 (58-96). In 1951 the Browns finished in the cellar (52-102) again, and Taylor was fired. The highlight of that

### 1938 Charles Evard "Gabby" "Old Sarge" Street

Street had been a fair manager with the Cardinals (1929-1933) before he was called in to take over the Browns in 1938. But that year the club finished in seventh place (55-97) and Street was fired. He died on February 6, 1951, in Joplin, Missouri.

### 1939-1941 Fred Girard "Pudge" Haney

Haney, born on April 25, 1898, in Albuquerque, New Mexico, had been a good first baseman with the Tigers (1922-1925), the Red Sox (1926-1927), the Cubs (1927) and the Cardinals (1929). Haney continued the Browns' losing tradition, coming in eighth (43-11) in 1939, sixth (67-87) in 1940,

and, with the club in seventh (15-29) again in 1941, he was let go. He would return to managing in 1953, with the Pirates.

### 1941-1946 James Luther "Luke" Sewell

Sewell was born on January 5, 1905, in Titus, Alabama, and had been a catcher in the American League for 19 years before he joined the Browns, playing for the Indians (1921-1932), the Senators (1933-1934), the White Sox (1935-1938) and the Indians again (1939). He took over the Braves when they were in seventh place (15-29) and, by winning 55 and losing 55, he was able to lift them to sixth place (70-84 overall). Amazingly, he brought the Browns in in an unaccustomed third place (82-69) in 1942. It

**Above:** *Three views of Marty Marion.*
**Top right:** *General and Mrs. Douglas MacArthur, Casey Stengel and Zack Taylor.*

miserable season was the appearance of Eddie Gaedel. On August 20, at the urging of club President Bill Veeck, Taylor inserted Gaedel into the lineup as a pinch hitter. The unusual thing about it was that Gaedel was a midget – only three feet, seven inches high. After screams from the Browns' opponents, the Tigers, a valid contract was produced and Gaedel was allowed to bat. He marched up to the plate wearing Number 1/8. Bob Cain, the Detroit pitcher, could not find Eddie's tiny strike zone and walked him in four pitches. Gaedel took first, was replaced by a pinch runner and never made another appearance in a baseball uniform. Taylor died on July 6, 1974, in Orlando, Florida.

### 1952 Rogers "Rajah" Hornsby

Hornsby was brought back to manage at the beginning of the 1952 season. But after 50 games, with the Browns in seventh place (22-28), he left to manage the Reds.

### 1952-1953 Martin Whitford "Marty" "Slats" "The Octopus" Marion

Marion had been the manager of the Cardinals in 1951 and came to the Browns in 1952 to finish the season for them. The club was in seventh (22-28) after 50 games, and he was able to win only 42 games, while losing 62. The Braves ended in seventh place (64-90 overall). The team was really bad. Ned Garver, the star pitcher of the club, was also their best hitter. And the crowds were pitifully small. Garver said, "The crowd didn't boo us because we had them outnumbered." Nineteen fifty-three was still another miserable year. In that year the Browns had lost 14 games in a row. Marion ran into sportswriter Milt Richman of the UPI in the clubhouse. Marion was so discouraged that he handed Richman his empty line-up card and said, "Here, you make it out." Richman declined, but Marion was insistent. "Pick out any one you like." Richman did, and the Browns won the game. The Browns finished last (54-100) once again that year, and Marion was on his way to a better managerial job with the White Sox. He wasn't the only one to leave. The Browns themselves were also on the move – the franchise was transferred, as the Orioles, to Baltimore (which had had an American League team, also known as the Orioles, in 1901-2).

# INDIANS
## Cleveland (1901- )

## Called **BLUES** (1901)

### 1901 **James Robert "Jimmy" McAleer**

Amid skepticism that the new American League could provide the kind of competition Cleveland was accustomed to seeing from the old National League, former outfielder Jimmy McAleer (born in Youngstown, Ohio, on July 10, 1864) struggled to assemble a respectable team. But the Blues finished next to last in their opening year. McAleer afterwards took a position managing the Browns.

## Called **BRONCHOS** (1902-1904)

### 1902-1904 **William R "Bill" Armour**

Desperate to enlist capable players, Bill Armour persuaded a *Cleveland Plain Dealer* writer on one occasion to announce openings for pitchers who might be qualified. One of the applicants, a lean left-hander from a semi-professional team in central Ohio, pitched his first game against the Senators the day he signed. Eventually Otto Hess became a 20-game winner.

Armour, who had never played in the majors, directed the Bronchos (changed from Blues in the team's first spring training camp) through three .500-plus seasons, but he led them to a position no better than third in 1903. Armour, born on September 3, 1869, in Homestead, Pennsylvania, closed 1904, his last season in Cleveland, with the team in fifth spot, although writers had earlier selected them to rival the Red Sox as the league's best. He went on to manage Detroit the following year.

## Called **NAPS** (1905-1914)

### 1905-1909 **Napoleon "Larry", "Nap" Lajoie**

Graced with extraordinary abilities as a player and enormously popular with fans, Nap Lajoie came to Cleveland as a returned favor from Connie Mack to owner Charley Somers. Lajoie's brilliance in the infield, at

*Nap Lajoie as a player.*

the plate and as strategist quickly won him devotion in Cleveland, to the extent that the team nickname became the "Naps."

Alas, Lajoie's achievements as player did not improve the team's performance. In Nap's first year managing and playing the Naps ended in fifth place, the slot they had held the year before when Bill Armour quit, unable to work with Lajoie.

A Rhode Islander, born on September 5, 1875, in Woonsocket, Lajoie missed winning the pennant by one-half game in 1908, but the next year a sixth place in the standings in August was intolerable for the perfectionist and impatient Lajoie, and he resigned as manager. He continued playing,

though, with the same elan that had become his trademark. One of the original inductees into the Hall of Fame (1937), Lajoie lived to be 85, dying on February 7, 1959, in Daytona Beach, Florida.

### 1909-1911 **James Thomas "Deacon" McGuire**

After completing the 1909 sixth-place season begun by Nap Lajoie, Deacon McGuire, who had been managing the Red Sox the year before, was able to advance the Naps only one position, to fifth, in his first (and last) full season in 1910. Target of unflattering newspaper stories, McGuire's Cleveland teams received the nickname "Molly McGuires." Before he resigned early in the 1911 season, with the team mired in fifth place, McGuire could, however, claim the distinction of having managed in Cleveland's first Sunday game (May 11, 1911). Also, he had had the privilege of working with "Shoeless" Joe Jackson the year he entered the major leagues. McGuire did not manage in the big leagues after 1911. He died on October 31, 1936, in Albion, Michigan.

### 1911 **George Thomas "Firebrand" Stovall**

With the aid of Joe Jackson's hitting former first baseman George Stovall moved a team with only six wins in its first 17 games in 1911 into third place by season's end. Cleveland fans were outraged to learn, however, that Missouri-born Stovall (Independence, November 23, 1878) was never intended by owner Somers to work as manager of the Naps after 1911. He went on to manage in St. Louis the following year.

### 1912 **Harry "Jasper" Davis**

Entering Cleveland amid the anger of fans and players who felt George Stovall should continue managing, former first baseman Harry Davis did not complete the 1912 season, but quit in August with the team in sixth place. Davis, born in Philadelphia on July 10, 1873, did not manage in the major leagues again. He died on August 11, 1947, in Philadelphia.

### 1912-1915 Joseph Lee "Joe" "Dode" Birmingham

Unintimidated by Nap Lajoie, outfielder Joe Birmingham instead benched him in June, 1913, when he wasn't hitting. He then directed the Naps to third place in his first full season. Birmingham was unable, though, to prevent the team's worst showing in history when, in 1914, they won only 51 games and lost the support of loyalists. In May, 1915, owner Somers sacked Birmingham, (born on August 6, 1884 in Elmira, New York). He did not manage in the major leagues after 1915, and he died on April 24, 1946, in Tampico, Mexico.

## Called INDIANS (1915-present)

### 1915-1919 Leo Alexander "Lee" Fohl

Entering Cleveland's baseball history at a momentous time, former catcher Lee Fohl watched as, during the space of a few months, the team changed owners and name, becoming the Indians after Somers traded the embittered Nap Lajoie. A third change eventually became the most influential in the Indians' performance over the next decade. Adept at recognizing and making use of a player's natural abilities, Fohl readily sealed a bond with a brilliant outfielder acquired from the Red Sox, Tris Speaker.

Fohl, born on November 28, 1970, in Lowell, Ohio, and Speaker worked together almost as though they were co-managers – to the point that Speaker sometimes influenced the manager's choice of starting pitcher. Meanwhile, fans responded to the change by returning to watch the Indians – 21,000 on opening day of 1917, the largest first-day attendance in Cleveland's history. Fohl's term with the Indians ended, however, when he resigned after Babe Ruth hit one of his longest recorded home runs to beat the Indians in the ninth inning of a crucial game for first place about half way through the 1919 season. He returned to managing in 1921 in St. Louis.

### 1919-1926 Tristram E "Tris" "The Gray Eagle" "Spoke" Speaker

When Tris Speaker learned that he had been named new Indians manager upon the resignation of Lee Fohl, he protested that he preferred playing the outfield to managing. Under Spoke the Indians won 39 of the remaining 60 games of 1919 and overtook

the Yankees to finish 3½ games behind the White Sox.

1920 was the year of dismay in Chicago and throughout much of baseball after news of the 1919 World Series scandal, but it was a season of jubilation for Cleveland fans. The Indians won 98 games, the pennant, and the World Series in Tris Speaker's first complete season. The Texan (born on April 4, 1888, in Hubbard) had only two more strong years – second place in 1921 and second again in his last year managing in the major leagues, 1926. Speaker was elected to the Hall of Fame in 1937, notwithstanding allegations that he had participated in the scheme to blow the 1919 Series. He died on December 8, 1958, in Lake Whitney, Texas.

### 1927 Jack McCallister

Less attention went to Jack McCallister's sixth-place 1927 season than to rumors about causes of Tris Speaker's suspicious resignation in December the year before. McCallister (born on January 19, 1879, in Marietta, Ohio) had never played in the majors and did not manage in the major leagues after his year with the Indians. He died on October 18, 1946.

### 1928-1933 Roger Thorpe Peckinpaugh

Elected to manage the Indians in 1928 almost by birthright, and not necessarily on merit, Roger Peckinpaugh was one of a host of candidates considered for the job. Peckinpaugh, however, had entered the big leagues in Cleveland directly from a high school in the city (though he was born in Wooster, Ohio, on February 5, 1891), and,

having had some managerial experience with the Yankees in 1914, held a decided edge on the other nominees at a time when new owners were Clevelanders. Peckinpaugh discovered soon that civic pride and cash were not substitutes for promising players: the 1928 team finished seventh. Next year's third place inflated hopes that the Indians were becoming a team with a future, but fourth-place closings in 1930 and 1931 exasperated the millionaire owners, who continued to spend with abandon. Fans became disillusioned, despite the dedication of an extravagant new park named Cleveland Stadium with 80,000 seats. Early in June, 1933, the team president announced that the fans had decided it was time for a new manager, and "Peck" was let go for the remainder of the 1930s (he would return in 1941).

### 1933-1935 Walter Perry "The Big Train" "Barney" Johnson

Six years after retiring from pitching and compiling 416 wins (second best in major league history), Walter Johnson came to Cleveland after a managerial stint in Washington. His hitters were no more able to produce runs, however, than were the others who had rattled around in the enormous Cleveland Stadium, where the league's best hitters fumed when a 400-foot drive was not long enough to clear the centerfield wall. The Indians' hitting averages plummeted 50 to 100 points, but Johnson's 1934 team finished third some-

**Above:** *Manager Roger Peckinpaugh.*
**Top:** *Manager Tris Speaker.*
**Opposite:** *Walter Johnson, scout Joe Engel.*

how, even though the players quarrelled with the unyielding manager and among themselves. In his last season at Cleveland, and as a big league manager, Johnson lost his job after the first 96 games, with the team in fifth spot. He died on December 10, 1946, in Washington, DC, having been elected to the Hall of Fame in 1936.

## 1935-1937 Stephen Francis "Steve" O'Neill

Arriving two-thirds of the way into the 1935 season, former catcher Steve O'Neill improved the team's performance and advanced its position in the standings from fifth to third. Nevertheless, an 80-win 1936 season in 1936 brought no better than fifth place; and in his last year at Cleveland, the Pennsylvanian (born on July 6, 1891, in Minooka) directed the Indians to 83 victories, but only fourth place. He next showed up managing the Tigers in 1943.

## 1938-1940 Oscar "Ossie" Vitt

In small increments the Indians' winning percentage improved under Ossie Vitt, and in 1940 the team lost the pennant in a final series with Detroit. Vitt had earned a reputation for feverish playing at third base while with the Tigers (1912-1918), and he promised to build a fire under the Indians on the occasion when he formally accepted his appointment. "Ol' Os" did stir up the team – but not always productively when he leaked accounts of problems within their ranks. Vitt's continued abrasive behavior cost him the few remaining loyalties there were in his final season managing in the major leagues. Vitt was born in San Francisco on January 4, 1890. He died in Oakland, California, on January 31, 1963.

## 1941 Roger Thorpe Peckinpaugh

Elected to secure the elusive pennant lost to Detroit the year before, Roger Peckinpaugh, fired eight years earlier, directed a team that remained contenders through June, but fell to four games under .500 by season's close. Peckinpaugh received a promotion to a front office job and did not manage again; he died on November 17, 1977, in Cleveland.

## 1942-1950 Louis "Lou" Boudreau

A mere 24 years old when offered the position of Indians manager, Lou Boudreau had already lived enough episodes to qualify for a Horatio Alger hero. An all-state high school athlete in Illinois (born in Harvey, Illinois, on July 17, 1917), young Boudreau received a modest financial aid college scholarship, but lost his eligibility when he accepted $100 a month from the Indians while still in school.

He left after his junior year and became a shortstop with the Indians in 1938. Four years later, as manager and player, he again became victim of misfortune when his team was decimated by the wartime draft. Boudreau managed the team through the discouraging war period when the Indians were not competitive, finishing fifth in 1944 and 1945.

Within three seasons, though (1946-1948), the Indians under Boudreau advanced from sixth to pennant winners and then World Champions. Boudreau (Hall of Fame, 1970) led Cleveland to 89 victories in 1949 and 92 in his last year with the Tribe, but they ended in third and fourth places respectively. In 1952 Lou became the manager of the Red Sox.

### 1951-1956 Alfonso Raymond "Al" Lopez

Ranking ninth in all-time winning percentage for managers, former catcher Al Lopez worked six years in Cleveland, and they were brilliant years. His Indians averaged better than 93 wins per season and a .616 winning percentage. A single rival pre-

**Opposite:** *Al Lopez argues.*
**Below:** *Bob Feller (l.), Lou Boudreau.*

vented the Indians from dominating the league during most of Lopez's term – the Yankees, during some of Casey Stengel's best years.

The Indians crushed the Yankees and outclassed every other team in the league in 1954, however, with 111 wins – the most for any team in league history. In a bitter disappointment, however, Leo Durocher's Giants swept the World Series.

Born on August 20, 1908, in Tampa, Florida, Lopez had come to Cleveland at a time when the team was its strongest since the years of Tris Speaker. Their poorest showing under Lopez was in his last year, when they won 88 games, but finished

second – again to Stengel's Yankees. Al Lopez, who went on to manage the White Sox in 1957, was elected to the Hall of Fame in 1977.

### 1957 Major Kerby Farrell

Struggling through a season when most of the names who had led the league only three years earlier in hitting and pitching were either gone or achieving below expectations, former first baseman Kerby Farrell (born in Leapwood, Tennessee on September 3, 1913), in his only year managing a big-league team, led the Indians to a sixth-place conclusion. Farrell died in Nashville on December 17, 1975.

### 1958 Robert Randall "Bobby" Bragan

Called on to stop the hemorrhaging that had begun the year before, Bobby Bragan, who had earlier managed the Pirates, worked only 67 games, winning 36 for fifth spot by early June before being released. He became Milwaukee's manager in 1963.

### 1958-1960 Joseph Lowell "Joe," "Flash" Gordon

Working in the last two-thirds of the 1958 season, former second baseman Joe Gordon sustained the improvement begun by Bobby Bragan and elevated the Indians one more notch to fourth. Continued advancement under the Californian (Los Angeles, born on February 18, 1915) in his first full year of managing produced a second-place finish in 1959. The ascent did not continue, however, and in Gordon's final opportunity in Cleveland, the first 95 games of 1960, the

Indians dropped to fourth. Gordon became the Tigers's manager that year.

### 1960 Joyner Clifford "Jo-Jo" White

Standing in for a single game in August, 1960, former outfielder Jo-Jo White (born on June 1, 1909, in Red Oak, Georgia) directed the Indians to a victory. White did not manage in the major leagues again. He died on October 9, 1986.

### 1960-1961 James Joseph "Jimmy" Dykes

Jimmy Dykes came to Cleveland from Detroit to work in the last 58 games of the 1960 season, leading the team to 26 wins and a fourth-place finish. He managed in all but the final game in 1961, when the Indians fell to fifth. Dykes died in Philadelphia on June 15, 1967.

### 1961 Melvin "Mel", "Chief" "Wimpy" Harder

Assigned the inglorious task of closing a dismal 1961 season, former pitcher Mel Harder, a native Nebraskan (born on October 15, 1909, in Beemer), directed the Indians in their final game – a loss that maintained them in fifth place. That was Harder's only appearance as a manager.

### 1962 Fred Melvin "Mel" McGaha

Even though the Indians under Mel McGaha, who had never played in the majors, won more games than they had each of the previous two seasons, they fell further in the standings to sixth. McGaha, born in Bastrop, Louisiana, 26 September, 1926, not surprisingly did not manage the Indians the next year, but he did turn up managing the A's in 1964.

### 1963-1966 George Robert "Birdie" Tebbetts

In Tebbetts' first year managing the Indians (he had come to them after a two-year stint of managing in Milwaukee), Cleveland finished the season with the league's second-lowest team hitting average and fourth-lowest pitching ERA, an achievement that won them fifth place. An identical record (79-83) in Tebbetts' second year produced sixth place, the second time in three years. Pitching improved in 1965 (Sam McDowell's 2.18 ERA was the league's best), but even Rocky Colavito's league-leading 108 RBI's could not keep the Indians out of fifth. Through September, 1966, the Tribe held fifth place again; and Tebbetts did not complete the season nor did he direct a major league team again.

### 1966 George Bevan "Bo" Strickland

Louisianan George Strickland, born on January 10, 1926, in New Orleans, had played shortstop and various bases for the Indians from 1953-1960 and was coaching when he was asked to manage in the remaining 39 games of 1966. The team won 15 and held onto fifth place. Strickland never managed thereafter.

### 1967 Joseph Wilbur "Joe" Adcock

The 1967 Indians lost only six more games under new manager Joe Adcock, a former first baseman, than they had the year before, but those six additional defeats dropped them to eighth place. Adcock, born in Coushatta, Louisiana, on October 30, 1927, did not manage again.

### 1968-1971 Alvin Ralph "Al" "Blackie" Dark

The 1968 Indians under Alvin Dark (brought over from managing in Kansas City) actually dropped in team hitting, and with one exception (Luis Tiant's brilliant 21-9 record and league-winning 1.60 ERA) pitching did not improve radically; yet the team surged to third after closing the year before in eighth.

In an absolute inversion, in 1969 (when the leagues divided into east and west contingents) Cleveland ended not only last in their division, but with the worst record in the league. No one player was accountable, but Tiant's record was 9-20 with an ERA of 3.71. Dark's last two years with Cleveland were equally disappointing and, after only 42 wins through early August in 1971, he was forced to look for a job managing elsewhere – which turned out to be Oakland, in 1974.

### 1971 John Joseph "Johnny" "Skids" Lipon

Born not far from Cleveland (Martin's Ferry, on November 10, 1922) former shortstop Johnny Lipon had never played for the Indians, but he did manage them – in the last 59 games of 1971, winning 18. "Skids" did not return the next year, nor did he manage in the major leagues again.

### 1972-1974 Kenneth Joseph "Ken" Aspromonte

The only offensive strength Cleveland could claim in former infielder Ken Aspromonte's first year managing was Chris Chambliss' .292 season hitting average – almost a full 40 points above the team's second best. Gaylord Perry's 24 wins were the league's best and did help lift the Indians out of last place in their division, but only for 1972. In 1973, the first 162-game season, Aspromonte's Indians

finished in their familiar sixth (last) place. And not withstanding a rally strong enough for fourth place, 1974 was the last season managing in the major leagues for the Brooklyn-born (September 22, 1931) Aspromonte.

### 1975-1977 Frank Robinson

Bearing the responsibility not only of bringing back a Cleveland team that had gone through an extended dry spell (21 years since the last pennant), but also of working under the scrutiny of the entire country as the major leagues' first black manager, Frank Robinson had not much to gain and a great deal to lose if he did not perform heroically.

Robinson, who was born in Beaumont, Texas, on August 31, 1935, had carved some impressive numbers for himself as an outfielder for Cincinnati and Baltimore. (He was the only player, for example, to win Most Valuable Player in both leagues.) As manager of the Indians, Robinson was not able to move the team any closer than fourth, but he at least kept them out of last place in his two full seasons. But he lost his chance to continue after 57 games in 1977, with the team back in sixth. Four years later he would be managing in San Francisco. He entered the Hall of Fame in 1982.

### 1977-1979 Jeffrey Allen "Jeff" Torborg

Completing Frank Robinson's 1977 season, former catcher Jeff Torborg was able to elevate the Indians from last place in their division to fifth. Born in Plainfield, New Jersey, on November 26, 1941, Torborg improved Cleveland's winning percentage in his first complete year, but the team still finished 21 games below .500 and in sixth spot in 1978. Forty-three wins in the first 95 games in 1979 was a further improvement, but it was still too little. Torborg lost his position with the Indians. Ten years later he was appointed manager of the White Sox.

### 1979-1982 David "Dave" Garcia

Under Dave Garcia, brought over from the Angels to reverse a season that had begun woefully, the Indians won 38 of their last 66 games in 1979 and ended the year one game

man Mike Ferraro (born on August 14, 1944, in Kingston, New York) led the team to 40 wins in their first 100 games in 1983, a last-place performance, at which point he was let go.

### 1983-1987 Patrick "Pat", "Ike" Corrales

When Pat Corrales arrived in Cleveland from Philadelphia, where he had managed the Phillies, there were little more than two months left in the season in 1983, and the Indians had come to represent the soft spot in the schedule for the rest of the league. Playing almost .500 for the 62 games in which Corrales managed, the team was still unable to move from the last spot. Proving that there was still life in a team that was now eliciting sympathy as an underdog, the Tribe finished ahead of the Brewers for sixth place in 1984; but only 60 victories the next year cancelled any doubts about the Indians' ineptitude. Corrales (born on March 20, 1941, in Los Angeles, California) nevertheless stayed on and completed the 1986 season, the first year above .500 since 1981. But a dreadful 31-56 pace through the middle of July 1987, concluded Corrales' term in Cleveland. He became a Yankee coach in 1989.

### 1987- Howard "Doc" Edwards

With little to lose (except the humiliation of getting kicked around by the rest of the league), Cleveland Indians planners chose an untested name to complete the 1987 season. Doc Edwards, born on December 10, 1937, in Varney, West Virginia, had played as stand-in catcher in 317 games in both leagues over five years from 1962 through 1970. After winning 30 of the 75 games in which he managed in 1987, Edwards began to mobilize old-time Cleveland baseball fever when the Indians started commandingly in 1988 and doggedly continued to be among the division leaders through May. Dishearteningly, they played in the season's second half much as the Indians teams of the past decade had played and ended in sixth place. The team's pugnacity at the beginning of the 1988 season had roused hopes for 1989, but again the year proved to be a disappointment.

over .500. Had they played as well throughout the season they would have finished in third place instead of sixth. Garcia's teams finished last each of the next three years, however, (except for fifth the second half of strike-split 1981) and he lost his position at the end of the 1982 season.

### 1983 Michael Dennis "Mike" Ferraro

Only one team in the American League East struggled more than Cleveland in the first years after expansion in 1977 – Toronto, the new franchise. As evidence of the Indians' struggles, former third base-

Left: *Jeff Torborg argues – 1977.*
**Opposite top left:** *Robinson discusses.*
**Opposite top right:** *Torborg discusses.*
**Opposite bottom left:** *Dave Garcia.*
**Opposite bottom right:** *Pat Corrales.*

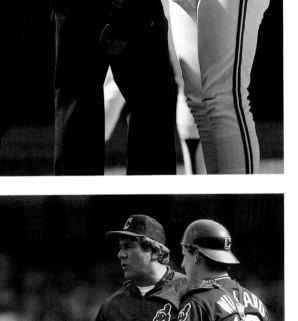

# MARINERS
## Seattle (1977-   )

## 1977-1980 **Darrell Dean Johnson**

The Blue Jays and the Mariners were the new American League teams in the expansion year of 1977, and Johnson was selected to manage the Mariners. He had been the manager of the Red Sox (1974-1976), and had done a quite respectable job, finishing first once and third twice. But the Mariners were, after all, an expansion team, and so he was able only to lead them to sixth place (64-98) in 1977. It was last place (56-104) in 1978 and sixth place (67-95) in 1979. In 1980, after 104 games and with the team in last place (39-65) again, he was fired. Johnson would turn up as manager of the Rangers in 1982.

## 1980-1981 **Maurice Morning "Maury" Wills**

Born on October 2, 1932, in Washington, DC, Wills had been an outstanding short-stop-third baseman for the Dodgers (1959-1966), the Pirates (1967-1968), the Expos (1969) and the Dodgers again (1969-1972).

For six years he had led the league in stolen bases and ended his career with 586 regular-season thefts and a .281 batting average. He took over a seventh-place (39-65) club in

1980 and, by winning 20 and losing 38, he kept them in last place (59-103 overall). In 1981 the Mariners were still in seventh place (6-18) after 24 games, and Wills was let go.

## 1981-1983 **Rene George Lachemann**

Lachemann, born on May 4, 1945, in Los Angeles, had been a catcher with the Athletics (1965-1966) and the A's (1968). He took over the last-place (6-18) Mariners in 1981, that strike-ridden year, and he was able to lead them to a sixth-place (21-36 overall) finish in the first half of the season by winning 15 and losing 18. In the second half of the season he brought them in in fifth (23-29). It was fourth place (76-86) in 1982, but in 1983, after 73 games and with the Mariners in seventh place (26-47), he was fired. Lachemann would manage the Brewers in 1984.

## 1983-1984 **Delmar Wesley "Del" Crandall**

Crandall had been the manager of the Brew-

146

ers (1972-1975) and was brought in in 1983 to manage the Mariners in mid-season, when they were in seventh place (26-47). By winning only 34, while losing 55, he kept them in last place (60-102 overall). In 1984, after 135 games, the Mariners were still in seventh place (59-76), and Crandall was fired.

### 1984-1986 Charles Keith "Chuck" Cottier

Born on January 8, 1936, in Delta, Colorado, Cottier had been primarily a second baseman with the Braves (1959-1960), the

**Above:** *Jim Lefebvre.*
**Opposite top:** *Maury Wills (r.) and son.*
**Opposite bottom:** *Manager Del Crandall.*

Tigers (1961), the Senators (1961-1965) and the Angels (1968-1969) before being brought in to finish the 1984 season with the Mariners. He inherited a seventh-place (59-76) club and, by winning 15 and losing 12, was able to push them up into sixth place (74-88 overall). In 1985 he kept them in sixth place (74-88), and in 1986, after 29 games, the club was still in sixth place (9-20), and Cottier was fired.

### 1986-1988 Richard Hirschfeld "Dick" Williams

Williams had had a long and fairly successful history as the manager of the Red Sox (1967-1969), the A's (1971-1973), the Angels (1974-1976), the Expos (1977-1981) and the Padres (1982-1985). He took over the Mariners in sixth place (9-20) in 1986 and managed to win only 58, while losing 75, sending them to seventh place (67-95 overall). In 1984 he led them to the heady heights of fourth place (78-84), but in 1988, after 56 games and with the team at 23-33, he was fired.

**Above:** *Manager Chuck Cottier.*
**Right:** *Manager Dick Williams.*

### 1988 James Robert "Jim" Snyder

Snyder, born on August 13, 1932, in Dearborn, Michigan, had been a second baseman for the Twins (1961-62, 1964), but appeared in only 41 games in those three years. He took over the Mariners with the team having lost 33, while winning only 23. Snyder managed to win 45, while losing 60, but the team ended the season in last place (68-93), and he was fired.

### 1989- James Kenneth "Jim" "Frenchy" Lefebvre

Born on January 7, 1943, in Hawthorne, California, Lefebvre had been primarily a second baseman for the Dodgers (1965-72), and after various coaching positions he was given his first crack at managing in 1989.

# ORIOLES
## Baltimore (1901-1902)

### 1901-1902 John Joseph "Little Napoleon" McGraw

The year 1901 was the first year of existence for the American League, and future Hall of Famer (1937) McGraw was appointed player-manager of the Baltimore Orioles. Born in Truxton, New York, on April 7, 1873, he had played mainly third base for Baltimore of the American Association (1891) and for Baltimore of the National League (1892-1899), where he had been player-manager, before coming to the Orioles. In 1901 he brought the team in in fifth place (68-65) and in 1902, after 62 games and with the club in seventh place (28-34), he left to become manager of the Giants.

### 1902 Wilbert "Uncle Robbie" Robinson

Robinson, born on June 2, 1863, in Bolton, Massachusetts, had been a Hall of Fame (1945) catcher with Philadelphia of the American Association (1886-1890), Baltimore of the American Association (1890-1891), Baltimore of the National League (1892-1899), the Cardinals (1900) and the Orioles (1901-1902) before taking over the seventh-place (28-34) Orioles in 1902. He won only 22, while losing 54, and the club sank to eighth place (50-88 overall). Robinson was fired but would turn up as manager of the Dodgers in 1914. The Orioles left town at the end of the season, too, and became the New York Highlanders (later the Yankees) in 1903.

# ORIOLES
## Baltimore (1954-    )

**1954 James Joseph "Jimmy" Dykes**

Dykes had been the manager of the White Sox (1934-1946) and the Athletics (1951-1953), and now it was his job to lead the sorry Browns to Baltimore to become the equally sorry Orioles. Before the game began on opening day the city had a huge parade that attracted 500,000 people. It was graced by the presence of then-Vice President Richard M. Nixon, who rode in an open car. Oldtimers Connie Mack and Clark Griffith were also in open cars. There were floats and marching bands. After the parade, the Orioles went on to lose the first of the 100 games they would lose that year. Dykes brought them in in seventh place (54-100) and was fired. He was to reappear as manager of the Reds in 1958.

**1955-1961 Paul Rapier Richards**

Richards had been one of the most successful managers that the White Sox had ever had, but in his first year in Baltimore in 1955 it was another seventh-place (57-97) finish for the club. Things improved slightly in 1956, with a sixth-place (69-85) finish, and then it was fifth place (76-76) in 1957. Following that came two consecutive sixth-place finishes in 1958 (74-79) and 1959 (74-80). Then it was second place (89-65) in 1960. But with the club in third place (78-

**Above:** *Manager Joe Altobelli.*
**Left:** *Manager Frank Robinson.*
**Far left:** *Manager Cal Ripken, Sr.*

57) in 1961 after 161 games, Richards was gone. He showed up again as White Sox manager in 1976.

**1961 Chalmer Luman "Lum" Harris**

Harris, born on January 17, 1915, in New Castle, Arkansas, had been a right-handed pitcher for the Athletics (1941-1946) and the Senators (1947). He was brought in to finish the last 27 games for the Orioles. Harris kept them in third place (95-67 overall) by winning 17 and losing ten, but he was let go. He later became the manager of the Colt .45s in 1964.

### 1962-1963 William Clyde "Billy" Hitchcock

Hitchcock had been a manager for only one game before he joined the Orioles – with Detroit in 1960, and he won the game. In 1962 he let the Orioles fall to seventh place (77-85), but in 1963 he brought them up to a fourth-place (87-76) finish. Still, it was not good enough, and he was let go, only to show up as manager of the Braves in 1966.

### 1964-1968 Henry Albert "Hank" Bauer

Bauer had been a not-too-successful manager with Kansas City in 1961 and 1962, but he was a stern disciplinarian, and that was what the Orioles needed. He was able to turn the team around, finishing third (97-65) in 1964. In 1965 it was another third-place (94-68) finish. Then came the miracle of 1966. He led the Orioles to the pennant (97-63) and beat the Dodgers in the World Series, four games to none. The next year, 1967, was a downer, with the team finishing sixth (76-85), and, with the Orioles in third place (43-37) in 1968, Bauer left. He would be back as manager of the Athletics in 1969.

### 1968-1982 Earl Sidney Weaver

Weaver, a feisty, umpire-baiting, feuding manager, was born on August 14, 1930, in St. Louis. He had never played a game in the big leagues, although he had attended spring training with the Cardinals in 1952. Weaver had managed in the Orioles farm system for 11 years before moving up to become first base coach in 1968. Then he was chosen to finish off the 1968 season for Baltimore. By winning 48 games and losing 34 he moved them from third place to second (91-71 overall).

Then it was first place (109-53) in the Eastern Division in 1969, ending 19 games in front of the field. The Orioles won three straight in the League Championship Series over the Twins. In the World Series they came up against the "Miracle Mets" and lost, four games to one. Another Eastern Division Championship (108-54) came in 1970. Once again the Orioles wiped out the Twins in the League Championship Series in three straight games. In the World Series the Orioles beat the Reds four games to one. Still another Eastern Division title (101-75) followed in 1971. In the League Championship Series their opponents were the Royals, and once more the Orioles swept the series, three games to none. But the

Pirates beat them in the World Series four games to three.

Weaver had an off year in 1972, finishing third (80-74). But then he brought them back to first place (97-65) in 1973, eight games ahead of the Red Sox. In the League Championship series they lost to the A's three games to two. Then came another divisional championship (91-71) in 1974, and once again the Orioles faced the A's, this time losing the League Championship Series three games to two.

Weaver now began to have some minor problems with the team and guided them to three straight second-place finishes in 1975 (90-69), 1976 (88-74) and 1977 (97-64). Then it was fourth place (90-71) in 1978. But the team roared back in 1979 to finish first (102-57) again, beating out the Brewers by eight games, as Weaver won his sixth division title in 11 years. This time they didn't drop the League Championship Series, beating the Angels three games to one. Unfortunately, they lost to the Pirates in a thrilling World Series, four games to three. Then it was second place in 1980 (100-62).

The next year, 1981, was that terrible year of the players' strike when the season was divided into halves. The Orioles came in second (31-23) in the first half and fourth (28-23) in the second. Weaver brought his team in in second place (94-68) in 1982 and then decided to retire "to tend his garden." But he was to return in 1985.

## 1983-1985 Joseph Salvatore "Joe" Altobelli

Altobelli had been the manager of the Giants from 1977 to 1979 but had little success. Then he came to Baltimore and was an immediate mastermind. He took them to first place (98-64) in 1983, his very first year. Then they went on to sweep the White Sox three games to none in the League Championship Series. In the World Series the Orioles took the Phillies four games to one. But it was fifth place (85-77) in 1984, and, with the Orioles mired in fifth place (29-26) after 55 games in 1985, Altobelli was out.

## 1985 Calvin Edward "Cal" Ripken Sr.

Ripken, born on December 17, 1935, in Aberdeen, Maryland, had had no major

**Above:** *Hank Bauer with two coaches.*
**Opposite top:** *Jimmy Dykes in a Browns cap.*
**Opposite center:** *Stengel, Paul Richards.*
**Opposite bottom:** *Weaver, Robinson.*

league playing experience when he took over the Orioles for one game. He won the game, and then made way for Weaver.

## 1985-1987 Earl Sidney Weaver

Weaver left his garden to come back and try to save the fortunes of the Orioles in 1985. It didn't work. He took over the fifth-place (30-26) club and, by winning 53 and losing 52, was able to raise them to fourth place (83-78 overall). In 1986 things got much worse: the club came in in seventh (73-89), and Weaver headed back to his garden.

## 1987-1988 Calvin Edward "Cal" Ripken Sr.

Ripken was brought back in 1987, but things did not improve much. He led the Orioles to a sixth-place (67-95) finish. Then, in 1988, on April 12, after the team had lost its first six games, Ripken was fired. He was to return to the club as third base coach in 1989.

## 1988- **Frank Robinson**

Robinson had been the manager of the Indians (1975-1977) and the Giants (1981-1984) and had also been the first black manager in the major leagues when he was appointed to the Cleveland managership in 1975. But things did not go well for him in Baltimore, since the Orioles set a new

Amerian League record under his stewardship: they went on to lose the first 15 games under his leadership, and that, added to the losses under Ripkin, was the worst start in league history – 21 straight losses at the beginning of the season. An embarrassing thing popped up during this awful streak when a newspaper advertisement appeared

*Earl Weaver in a discussion.*

for the Cal Ripken Baseball School: "Learn to play baseball the Oriole way." Robinson was able to win only 54 games, while losing 101, and the club finished in last place (54-107) – the worst record in the major leagues and the worst in the Orioles' history.

# PILOTS
## Seattle (1969)

**1969 Joseph Charles "Joe" "Dode" Schultz Jr.**
Seattle and Kansas City were granted new American League franchises in this expansion year, and the Pilots chose Joe Schultz to be their first manager. Schultz, born on August 29, 1918, in Chicago, had been a back-up catcher with the Pirates (1939-1941) and the Browns (1943-1948). As the manager of the Pilots he was able only to bring them in in sixth place (64-98). Then he was fired, to turn up in 1973 as the Tiger manager. At the end of the season the team had been so bad and the crowds had been so small that the Pilots were moved to Milwaukee and became the Brewers. Exactly why Seattle had expected a first-year expansion team to do any better is unclear.

# RANGERS
## Texas (1972-   )

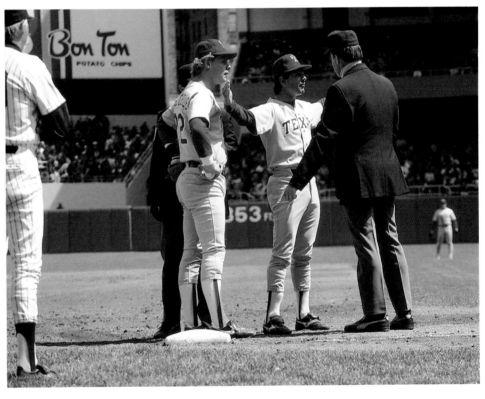

**1972 Theodore Samuel "Ted" "The Splendid Splinter" "The Thumper" Williams**
Williams, who had been managing the Senators, followed them to Texas in 1972, when they became the Rangers. He could do no better than a sixth-place (54-100) finish and thereupon retired from baseball.

**1973 Dorrel Norman Elvert "Whitey" "The White Rat" Herzog**
Herzog, born on November 9, 1937, in New Athens, Illinois, had been an outfielder for the Senators (1956-1958), the Athletics (1958-1960), the Orioles (1961-1962) and the Tigers (1963). He took over the Rangers in 1973 and lasted only 138 games. With the team in sixth place (47-91), he was fired. Herzog turned up as manager of the Royals in 1975.

**Above:** *Bobby Valentine in a rhubarb.*
**Above left:** *Manager Don Zimmer.*
**Below left:** *Manager Doug Rader.*

153

**Above:** *Manager Ted Williams tries out his new Texas hat.*
**Above right:** *Manager Eddie Stanky.*

## 1973 Delbert Quentin "Del" "Babe" Wilber

Wilber was born on February 24, 1919, in Lincoln Park, Michigan, and had been a catcher for the Cardinals (1946-1949), the Phillies (1951-1952) and the Red Sox (1952-1954) before becoming a coach. He was called in by the Rangers to manage one game in 1973, which he won.

## 1973-1975 Alfred Manuel "Billy" Martin

Martin had been the manager of the Twins (1969) and the Tigers (1971-1973), and he took over the Rangers in 1973 when they were in sixth place (48-91) after 139 games. He was able to win nine and lose 14, and the team fell to last place (57-105). Martin turned the team around in 1974, bringing them in in second place (84-76). He had them in third place (44-51) after 95 games in 1975, when he got a summons from his dream team – the Yankees – and was off to New York to manage.

## 1975-1977 Frank Joseph Lucchesi

Lucchesi had been the manager of the Phillies (1970-1972), and he came to the Rangers with the team in third place (44-51) after 95 games. He won 35 and lost 32 to keep them in third (79-83 overall). In 1976 the team fell to fifth (76-86) and after 62 games in 1977, with the team in fourth place (31-31), he was fired. Lucchesi was to surface as the manager of the Cubs in 1987.

## 1977 Edward Raymond "Eddie" "The Brat" "Muggsy" Stanky

Stanky, a coach who had been the manager of the Cardinals (1952-1955) and the White Sox (1966-1968), was brought in as interim manager for one game, which he won, raising the club to second place.

## 1977 Cornelius Joseph "Connie" Ryan

Ryan took over the team for six games in 1977. He had been the manager of the Braves in 1975. Ryan took a second-place (32-31) club, won two and lost four, and left the team in fourth place (34-35).

## 1977-1978 Gordon William "Billy" Hunter

Hunter, born on June 4, 1928, in Punxsutawney, Pennsylvania, had been a short-stop with the Browns (1953), the Orioles (1954), the Yankees (1955-1956), the Athletics (1957-1958) and the Indians (1958). He was brought in to manage the Rangers with 93 games to go in the season. He led them to 60 wins and 33 losses, which raised the team from fourth place to second (94-68 overall). In 1978 came another second-place (87-75) finish, but after that Hunter was gone.

## 1979-1980 Patrick "Pat" "Ike" Corrales

Born on March 20, 1941, in Los Angeles, Corrales had been a catcher with the Phillies (1964-1965), the Cardinals (1966), the Reds (1968-1972) and the Padres (1972-1973). In 1979 he was able to guide the Rangers to a third-place (83-79) finish, but the team fell to fourth (76-85) in 1980, and Corrales was fired. He would become the manager of the Phillies in 1982.

## 1981-1982 Donald William "Don" Zimmer

Zimmer had been the manager of the Padres (1972-1973) and the Red Sox (1976-1980) before he was brought in to manage the Rangers in that strike-split season of 1981. In the first half of the season he led them to a second-place (33-22) finish, and it was third place (24-26) in the second half. In 1982, with the team in sixth place (35-58) after 96 games, he was fired. Zimmer became the manager of the Cubs in 1988.

## 1982 Darrell Dean Johnson

Johnson, who had managed the Red Sox (1974-1976) and the Mariners (1977-1980), was brought in as interim manager to finish the 1982 season. With the team in sixth place (38-58), he was able to win only 26, while losing 40; the team stayed in sixth place (64-98 overall), and Johnson was fired.

## 1983-1985 Douglas Lee "Doug" "Rojo" "The Red Rooster" Rader

Rader, born on July 30, 1944, in Chicago, had been a third baseman with the Astros (1967-1975), the Padres (1976-1977) and the Blue Jays (1977). As the Rangers' manager he was able to lead them to a third-place (77-85) finish in 1983. But then it was seventh (69-92) in 1984, and in 1985, with the team still in last place (9-23) after 22 games, he was fired. Rader would become the White Sox manager in 1986.

## 1985- Robert John "Bobby' Valentine

Valentine was born on May 13, 1950, in Stamford, Connecticut, and had been a fiery utility player in the outfield and the outfield (he even caught for two games) for the Dodgers (1969, 1971-1972), the Angels (1973-1975), the Padres (1975-1977), the Mets (1977-1978) and the Mariners (1979). At the age of 29 he had been such an aggressive player that he had smashed his legs so badly that he could no longer play. He was a restaurateur in his home town when he was called to finish the 1985 season as manager of the Rangers. He was still only 35 years old. He inherited a seventh-place (9-23) team and could not improve their standing (62-99 overall) by winning 53 and losing 76. But in 1986 he brought them in in second place (87-75). Then it was sixth place (75-87) in 1987. In 1988 he again led the team to a sixth-place finish (70-91).

# RED SOX

Boston (1901-    )

## Called **SOMERSETS** (1901-1904)

### 1901-1904 **James Joseph "Jimmy" Collins**

Regarded as the premier third baseman in the major leagues when he came to the Boston Somersets from the Boston Beaneaters across the tracks, Jimmy Collins (Hall of Fame 1945) lost no time in establishing the junior league team as a contender. In his first season as manager Collins, born in Buffalo, New York, on January 16, 1870, directed the Somersets to a second-place finish, four games behind the White Sox; and Collins's play as third baseman was an indispensable reason for the team's success: he batted .332, with 94 RBI's.

After dropping to third place the next year (1902), Collins moved the team to league championships in 1903 and 1904. In the 1903 World Series, the first ever played between the American and National Leagues, the Somersets humiliated the Pittsburgh Pirates by winning five games to three after Boston had fallen behind three games to one. Because of the embarrassment, the National League refused a second contest the next year.

## Called **PURITANS** (1904-1906)

### 1905-1906 **James Joseph "Jimmy" Collins**

Continuing to play third base, Collins managed the team to a disappointing fourth place in 1905, and in his last year, when he did not play, the team (renamed Puritans in 1904) had plummeted to last place before Collins left with only 18 games remaining. Despite winning only 44 of 136 games in his final year, Collins finished his term in Boston with a .544 won-lost percentage.

In May, 1901, the Somersets had made their first road trip, an unnerving tour that resulted in seven losses out of nine games. But when the team returned fans in Boston had left no doubt that they favored the American League team over the Beaneaters: on May 8, 1901, the Somersets had

drawn 11,500 spectators, while the Beaneaters had attracted less than half that many, 5500. Jimmy Collins survived his retirement by 37 years, dying in Buffalo on March 6, 1943.

### 1906 **Charles Sylvester "Chick" Stahl**

"Chick" Stahl managed the Puritans for only 18 games to close out the 1906 season after the retirement of Jimmy Collins. An outfielder for the team – he had played in Boston for both leagues since 1897 – Stahl (born in Avila, Indiana, on January 10, 1873) stepped into a hopeless set of circumstances, with a team in the cellar in the standings and in morale, and won only five games. The following spring, on March 28, in West Baden, Indiana, Stahl for some unknown reason drank some carbolic acid that a doctor had prescribed for a leg injury and died within minutes.

**Above:** *Manager Cy Young.*
**Above left:** *Manager Jimmy Collins.*

## Called **RED SOX** (1896-)

### 1907 **Denton True "Cy" Young**

Acting as interim manager until team owner John I. Taylor could find someone permanent for the job, Cy Young, born in Gilmore, Ohio, on March 29, 1867, directed the team during its first seven games, winning three. Young died in Newcomerstown, Ohio, on November 4, 1955, after setting some of the most durable standards for pitching in baseball history, an achievement which won him Hall of Fame honors in 1937.

### 1907 **George A. Huff**

Second of four managers to appear within months after the stunning death of "Chick"

Stahl in the spring of 1907, George Huff, born in Champaign, Illinois, on June 11, 1872, had only eight games to prove himself (three wins) before owner John Taylor sacked him. Huff, who had never played in the majors and who would not manage in them again, died on October 1, 1936, also in Champaign.

### 1907 Robert Alexander "Bob" Unglaub

After coming from the New York Highlanders to play at first base with the Red Sox, Bob Unglaub (born in Baltimore on July 31, 1881) became Boston's second "permanent" manager in less than two months. Twenty-eight games (20 losses) later, however, he was retired to his original position of first baseman where he finished the season. His playing career ended in 1910, and Unglaub died in Baltimore on November 29, 1916.

### 1907-1908 James Thomas "Deacon" McGuire

A 42-year-old catcher from the New York Highlanders, "Deacon" McGuire, born in Youngstown, Ohio, on November 2, 1865, was the fourth Red Sox manager in 1907 to try to stabilize the team. McGuire managed in 111 games, and the team finished seventh. In 1908 he directed in the first 115 games to sixth in the standings before Taylor fired him. McGuire turned up managing in Cleveland the following year.

### 1908-1909 Frederick Lovett "Fred" Lake

Managing in only the last 39 games of the 1908 season, catcher Fred Lake, from Nova Scotia (born October 16, 1866), improved the team's position by one spot, to fifth. Continued improvement the following year was good enough to win third place in the standings – the best finish since the 1904-1905 pennant-winning years, yet Lake was victim to Taylor's dissatisfaction and sentence of termination. The next year found him across town managing the Boston Pilgrims (Braves).

### 1910-1911 Patrick "Patsy" Donovan

Patsy Donovan's two years of managing were only modestly successful if measured by the team's place in the standings (fourth in 1910 and fifth the following year), but they proved to be the base for some spectacular years to come. Donovan, who had

come to Boston after a managerial stint in Brooklyn, had an impressive roster of young players who later became giants for the Red Sox. Among them were "Smokey" Joe Wood, Tris Speaker, Bill Carrigan, Jake Stahl, and Harry Hooper. But Donovan's managing career ended after 1911. He died on Christmas day, 1953, in Lawrence, Massachusetts.

### 1912-1913 Garland "Jake" Stahl

In 1912, Fenway Park's inaugural season, former Washington manager Jake Stahl directed the Red Sox to 105 wins (league

*Above: Manager Don Zimmer.*
*Opposite: Manager Ralph Houk.*

best until 1927 Yankees' 110) and, in the World Series, to a conquest of John McGraw's Giants, four games to three. Stahl's time as manager was cut short, however, when new owner Jimmy McAleer fired him midway through the 1913 season as a result of rumors that the player/manager had ambitions to usurp the owner's position as president of the team. Stahl's managing career ended at this point. He died in Los Angeles on September 18, 1922.

## 1913-1916 **William Francis "Rough" Carrigan**

Having left Holy Cross College only seven years before becoming manager of the Red Sox, catcher Bill Carrigan shouldered his new responsibility with unusual balance. His players described him as intelligent, rugged, unintimidated by anyone on the team or among opponents. Babe Ruth, in fact, spoke of Carrigan as the best manager he ever had.

A native of Lewiston, Maine (born October 22, 1883), "Rough" managed during the last 70 games of the 1913 season after the firing of Jake Stahl, a year of rancor that resulted in a fourth-place finish. In 1914 new owner Joe Lannin acquired Babe Ruth from cash-poor Baltimore for $2900, and "Rough" did not hesitate to thrust him into service. Before the 19-year-old rookie was sent to the Red Sox' Providence club he won two games and lost one, and Carrigan's team improved to a second-place spot at the end of the season.

The Red Sox were pennant winners in 1915 and 1916 under "Rough," and both years the team beat their National League rivals for the World Championship (four games to one in 1915 against the Phillies and the same margin the next year against the Dodgers). Impressive as Carrigans' work was, owner Lannin did not invite him to return the next season (although ten years later the Red Sox would call for his help again).

## 1917 **John Joseph "Jack" Barry**

A former shortstop in Connie Mack's "$100,000 infield" of 1911, in 1917 Jack Barry both played second base and managed the Sox to a second place in the standings. Barry, a World War I veteran from Meriden, Connecticut (born on April 26, 1887), was indirectly responsible for one of six perfect games pitched in the American League when he called on Ernie Shore to relieve Babe Ruth (ejected after facing only one batter and arguing the umpire's judgment of a pitch). Barry decided to let Shore continue pitching after that first inning emergency, and Shore completed the game after having faced only 26 batters. This was Barry's only season as a manager. He continued playing through 1919 and died 42 years later, on April 23, 1961, in Shrewsbury, Massachusetts.

## 1918-1920 **Edward Grant "Cousin Ed" Barrow**

In a 1918 season shortened by the Secretary of War to end on September 2, Ed Barrow, who had earlier managed in Detroit, directed the Red Sox to their fourth pennant and fourth World Series win in seven years. An iron-clad manager who refused to take sass from any of his players, including Babe Ruth, Barrow nonetheless listened to one of his coaches (Harry Hooper) and agreed to play Ruth in the outfield when he was not pitching. As a result of Barrow's decision Ruth began to get more attention as a hitter and quickly decided he preferred fielding to pitching. Barrow (elected to the Hall of Fame in 1953) once fined and suspended Ruth for violating curfew, but since it had no effect on the temperamental player's habits and demoralized the rest of the team, Barrow compromised and insisted only that Ruth report to him each morning the time he had gone to bed the night before. This may not have accomplished much, but it saved face all around. In 1920 Barrow retired as Red Sox manager to become General Manager of the Yankees. He died on December 15, 1953, in Port Chester, New York.

## 1921-1922 **Hugh Duffy**

Once an outfielder for the Boston Bean-eaters (1894), for whom he batted the highest percentage in all baseball history, .438, Hugh Duffy had managed the White Sox in 1910-1911 and now had to suffer the disgrace of passively participating in the progressive dismantling of the Red Sox under owner Harry Frazee, who used income from the team to pay for his bad theater investments. The team ended in fifth place in 1921 but dropped to last place the next year and remained perennial losers until 1930. Under Duffy's management the team lost not only games, but fans as well. Nevertheless, Duffy was chosen to the Hall of Fame in 1945, nine years before his death in Boston on October 19, 1954.

*Above: Deacon McGuire in 1900.*
*Left: Manager Jake Stahl.*

## 1923 **Frank LeRoy "Husk" "The Peerless Leader" Chance**

A proven winner managing the Cubs (four pennants and two World Championships between 1905 and 1912), Hall of Fame member (1946) Frank "Husk" Chance was unable to perform his magic with only the ghost of a once-championship team that had been destroyed by the reckless trading of owner Harry Frazee. The team remained in the cellar, and Chance's managing career came to an end. He died in Los Angeles a year later, on September 14.

## 1924-1926 **Leo Alexander "Lee" Fohl**

After managing contenders in Cleveland and St. Louis (Browns), Lee Fohl entered the graveyard of Fenway Park and in his first year (1924) became the last manager in the decade of the 1920s to finish higher than last place for the Red Sox – seventh position (½ game ahead of the White Sox). Fohl did not manage after 1926. He died on October 30, 1965, in Cleveland.

## 1927-1929 **William Francis "Rough" Carrigan**

"Rough" Carrigan returned to the Red Sox in 1927 after the team had suffered last-place finishes the two previous years, but he was unable to change the performance of a demoralized team. The Bosox remained in last place during all of Carrigan's final three years of managing. "Rough" died in Lewiston, Maine, on July 8, 1969.

## 1930 **Charles F. "Heinie" Wagner**

The sixth manager in ten years, "Heinie" Wagner was unable to alter the pattern of drought which beset the team through the 1920s. Having played shortstop for the Red Sox (1907-1915), the New York-born Wagner (September 23, 1880) as manager compiled only 52 wins, and the team remained in eighth place. He was fired and did not manage again. He died in New Rochelle, New York, on March 20, 1943.

## 1931-1932 **John Francis "Shano" Collins**

After rescuing the team from the cellar (the first time in seven years) and bringing it to sixth place in 1931, former outfielder Shano Collins and the Red Sox staggered through 1932, the worst year in the team's history, winning 43 and losing 111. Collins, born in Charlestown, Massachusetts, on December 4, 1885, directed only the first 57 games (winning 11) and was the last manager to work under owner Bob Quinn before he sold the team to Tom Yawkey in February, 1933. Collins, who never managed in the majors again, died in Newton, Massachusetts, on September 10, 1955.

## 1932-1933 **Martin Joseph "Marty" McManus**

Substitute third baseman Marty McManus completed the 1932 season begun by Shano Collins (last 97 games) but was unable to keep the Red Sox out of last place again. McManus, born in Chicago on March 14, 1900, remained through the 1933 season (the first of Tom Yawkey's ownership) and the team moved into seventh position. McManus did not manage after 1933 and died at the age of 65 on February 18, 1966, in St. Louis.

## 1934 **Stanley Raymond "Bucky" Harris**

The "Boy Wonder" manager who had outwitted John McGraw in the 1925 World Series' seventh game to win the Washington Senators their sole World Championship, Bucky Harris (inducted into the Hall of Fame in 1975) was the beneficiary of Tom Yawkey's determination to buy a winning team instead of waiting for one to emerge systematically. Nevertheless, the Red Sox finished an even .500 and in fourth place. Harris, who had come to Boston after five years with Detroit, now went back to managing the Senators.

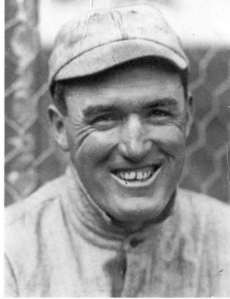

Above: *Bill "Rough" Carrigan brought the Red Sox to two pennants and two Series victories.*

Above: *Manager Bill Carrigan (l.).*
Below: *Hugh Duffy in his playing days.*

## 1935-1947 Joseph Edward "Joe" Cronin

When millionaire Tom Yawkey bought the Red Sox in 1933 he had no shortage of cash and acquired Joe Cronin from Clark Griffith, owner of the Senators. Cronin had been player-manager at the age of 28 when Washington won the pennant in 1933, and he had been a steady .300-range hitter, with over 100 RBI's, during the four previous years.

The new manager's first year (1935) featured good hitting, but the pitching did not hold up; and the team finished in fourth place behind Detroit, the Yankees and Cleveland. Cronin tolerated no nonsense from his players, including some talented ones who didn't last long when they challenged his judgement. Once Ben Chapman, for example, hit into a double play after being told to bunt; his explanation was simply that he didn't bunt; he was subsequently traded to Cleveland, even though he was hitting .340.

In 1938 the team finished in second place (its best performance since 1918), and Cronin batted .325. In 1939 Ted Williams began his assault on every batting record in baseball history and was one reason Boston led the league in hitting for the next three years. But the hitting strength was not matched by pitching, and the team was unable to rise above second place behind the Yankees.

Cronin retired as a player in 1945, the year all the big hitters returned from service in the war. The pressure on Cronin was now intense, for it was obvious that both the fans and Yawkey expected him to deliver at least a pennant as manager of one of the best, if not *the* best, hitting line-ups in the league. He also had, at last, support from a durable pitching roster.

Despite Cronin's concentrating on managing exclusively, only Connie Mack's Athletics had a worse record than the Red Sox in 1945, but in 1946, the first season after the war, Cronin's managing and an exceptionally talented team trounced second-place Detroit by a margin of 12 games and closed 17 ahead of the Yankees in winning 104 games, the most wins since the Yankees' 106 in 1939.

The World Series went a full seven games, with Boston losing to St. Louis by a 4-3 score in the last game. Not for 21 more years did the Red Sox play again in a World Series, and again they lost to the Cardinals in seven games. Cronin's final year as manager, 1947, was a season of injuries to pitchers' arms, and the team dropped to third place. After 13 years, the longest stay in the team's history, field manager Cronin became general manager, and nine years later he was elected to the Hall of Fame.

It was no secret that playing and managing was a trying combination for Cronin. Williams recognized the effects of the in-

**Above:** *Manager Joe Morgan.*
**Left:** *John McNamara (center).*
**Opposite top:** *Bucky Harris and Joe Cronin.*
**Opposite bottom:** *Joe McCarthy and Ted Williams.*

compatibility of the two responsibilities and acknowledged that Cronin's managing improved when he stopped playing. The legendary hitter also called Cronin a manager for hitters. Williams was certainly in a position to offer insight about the manager's concern for his batters: in one famous instance, Cronin had offered to help protect Williams' .3995 (*ie* .400) average in 1941 by allowing him to decline to play in the season's final two games. But Williams had insisted on playing and finished the year with a record .406. Cronin died in Osterville, Mass., on September 7, 1984.

### 1948-1950 **Joseph Vincent "Marse Joe" McCarthy**

Persuaded to come to Boston after retiring (for health reasons) as a triumphant Yankee manager, Joe McCarthy lost the pennant to Cleveland in a single-game playoff in 1948, and in 1949 he lost to Casey Stengel's Yankees in the season's last game, and the Sox finished second again. Renowned for enforcing lofty standards for his players' appearance and manners outside the ball park, McCarthy, nevertheless, was the favorite manager of Ted Williams, who insisted on casual attire.

By the middle of June, 1950, "Marse Joe" decided to retire permanently. The Red Sox were then in fourth place – 8½ games behind New York. McCarthy entered the Hall of Fame in 1957, 21 years before his death in Buffalo, New York, on January 3, 1978.

### 1950-1951 **Stephen Francis "Steve" O'Neill**

Steve O'Neill completed the last two-thirds of the 1950 season after Joe McCarthy's resignation and improved the team's place one position to third. Coming to the Red Sox with imposing managerial credentials (World Series victor with Detroit in 1945), he nonetheless was unable to finish better than third in either 1950 or 1951. In 1952 he became the manager of the Phillies.

### 1952-1954 **Louis "Lou" Boudreau**

Lou Boudreau, who had signed with the Red Sox as a shortstop under Steve O'Neill, had managed in Cleveland since 1942. When he took over as manager of the Sox in 1952 he announced that he would produce a winner even if it meant trading everyone on the team – including Ted Williams. There were rumors that Williams was set to retire after the 1954 season (upon returning from

Korea) if Boudreau remained. Boudreau (Hall of Fame, 1970) moved on to Kansas City after three mediocre seasons (sixth in 1952 and fourth his last two years), much to the delight of the Red Sox and their fans.

### 1955-1959 Michael Franklin "Pinky" Higgins

The only manager to direct the Red Sox to a first-division finish between 1958 and 1967, "Pinky" Higgins led the team in 1957 and 1958 to third place finishes. Higgins, a Texan, born in Red Oak on May 27, 1909, had once played third base (1937-38) for the Red Sox. He was chosen to manage after having led the Louisville Colonels, a Red Sox affiliate, to the championship in the Little World Series in 1954. When Higgins could manage to win only 31 of the first 73 games of the 1959 season, he was dismissed.

### 1959 Rudolph Preston "Rudy" York

A first baseman on Joe Cronin's 1946 World Series team (hitting two home runs, one double, and one triple in seven games), Rudy York managed only one game between Higgins' departure and Billy Jurges's arrival. York was born in Ragland, Alabama, on August 17, 1913. He died in Rome, Georgia, on February 2, 1970.

### 1959-1960 William Frederick "Billy" Jurges

Born in the Bronx, New York City, on May 9, 1909, former shortstop Jurges took over at mid-season in 1959 and won 44 of the final 80 games, improving the team's standing from 8th (last) to 5th place. Notable in this 1959 season is that in July the Red Sox signed their first black player, Elijah "Pumpsie" Green. As the 1960 season progressed, Jurges could win only 34 of the first 81 games, and he was dismissed.

### 1960-1962 Michael Franklin "Pinky" Higgins

Higgins returned to finish out the 1960 season, winning 31 of the 73 games left. He stayed on to win 76 games in each of the next two years, finishing in sixth and eighth place respectively, and he was not asked to come back for 1963. But Higgins was second only to Joe Cronin in the total number of years he managed the Red Sox, and his tenure included the year Ted Williams retired (1960) and the debut of Carl Yastrzemski (1961). Higgins died in Dallas, Texas, on March 21, 1969.

### 1963-1964 John Michael "Johnny" Pesky

Trying to recover at least first-division status after the team's poor performances in the previous two years, Pesky instead found himself managing a mediocre team, ending the 1963 season in 7th place and the 1964 season in eighth place. Born John Michael Paveskovich in Portland, Oregon, on September 27, 1919, Pesky had been a hero in his playing years with the Red Sox when he hit over .300 in six of his first seven years, but this was not enough to hold him as manager, and he was let go with two games to play in 1964.

### 1964-1966 William Jennings Bryan "Bill" "Bryan" Herman

Billy Herman, born in New Albany, Indiana, on July 7, 1909, had been a 15-year veteran second baseman with an assortment of National League teams. He had not managed since directing the Pirates in 1947. In Boston he won the only two games he worked in 1964, when he completed Johnny Pesky's last year. But then he lost 100 games in 1965, his first full season. Even though the Red Sox finished ninth in 1966, second to last-place (owned by the Yankees), Billy Herman credited himself with building the base for the 1967 pennant-winning team. The team's record in the second half of 1966

**Above:** *Manager Pinky Higgins.*
**Top:** *Boudreau (center) and rookies – 1952.*

was, in fact, second only to that of Baltimore, the World Champions that year. But Yawkey fired him with 16 games remaining in 1966. Herman entered the Hall of Fame in 1975.

### 1966 James Edward "Pete" Runnels

Pete Runnels, a Texan (born on January 28, 1928, in Lufkin) had played infield for the

Red Sox from 1958-1962 and had beaten Ted Williams for the league batting title in 1960 with a .320 average. Managing the final 16 games of the 1966 season after Billy Herman's dismissal, he won eight and lost eight.

### 1967-1969 Richard Hirshfield "Dick" Williams

A native of St. Louis (born May 7, 1928), Dick Williams moved a team that had finished in ninth place in 1966 (and was given 100 to 1 odds to win the pennant when spring training began in 1967) through an exhilarating season to an unforgettable seven-game World Series with St. Louis.

Applying the simple formula of work, concentration and repetition, Williams had cultivated confidence and expectation in his young team (the average age was 25). But the next year they couldn't stand their prosperity, became peevish with one another and dropped to fourth. When asked, after being sacked by Yawkey in his third year, why he was being tagged as the villain, Williams said he had been accused of being too demanding of his players. Be that as it may, the Dick Williams years in Boston had attracted the most fans in the team's history. In 1971 Williams became the (spectacularly successful) manager of the Oakland A's.

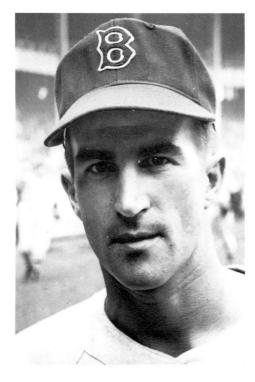

Above: *Manager Johnny Pesky.*
**Right:** *Manager Dick Williams.*
**Below:** *Billy Herman in his playing days.*

## 1969 Edward Joseph "Pop" Popowski

With only nine games remaining in 1969, Eddie Popowski, born in Sayreville, New Jersey, on August 20, 1913, stood in to relieve Dick Williams. Popowski, who had never played in the majors, maintained a third-place stand – only three games behind Detroit, but 22 away from first-place Baltimore.

## 1970-1973 Edward Michael "Eddie" Kasko

Eddie Kasko, from Linden, New Jersey (born June 27, 1932), maintained the team's standing in the first division in his four years, but he was unable to come closer to winning the pennant than ½ game behind Detroit, which won the title in a final three-game series in 1972.

An infielder for the Red Sox (mostly shortstop) for 58 games in 1966 (the year before the Sox won the pennant and a season for testing new players), Kasko knew what it was to encourage promising rookies. Carlton Fisk was one of those rookies in Kasko's first year, and Louis Tiant pitched his first time for the Red Sox under Kasko in 1971. Though Boston again finished in second place in 1973, Kasko was gone after the season's end. He did not manage again in the major leagues after that.

## 1974-1976 Darrell Dean Johnson

The year 1974 boasted an abundance of exceptional new prospects for the Red Sox, as well as a new manager, Darrell Johnson. In his debut as a major league manager, 45-year-old Johnson, born in Horace, Nebraska, on August 25, 1928, faced the privileges and demands of directing a stellar cast of young, ambitious and brilliant individual performers (Dwight Evans, Jim Rice, Rick Burleson, Fred Lynn, and Cecil Cooper) toward a single ambition – to play and win as a team. Former catcher Johnson was up to the task, and in 1975 the young team swept Oakland in three games for the league championship and then played one of the best teams in two decades, the Reds, to a deadlock in the World Series before losing game seven.

Characteristically, the Red Sox could not repeat as contenders the following year (1976), the year owner Tom Yawkey died unexpectedly of leukemia, and finished third. Johnson himself was finished at Boston by the end of July that year. The following year he was managing the newly-formed Mariners in Seattle.

## 1976-1980 Donald William "Don" Zimmer

After two glamourless years of managing in San Diego Don Zimmer came to Boston to salvage the 1976 season for a team laden with talent but running in place. The Red Sox played eight games over .500 in Zimmer's first three months (76 games) and did not improve in the standings (third).

In Zimmer's first full year, 1977, the team tied for second place with the Orioles – two and one-half games behind New York; but such a surge was merely prelude to the performance of 1978, when the Red Sox fielded the most lethal hitting and pitching balance they had been able to boast of in a decade. Leading the quarrelsome Yankees by 14 games and second-place Milwaukee by 10 in mid-July, the Sox cruised through August. Then came a colossal collapse – 14 losses in 17 games between August 30 and September 14. Recovering, they finished the season in a tie with the Yankees but lost the one-game playoff.

A disheartening third-place finish in 1980 spelled the gallows for Zimmer, who had won 411 of his 715 games in Boston but had failed to capture a flag. Zimmer then moved on to manage the Texas Rangers.

## 1981-1984 Ralph George "Major" Houk

Military hero Ralph "Major" Houk could not resist the Red Sox' appeal in 1981 after two years of retirement from managing in Detroit. He arrived just in time for the season ruined by the strike. Houk, winner of two World Series with the Yankees, now directed a team that remained in contention for the pennant throughout most of 1982 but that came to rest in third place, six games behind Milwaukee.

A perpetual optimist and players' manager, Houk would always stand in defense of his players when they were under fire. Working with a pitching staff that had fallen apart under Zimmer, the patient Houk nurtured them through a period of rehabilitation while finishing in fourth place in his last year (1984) of managing.

## 1985-1988 John Francis McNamara

Despite an even .500 record in 1985, his first year with the Red Sox (fifth place), John McNamara, who had come to Boston from a second-place finish managing the Angels in 1984, was catapulted into Manager-of-the Year honors in 1986. He led a team picked in pre-season to occupy a spot in the second division to an astonishing pennant win over Oakland in seven games and then to an exhilarating seven-game cliff-hanger World Series that was finally and disappointingly won by the Mets.

McNamara fell into disfavor in the following season, however, when the near-World Championship team seemed afflicted with inertia, despite brilliant performances by Cy Young-winner Roger Clemens and other pitchers. The veteran manager was inclined to favor safe, proven players, even when they did not perform, and he lost his job after the All-Star break in 1988.

**Above:** *Manager Darrell Johnson.*
**Opposite:** *Manager Ralph Houk.*

## 1988- Joseph Michael "Joe" Morgan

A Red Sox team in a state of torpor and disharmony at the time of the All-Star game exploded with 12 straight wins under new manager Joe Morgan. Toppling one record after another, the team moved from fourth place, nine games out, on July 13 to a division lead of three and one-half games by the middle of September.

The unflappable Morgan, a former third baseman, had been third-base coach for the Red Sox until called to stand in for the departed McNamara. Recognized for his Yankee resourcefulness (including driving snowplows to pick up extra cash and pay the rent when his income from coaching baseball wouldn't get him through the long winter), Morgan, a native of Walpole, Massachusetts (born on November 19, 1930) completed the regular season in first place in the East Division. The Red Sox, alas, were in a hitting slump and lost 11 of their last 12 games – including a four-game sweep by the Athletics for the pennant. Morgan, nonetheless, was runner-up for American League Manager of the Year.

*Manager Eddie Kasco.*

*Manager Don Zimmer.*

# ROYALS
## Kansas City (1969-    )

### 1969 Joseph Lowell "Joe" 'Flash' Gordon

Nineteen sixty-nine was another expansion year, and the American League added two teams, the Padres and the Royals. Joe Gordon, who had been manager of the Indians (1958-1960), the Tigers (1960) and the Athletics (1961) became the Royals' first manager. In 1969 the team finished in fourth place (69-93), and he was gone. It was his last managing job in the majors. Gordon died on April 14, 1978, in Sacramento, California.

### 1970 Charles "Charlie" Metro

Metro had been one of the coach-managers with the Cubs (1962) before taking over the Royals. After 54 games into the 1978 season, and the club in sixth place (19-35), he was fired.

**Above:** *Bob Lemon in his playing days.*
**Top:** *Manager Whitey Herzog.*

### 1970-1972 Robert Granville "Bob" Lemon

Lemon, born on September 22, 1920, in San Bernardino, California, had been a Hall of Fame (1976) pitcher with the Indians (1941-1942, 1946-1958). He carried a lifetime record of 207 wins and 128 losses and an awesome earned run average of 3.23. He had led the league in wins in three years and in complete games in five years. He was brought in to finish the 1970 season for the Royals and was able to win only 46 and lose 62, but that was enough to boost the team from sixth to fourth (65-97 overall). In 1971 he managed a miraculous second-place (85-76) finish. But then, in 1972, the team fell to fourth place (76-78), and Lemon was let go. He was to appear as manager of the White Sox in 1977.

### 1973-1975 John Aloysius "Jack" McKeon

Born on November 23, 1930, in South Amboy, New Jersey, McKeon had had no major league playing experience when he joined the Royals as manager in 1973. He was able to bring them in in second place (88-74) that year, but then it was fifth place (77-85) in 1974 and, after 96 games and a second place (50-46) standing in 1975, he was gone. McKeon showed up as manager of the A's in 1977.

### 1975-1979 Dorrell Norman Elvert "Whitey" "The White Rat" Herzog

Herzog had been the manager of the Rangers in 1973, and he was brought in to skipper the Royals for the last 66 games of the 1975 season. The team was in second place (50-46) at the time, and Herzog won 41 games while losing only 25, keeping them in second (91-71 overall). In 1976 he brought them in in first (90-72), two games ahead of the A's. The League Championship Series went the full five games, but the Royals lost to the Yankees three games to two.

Herzog repeated in 1977 – another first-place (102-60) finish. This time they beat out the A's by eight games. The League Championship Series again went the full five games, but again the Yankees won it three games to two. In 1978 Herzog led them to their third consecutive first-place (92-70) finish – five games ahead of the A's. But for the third straight year, the Yankees beat the Royals in the League Championship Series, this time by three games to one. In 1979 the team slipped to second place (85-77), and Herzog left to manage the Cardinals in 1980.

### 1980-1981 James Gottfried "Jimmy" Frey

Born on May 26, 1931, in Cleveland, Frey had had no major league playing experience before he was called to be the Royals manager in 1980. But he brought them in in first place (97-65) in his first year – 14 games ahead of the A's. In the League Championship Series, the Royals met the Yankees for the fourth time in five years, and this was the revenge year, with the Royals triumphing in three straight games. But it was the Phillies' year in the World Series, and they beat the Royals four games to two. In 1981, that strike-split season, Frey could do no better than fifth place (20-30) in the first half of the season, and, with the team in second (10-10) after 20 games, Frey was fired. He went on to manage the Cubs in 1984.

**Opposite:** *A Jim Frey tantrum.*

### 1981-1986 **Richard Dalton "Dick" Howser**

Howser had been the manager of the Yankees (1978, 1980) before coming to the Royals as manager. He inherited the team in second place (10-10) in the second half-season in 1981, and, by winning 20 and losing 13, he brought them in in first place (30-23 overall). But the A's swept the Divisional Playoff Series three games to none. Then came a second-place finish in 1982 (90-72), which was quite a triumph considering that four Royal players were found guilty of cocaine use that year. It was second (79-83) again in 1983.

Howser won the pennant (84-78) in 1984, three games ahead of the Angels. But the Royals were swept in three straight games by the Tigers in the League Championship Series. It was another pennant (91-71) in 1985, one game ahead of the Angels. In the League Championship Series, the Royals beat the Blue Jays four games to three. And finally the club was able to win a World Series, beating the Cardinals four games to three. After 88 games into the 1986 season and with the team in fourth place (40-48), Howser knew he was dying and left the club. Death came a year later, on June 17, 1987, in Kansas City.

### 1986 **Michael Dennis "Mike" Ferraro**

Ferraro had been the manager of Cleveland in 1983, and he was brought in as interim manager to finish the 1986 season with the Royals. He took over a fourth-place (40-48) team and, by winning 36 and losing 38, brought them in in third place (76-86 overall). Then he was let go.

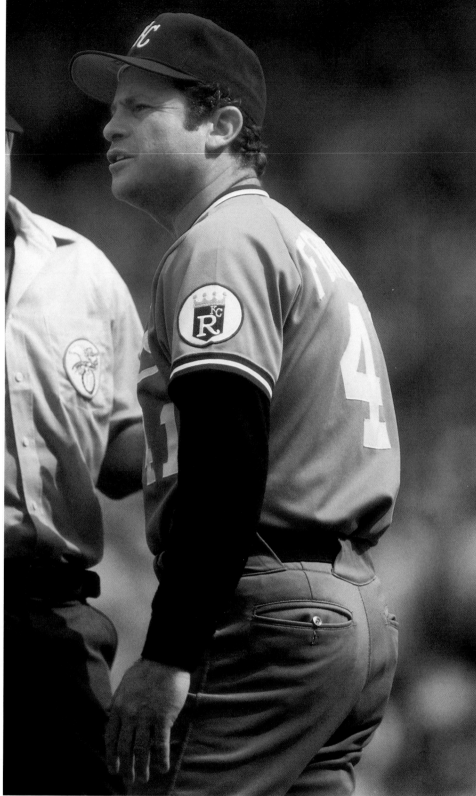

*Above: Manager Mike Ferraro.*
*Top left: Manager Dick Howser.*
*Opposite: Manager John Wathan.*

### 1987 **William Frederick "Billy" "Shotgun" Gardner**

Gardner had been the manager of the Twins (1981-1985) before becoming the Royals' manager in 1987. He lasted 126 games and was fired with KC in fourth place (62-64).

### 1987- **John David "Duke" Wathan**

"Duke" Wathan, who was born on October 4, 1949, in Cedar Rapids, Iowa, had been a catcher for the Royals (1976-1985) before he was invited to become the Royals' tenth manager. He took over a fourth-place (62-64) team and brought them in in second place (83-79 overall) by winning 21 and losing 15. In 1988, however, it was a third-place finish (84-77).

### 1901 **James H. "Jimmy" Manning**

Born on January 31, 1862, in Fall River, Massachusetts, Manning had been an outfielder for several clubs, all teams that no longer exist – Boston of the National League (1884), Detroit of the National League (1885-1987) and Kansas City of the American Association. In his five years in the majors he hit .215. His only season of managing, and the Senators' first year of existence, led to a sixth-place finish (61-73). Manning died on October 22, 1929, in Edinburg, Texas.

### 1902-1903 **Thomas Joseph "Tom" Loftus**

Loftus was brought over from Chicago, where he had been manager of the Cubs, and he kept the Senators in sixth place (61-75) in 1902. The next year was even worse, for he brought the team in in eighth (43-94) in 1903, after which Loftus was fired. He died on April 16, 1910, in Dubuque, Iowa.

### 1904 **Malachi J. Kittredge**

Kittredge, born on October 12, 1869, in Clinton, Massachusetts, had had a long career in the major leagues. He was a catcher for 16 years, but he also appeared as a pitcher in one game in 1896. He had played for the Cubs (1890-1897), Louisville of the National League (1898-1909), Washington of the National League (1899), the Boston Beaneaters (1901-1903), the Senators (1903-1906) and the Indians (1906). In 1904 he was appointed player-manager of the Senators. But after 17 games, with the team in last place (1-16), the Senators decided that an .059 record was not what they were looking for, so Kittredge was let go as manager and went back behind the plate full time. He died on June 23, 1938, in Gary, Indiana.

### 1904 **Patrick Joseph "Patsy" Donovan**

Donovan had been brought in from the Cardinals in 1904 to play the outfield for the Senators. He had been the player-manager of the Pirates (1887, 1899) and the Cardinals (1901-1903), so it seemed natural that he

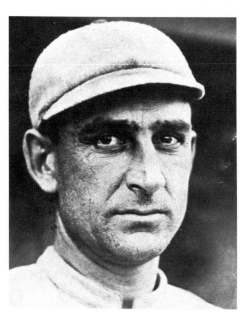

should take over from Kittredge. He finished the last 134 games, leading the club to only 37 wins, while losing 97, and the Senators remained in last place (38-113 overall). Donovan was gone as manager, but he was with the club in the outfield in 1905. In 1906 he became the manager of the Brooklyn Superbas.

### 1905-1906 **Garland "Jake" Stahl**

Stahl was born on April 13, 1879, in Elkhart, Illinois. He had entered big league baseball as a catcher with the Red Sox in 1903. In 1904 he went to the Senators to play first base and the outfield. Then, in 1905, this two-year man was named Washington's player-manager. Stahl was able to improve the standing of the club a bit – to seventh place in 1905 (64-87) and 1906 (55-95). But that wasn't enough of an improvement, so he was fired as manager but continued at first base through 1906. Stahl was then traded to the Yankees (1908) and next to the Red Sox (1908-1910, 1912-1913), a team that he would manage, beginning in 1912.

### 1907-1909 **Joseph D. "Joe" "Pongo" Cantillon**

Cantillon, born on August 19, 1861, in Janesville, Wisconsin, had had no major league playing experience when he was named to be manager of the Senators in

1907. He could do no better than his predecessors. It was eighth place (49-102) in 1907. Then it was seventh place (67-85) in 1908. The only highlight in that season occurred on September 7, when Washington's magnificent pitcher, Walter Johnson, pitched his third consecutive shutout in four days with a 4-0, two-hit victory over the New York Highlanders. He might have

**Above:** *Manager Joe Cantillon.*

the club. In his long tenure as president of the Senators he became an enthusiast for night baseball. In 1948 the Senators held a pre-game ceremony honoring Griffith for his distinguished service to baseball. President Harry S Truman, who was there, said of the Old Fox, "Mr. Griffith is a shining example of what this great country of ours can produce." Griffith died in Washington on October 27, 1955, after 67 years in professional baseball and 36 years as president of his team. Griffith Stadium in Washington was named after him.

### 1921 George Florian McBride

Born on November 20, 1880, in Milwaukee, McBride had been a shortstop with Milwaukee of the American Association (1901), the Pirates (1905) and the Cardinals (1905-1906). Then he was traded to the Senators in 1906 and was an active player until 1920. In 1921, his only year of managing, he brought them up to a fourth-place (80-73) finish. McBride died on July 2, 1973, in Milwaukee.

### 1922 Jesse Clyde "Deerfoot" Milan

Clyde Milan was born on March 25, 1887, in Linden, Tennessee. He spent his entire playing career in the outfield with the Senators (1907-1922) and had a career batting average of .285. In 1922, as player-manager, he led the team to sixth place (69-85) and left the club. Milan died on March 3, 1953, in Orlando, Florida.

### 1923 Owen Joseph "Donie" Bush

Born on October 8, 1887, in Indianapolis, Indiana, Bush was a slick-fielding shortstop for 16 years in the American League – with the Tigers (1908-1921) and the Senators (1921-1923). In his last playing year, 1923, he was made player-manager, and brought the Senators in fourth place (75-78). But he was released and later resurfaced as manager of the Pirates in 1927.

### 1924-1928 Stanley Raymond "Bucky" Harris

All teams have their miracle years, and 1924 was that for the Senators. Bucky Harris was the man who presided over the miracle. Harris was born on November 8, 1896, in Port Jervis, New York, and this Hall of Fame (1975) second baseman, who had

done this on three consecutive days, but the Senators had had the previous day off on Sunday, September 6, In eighth again (42-110) in 1909, Cantillon was fired at the end of the season. He died on January 31, 1930, in Hickman, Kentucky.

### 1910-1911 James Robert "Jimmy" McAleer

McAleer had been the manager of the Indians (1901) and the Browns (1902-1909) before he was brought in to manage the Senators in 1910. On April 14, 1910, 12,226 paid customers attended the opening day game in Washington. It was at this game that President William Howard Taft, a baseball fan, threw out the first ball, thus starting a tradition that was not broken by any president until Jimmy Carter took office. Despite this seeming presidential endorsement, McAleer was able only to bring in his club in in seventh place (66-85). It was seventh again (64-90) in 1911, and McAleer was fired. He died on April 29, 1931, in Youngstown, Ohio.

### 1912-1920 Clark Calvin "The Old Fox" Griffith

Griffith had been the manager of the White Sox (1901-1902), the New York Highlanders (1903-1908) and the Reds (1909-1911), and he was brought in to turn the Senators' fortunes around – and turn them around he did. He led them from seventh place the year before to a second-place (91-61) finish in 1912. In 1913 he once again brought them in second (90-64). But then things started slowly to go downhill. It was third (81-73) in 1914 and fourth (85-68) in 1915. Still, he had given the team four straight finishes in the first division and the only four years in which the Senators had had winning records. But they slipped to seventh (76-77) in 1916 and fifth (74-79) in 1917. After a brief appearance in the first division again, with a third place (72-56) finish in 1918, it was seventh place (56-84) in 1919 and sixth (68-84) in 1920.

In 1919 Griffith and William Richardson had gained a controlling interest in the Senators and Griffith became president of

begun his career with the Senators in 1919, was appointed player-manager of the club in 1924. In his first year as manager he won the pennant with a 92-62 record – Washington's first ever. The season was so exciting that even President and Mrs Calvin Coolidge came out to three games that year.

The Senators faced the Giants in the World Series and traded games back and forth until it was a tie series, three games to three, going into the final game. The Giants scored three runs in the sixth inning to take a 3-1 lead. But then came the fateful eighth inning. Washington's second baseman and boy-manager, the 28-year old Harris, hit a grounder to third baseman Fred Lindstrom that bounced over Lindstrom's head. There were two men on at the time, and both of them scored, tying the game. With the score still tied in the ninth inning, the great Washington pitcher, Walter Johnson, who so far had had a terrible Series, was sent in to pitch. He held on for four gruel-

ing innings, giving up a mere three hits and striking out five. In the bottom of the twelfth inning Giant catcher Hank Gowdy caught his foot in his mask, which was lying on the ground, while trying to catch Senator catcher Herold "Muddy" Ruel's routine foul fly. Ruel celebrated his good fortune by promptly hitting a double – only his second hit of the Series. Then Earl McNeely, the Senators' centerfielder, hit another ball to Lindstrom. Once again the ball took a bad hop, and the Senators won the game 4-3, and with it the Series, four games to three.

But the miracle was not quite over yet. In 1925 Harris won another pennant (96-55), aided by Walter Johnson, who had a 20-7 pitching record that year, his twelfth 20-game year. In the World Series the Senators faced the Pirates, and again it went to seven games. Johnson had won the first and fourth games, holding the Pirates to one run in each contest. He was also the pitcher

in the seventh and deciding game, but now he gave up 15 hits, and the Pirates won the game 9-5, and the Series four games to three. Harris, knowing that he owed the pennant to Johnson, had kept him in for the whole game, and he was severely criticized by American League President Ban Johnson, who accused the Washington manager of losing the Series for the sake of "maudlin sentimentality."

Then came three less-than-great years, although before Harris arrived, they would have been good one for the Senators. He brought them in in fourth (81-69) in 1926, third (85-69) in 1927, and fourth again (75-79) in 1928. Harris was banished to second base and relieved of his managerial duties in 1928, then left to manage the Tigers (1929-1933) and the Red Sox (1934). He was to come back to Washington in 1935.

## 1929-1932 Walter Perry "The Big Train" "Barney" Johnson

Johnson, the Hall of Fame (1936) right-handed pitcher, was born on November 6, 1887, in Humboldt, Kansas. He had thrown for the Senators from 1920 to 1927, and he had won 416 games and lost but 279 for a usually terrible ballclub. Johnson had had 12 20-game seasons, led the league in strikeouts 12 times and six times led the league in number of games won. His career earned run average was a mere 2.17. In his first year at the Senators' helm, 1929, he brought the club in in fifth place (71-81). The team finished second (94-60) in 1930. Two third-place finishes followed – in 1931 (92-62) and 1932 (93-61) – and Johnson was off to manage the Indians in 1933.

*FDR throws out the first ball – 1940. Bucky Harris is far right.*

## 1933-1934 Joseph Edward "Joe" Cronin

Once again a shining knight of a first-time manager came to the Senators to win a pennant in his first year at the helm. Cronin, born on October 12, 1906, in San Francisco, was to be elected to the Hall of Fame in 1956. He had been primarily a shortstop for the Pirates (1926-1927), and he was to continue to play for the Senators (1928-1934) and the Red Sox (1935-1945), carrying a .301 career batting average. In 1933 he was named player-manager of the Senators, and that was the year of their first-place (99-53) finish. It was also to be their last. In the World Series they faced the Giants and lost four games to one. The next year, 1934, was a disaster, with Cronin leading the team to a seventh–place (66-86) finish, and he was off to manage the Red Sox in 1935.

## 1935-1942 Stanly Raymond "Bucky" Harris

Harris was back as the manager of the Senators in 1935, but there were to be no miracles this time. He brought them in in sixth place (67-86) in 1935, and then the team soared to fourth (82-71) in 1936. But

then they fell to sixth again (73-80) in 1937, moved up to fifth (75-76) in 1938 and then it was sixth (65-87) in 1939. Nineteen forty saw them fall to seventh (64-90), it was sixth (70-84) in 1941, and in 1941 it was seventh again (62-89), and Harris was gone. He was to manage the Phillies (1943) and the Yankees (1947-1948) before returning once again to the Senators in 1950.

## 1943-1947 Oswald Louis "Ossie" Bluege

Bluege, born on October 24, 1900, in Chicago, had spent his entire 18-year career as a third baseman for the Senators, playing from 1922 to 1939. As a manager of the Washington club, he had an up and down

**Below:** *Dressen (l.) and Paul Richards.*

career. In his first year he took a seventh-place team and brought them in in second place (84-69). But in 1944 it was back to last place (64-90). Then it was back to second place (87-67) in 1945 and down to fourth (76-78) in 1946. In 1947 the Senators plugged down to seventh place (64-90), and Bluege was fired. He died on October 15, 1985, in Lewisburg, Pennsylvania.

## 1948-1949 **Joseph Anthony "Joe" Kuhel**

Born on June 25, 1906, in Cleveland, Kuhel had been a first baseman (except for a single game played at third base in 1936) in the American League for 18 years, first with the Senators (1930-1937), then the White Sox (1938-1943), the Senators again (1944-1946) and the White Sox again (1946-1947). His record as manager in Washington was far from distinguished, as in 1948 he took over a club that had finished in seventh place the year before, and he was able only to keep them in seventh place (56-97). In 1949 things got worse. The Senators won 50 and lost 104, to finish in last place, and Kuhel was let go. He died on February 26, 1984, in Kansas City, Kansas.

## 1950-1954 **Stanley Raymond "Bucky" Harris**

Harris was back in Washington for the third time in 1950. And, again, his magic didn't work, although things did improve a bit. He brought the team from eighth to fifth (67-87) in 1950, then fell to seventh (62-92) in 1951. Then it was two straight years in fifth place – in 1952 (78-76) and 1953 (76-76). The club fell to sixth place (66-88) in 1953 and Harris, unable to get the team out of the second division, left for the managership of the Tigers in 1955.

## 1955-1957 **Charles Walter "Chuck" Dressen**

Dressen had been the manager of the Reds (1934-1937) and the Dodgers (1951-1953) before being summoned to Washington in 1955. He had a worse time than most Senators' managers had had. In 1955 he was able only to win 53, while losing 101, and that was good for eighth place. The team zoomed up to seventh place (59-95) in 1956. Finally, with the club in eighth place (5-16) after 21 games in 1957, he was fired. Dressen became the manager of the Milwaukee Braves in 1960.

**Above:** *Lavagetto in his playing days.*
**Opposite top:** *Griffith, Ossie Bluege (r.).*

## 1957-1960 **Harry Arthur "Cookie" Lavagetto**

Lavagetto, born on December 1, 1912, in Oakland, had been a journeyman third baseman and second baseman for the Pirates (1934-1936) and the Dodgers (1937-1941, 1946-1947). Although he carried a lifetime batting average of .269, Lavagetto was probably best remembered for a hit he got in the fourth game of the 1947 World Series, in which the Dodgers were playing the Yankees; Yankee pitcher Floyd Bevans had held the Dodgers hitless until two were out in the ninth inning, only to have a pinch double by Lavagetto wreck his effort and beat the Yankees 3-2. Cookie took over the Senators in eighth place in 1957 (5-16) and, by winning 50 and losing 83, he kept them in last place (55-99 overall). In 1958 it was still an eighth-place (61-93) finish. Lavagetto was consistent in 1959, finishing last again (63-91). In 1960 there was a slight improvement – fifth place (73-81). Then Lavagetto and the club, now the Twins, were on their way to Minnesota.

# SENATORS
## Washington (1961-1971)

**1961-1963 James Barton "Mickey" Vernon**

Even though the old Washington Senators had moved to Minnesota after the 1960 season because of poor attendance, it was felt that the nation's capital needed a major league baseball team. So they got one, again called the Senators, in the expansion year of 1981. Vernon, the manager of the new club, was born on April 22, 1918, in Marcus Hook, Pennsylvania, and had been a star first baseman for 20 years with the Senators (1939-1943, 1946-1948), the Indians (1949-1950), the Senators again (1950-1955), the Red Sox (1956-1957), the Indians again (1958), the Braves (1959) and the Pirates (1960). In 1961, being an expansion manager, he brought them in in an expected last place (61-100).

In 1962 President John F. Kennedy threw out the first ball of the season as the Senators opened in their new $24 million stadium built at the taxpayers' expense. A throng of 44,383 watched the home team inaugurate their magnificent ballpark by beating the Tigers 4-1. Kennedy stayed for the whole game, leaving Laotian Ambassador Tiao Khampan back at the White House. But Vernon could do no better than another last-place (60-101) finish that year, and it was tenth place (14-26) again after 40 games in 1963, and Vernon was fired.

**1963-1967 Gilbert Raymond "Gil" Hodges**

Born Gilbert Ray Hodge on April 4, 1924, in Princeton, Indiana, he had played first base for 18 years with the Dodgers (1943, 1947-1961) and the Mets (1962-1963) before being named the manager of the Senators. He inherited a team in tenth place (14-26) in 1963, and was not able to improve its standing by winning 42 and losing 80, and the club ended with a 56-106 record overall. In 1964 President Lyndon B. Johnson threw out the first ball and confided to Hodges that he had played first base back in Texas. Thus encouraged, that year Hodges was able to elevate the Senators to ninth place (62-100). Then it was two years in eighth place – 1965 (70-92) and 1966 (71-88). In

**Above:** *Gil Hodges as a player.*
**Opposite:** *Ted Williams and fans.*

1967 he managed to raise the team to sixth (76-85), but after the season was over, he could not resist the offer to become manager of the Mets in 1968.

**1968 James Robert "Jim" Lemon**

Born on March 23, 1928, in Covington, Virginia, Lemon went on to play the outfield for the Indians (1950, 1953), the Senators (1954-1960), the Twins (1961-1963), the Phillies (1963) and the White Sox (1963). He managed the Senators for only one year, 1968. They came in last (65-96) again, and Lemon was gone.

**1969-1971 Theodore Samuel "Ted" "The Splendid Splinter" "The Thumper" Williams**

Williams joined the Senators as manager for a $1 million stock deal and a partnership with owner Robert Short – this made him end a nine-year self-imposed exile from

baseball. Born on August 30, 1918, in San Diego, Williams became a Hall of Fame (1966) outfielder for the Red Sox (1939-1942, 1946-1960). He not only went into service in World War II after the 1942 season, he also volunteered again for the Korean War after six games had been played in the 1952 season, returning to play in 37 games in 1953. Williams carried a lifetime batting averge of .344, he led the league in home runs four times, in doubles twice and three times batted .400 or better.

Williams took over the Senators in 1969 and performed a minor miracle by bringing them in in fourth place (86-76). He was voted the American League Manager of the Year for giving Washington its first winning season in 17 years. But the team finished in sixth place (70-92) in 1970 and fifth place (63-96) in 1971. Attendance was down, and despite all the rhetoric about the nation's capital needing a major league team, after the 1971 season the Senators left town and reappeared as the Texas Rangers in 1972.

# TIGERS
## Detroit (1901-    )

### 1901 George Tweedy "The Miracle Man" Stallings

Affording former catcher George Stallings the opportunity to manage without doubling as a player separated Detroit from other beginning American League teams. Former manager of Philadelphia in the original National League, Stallings (born in Augusta, Georgia, on November 17, 1867) was thus not inexperienced as he directed the Tigers to third place in their opening season. He did not return, however, moving on to lead the Yankees.

### 1902 John Francis "Frank" Dwyer

Dwyer had pitched for 12 years for an assortment of teams, mostly in the old National League. In 1902 he became Detroit's second manager. After directing the Tigers to seventh place among eight teams, Dwyer, born on March 25, 1868, in Lee, Massachusetts, did not return a second season. He died on February 4, 1943, in Pittsfield, Massachusetts.

**Above:** *Manager George Stallings.*
**Below left:** *Manager Hughie Jennings.*

### 1903-1904 Edward "Ed" "Cousin Ed" Barrow

Improved pitching and hitting brought about 13 additional wins (65) for Ed Barrow's Tigers in 1903 and an improvement of two notches in the standings (fifth place). Barrow, born in Springfield, Illinois, on May 10, 1868, did not complete his second season in Detroit, however, after 32 wins in the first 78 games. He would later manage the Red Sox. Barrow, who had never played in the majors, entered the Hall of Fame in 1953, the year of his death.

### 1904 Robert Lincoln "Bobby" "Link" Lowe

Lodged in seventh place when Bobby Lowe assumed leadership of the Tigers, the team continued to lose. Lowe, born on July 10, 1868, in Pittsburgh, Pennsylvania, was Detroit's first manager to play as well (second base). Unable to advance the Tigers from seventh place, Lowe did not return the next season. He died on December 8, 1951, in Detroit.

### 1905-1906 William R "Bill" Armour

A proven strategist, Bill Armour, who had previously managed the Indians, moved a Tiger team with few changes in personnel from seventh place in 1904 to third in his first season in Detroit. But in his second year with the Tigers, and his final in major league managing, Armour fell below .500 for the first time in his five years of directing, and the Tigers ended in sixth spot. He died in Minneapolis on December 2, 1922.

### 1907-1920 Hugh Ambrose "Hughie" "Ee-Yah" Jennings

The sixth manager of the Tigers, after only six years of team history, was Hughie Jennings, a baseball veteran who had played (mostly shortstop) for a varietry of teams since 1891. It was Jennings' good fortune to have on the team a rightfielder who, in his third year, finished the season as the league's best in total hits, in RBI's, in stolen bases, in hitting average and in slugging average. That stunning performance by Ty Cobb helped lift the Tigers to their first pennant. In the World Series, though, the Tigers lost to the Cubs 4-0.

Jennings led the Tigers to their second successive league championship in his second season of managing, but this time they were only one-half game ahead of the Cleveland Naps. In a World Series reprise Detroit lost to the Cubs again 4-1. Nonetheless, the Tigers had now become a fearsome team, and they proceeded to outrun Connie Mack's Athletics in 1909 for their third consecutive pennant. But the Pirates had finished the season with 110 victories and outmuscled the Tigers to win the World Championship in seven games.

Jennings, a Pennsylvanian (born in Pittston on April 2, 1869, and deceased on February 1, 1928, in Scranton), directed the Tigers 11 more years, but without another pennant. Twice he came close, with a second place in 1911 and again in 1915, when Detroit won 100 games but still lost to Bill Carrigan's Red Sox by four and one-half games. In only four of Jennings's 14 years with the Tigers (the only major-league team he managed) did his teams lose more games then they won. He was inducted into the Hall of Fame in 1945.

### 1921-1926 Tyrus Raymond "Ty" "The Georgia Peach" Cobb

In all but the first season of the six in which he managed the Tigers, Ty Cobb won more games than he lost. In all those years right fielder Cobb also played – and hit at a sizzling pace. In his first year of managing (1921), he batted .389. The team batting average of .316 that year was the highest in the league's history. The following year, 1922, Cobb batted .401.

Notwithstanding Cobb's performance at the plate throughout his managing year (and despite exceptional team hitting), the Tigers never were serious pennant contenders. Their best finish was second (1923), but then they were only one-half game ahead of Tris Speaker's Indians and 16 games behind Miller Huggins' Yankees.

A review of Ty Cobb's years of playing and then of working as player-manager documents that the Tigers finished better when he was not managing. Detroit won three pennants under Hughie Jennings, with Cobb running up spectacular hitting numbers (but modest by the standards of those he posted while managing). Yet as a player-manager Cobb was somehow unable to put together a winner. In his last year the Tigers fell to sixth – where they were in Cobb's first season. He did not manage after that, but played ball for two more sea-

*Ty Cobb (center) gets an award from the Michigan State Legislature.*

sons with the Athletics. Inducted into the Hall of Fame in 1936, "The Georgia Peach" was born in Narrows, Georgia, on December 18, 1886, and died in Atlanta on July 17, 1961.

### 1927-1928 George Joseph Moriarty

The Tigers were still among the league's best in team hitting and slugging during former third baseman George Moriarty's first year managing, but the Tigers nonetheless were outclassed by three better teams – the A's, the Yankees and the Senators. Detroit, consequently, advanced two positions from the previous year, but no better than fourth.

Moriarty (born in Chicago on July 7, 1884) returned for a second full season, but no more, after the Tigers dropped to sixth in 1928, in their first losing season since 1921. Moriarty did not manage again in the major leagues. He died on April 8, 1964, in Miami, Florida.

### 1929-1933 Stanley Raymond "Bucky" Harris

Bearing the credentials of a certified winner after five years managing the Senators (specifically his World Series theft from John McGraw's Giants in 1924), Bucky Harris came to the Tigers to direct a team which, by hitting standards, should have been a pennant contender.

For the past two years, however, Detroit had finished in sixth place and in 1928 had won only 68 games. Harris, in his first year, improved the winning total, but not the sixth spot in the standings, even though the Tigers led the league again in team batting. Harris's second year raised the Tiger's position to fifth, but the team was still playing under .500. The promise of improvement "The Boy Wonder" had brought along with him vanished altogether in his third season, when the team finished next to last, their poorest performance since 1904.

Harris would return to manage the Tigers again over 20 years later, but his inability to advance the team from fifth in his first five seasons meant the end of his first term, with only two games remaining in 1933. The following year would find him managing the Red Sox.

### 1933 Delmar David "Del" Baker

In his first appearance as Detroit manager, Del Baker, who had caught for Detroit between 1914 and 1916, gratuitously worked in the final two games of 1933, winning both but not raising the team from a third fifth-place finish. Baker (born on May 3, 1892, in

179

Sherwood, Oregon) would get a legitimate chance to prove his abilities in Detroit, but not for another five years.

### 1934-1938 Gordon Stanley "Mickey" "Black Mike" Cochrane

The year before famed catcher Mickey Cochrane began managing, the Tigers had lost fourth place to a Cleveland team whose best hitter batted .301. But "Black Mike" quickly became a catalytic force for the team. In his first year of playing and managing in Detroit, Cochrane's Tigers won 101 games and the pennant. Although they lost the World Series to the Cardinals in seven games, the Tigers put to rest any conjecture that Cochrane's triumph in his first year was abnormal. In 1935, his second season, he beat Joe McCarthy's Yankees for the pennant and then defeated the Cubs for the World Title.

Cochrane's influence as a player while managing became apparent in his third and fourth seasons, when the Tigers, without his .300-plus hitting, relinquished the pennant both times to the Yankees. Born in Bridgewater, Massachusetts, on April 6, 1903, Cochrane did not complete his last

year with the Tigers, but left in August when the team was in fourth place. He did not manage in the majors thereafter. Inducted into the Hall of Fame in 1947 (as a player, of course, rather than as a manager), "Black Mike" died on June 28, 1962, in Lake Forest, Illinois.

### 1938-1942 Delmar David "Del" Baker

In a second relief performance reminiscent of his first, Del Baker directed the Tigers to 37 wins in the 58 games that closed the 1938 season. The team did not advance in the standings from fourth, but the .649 win-loss percentage under Baker was all the more impressive when compared to the pennant-winning Yankees' .651.

Baker's first full season with the Tigers returned the pennant to Detroit for the third time in seven years, but the Tigers lost to Cincinnati in a seven-game World Series. In his last two seasons of managing (1941-1942) Baker led the Tigers to fourth- and fifth-place finishes respectively. He did not direct a major league team afterward. He died on September 11, 1973, in San Antonio.

**Opposite top:** *Jewel Ens (l.) and Harris.*
**Opposite bottom:** *Mickey Cochrane (l.).*

**Above:** *Manager Mickey Cochrane.*
**Below:** *McKechnie (l.) and Del Baker.*

## 1943-1948 Stephen Francis "Steve" O'Neill

If any playing position is akin to managing, catching would qualify. Steve O'Neill had caught for five different teams for 17 years (1911-1928) before he began managing. Coming along at a time when the prominent names synonymous with Tiger batting were either retired or had moved on (or had gone to war), O'Neill faced an assignment which is often the death knell for managers – the rebuilding cycle.

In his first season in Detroit O'Neill moved the Tigers above .500 again, though they still could not escape from fifth place. The same team needed only one more season of priming, however, before grasping the pennant and then the World Series from the Cubs in 1945, the last season influenced by the war.

The Tigers' performances under O'Neill over the next two seasons dispelled any suspicions that they were beneficiaries of a war-ravaged league. In both 1946 and 1947, with much the same roster that had won the Series in 1945, O'Neill played head to head against other teams strengthened by returning war veterans and firmly held second place both times. O'Neill, in his six full seasons with the Tigers, did not have a single losing year, even though his last season, 1948, ended in a fifth-place finish. He did not return the following year, and in 1950 he became the manager of the Red Sox.

## 1949-1952 Robert Abial "Red" Rolfe

Six years after retiring from playing third base for ten seasons with Joe McCarthy's Yankees (most of them World Series years), Red Rolfe began managing the Tigers. After finishing fourth in Rolfe's first year, Detroit ended only three games behind Casey Stengel's Yankees for second spot in 1950. Pitching collapsed, however, in 1951; and only George Kell batted over .300. As a result, the Tigers fell into the second division (fifth). Rolfe's last season with Detroit, and as a manager, was a disaster: he directed the team through early June, at which point the Tigers had won only 23 of 72 games. Rolfe died on July 8, 1969, in Gifford, New Hampshire.

**Above:** *Manager Red Rolphe.*
**Below:** *Manager Steve O'Neill (l.) and the Cubs' Charlie Grimm – 1945.*

## 1952-1954 Frederick Charles "Fred" Hutchinson

Accepting the dubious privilege of trying to rescue a Tiger team in jeopardy of compiling the worst season in all its history, Tiger pitcher Fred Hutchinson, in his introduction to managing, was able to accomplish no more than to improve the paltry winning percentage by .010. Detroit won only 50 games during the entire season – its lowest winning total ever and a last-place finish (the first time in team history).

Hutchinson (born in Seattle, Washington, on August 12, 1919) completed two full seasons with the Tigers after the washout in 1952, and the team improved each year. The best they were able to achieve with Hutchinson managing, however, was fifth place in his last season in Detroit. In 1956 he became the manager of the Cardinals.

## 1955-1956 Stanley Raymond "Bucky" Harris

Closing his 29 years as a manager (third highest in total games in major league history) in 1956, Bucky Harris, who had come to Detroit from Washington in 1955, boosted the Tigers' winning percentage more than .070 points over the previous year's mark, but they nevertheless remained in fifth place both years. Inducted into the Hall of Fame in 1975, Harris lived only two more years, dying in Bethesda, Maryland, on November 8, 1977.

## 1957-1958 John Thomas "Jack" Tighe

Still with little direction to go except up in the standings, the Tigers moved ahead one position to fourth in Jack Tighe's first year competing in the major leagues (as manager or player). Tighe (born on August 9, 1913, in Kearney, New Jersey) set off an alarm, however, when he opened the next year with only 21 wins in 49 games. He left with the Tigers back in fifth and did not manage a major league team again.

## 1958-1959 Henry "Bill" Norman

The second successive novice manager to direct the Tigers, former outfielder Bill Norman (born on July 16, 1910, in St. Louis, Missouri) confronted the same discouraging problems his predecessor had faced. Although the team improved their winning percentage to .533 under Norman, they finished in fifth place. Norman did not make it through April in his second season,

*Manager Jimmy Dykes.*

winning only two of 17 games before leaving with the team in last place. Norman died in Milwaukee on April 21, 1962.

## 1959 James Joseph "Jimmy" Dykes

Continuing a pattern that was becoming redundant for the Tigers (and for their managers), Jimmy Dykes accepted the challenge of trying to restore order to a team that was desperate for leadership. Dykes had applied similar tourniquets twice earlier, for the White Sox in 1946 and for the Reds in the season before he came to Detroit.

Dykes inherited a team that had won only two of its first 17 games in 1959, and he directed them at a .540 pace for the remainder of the season – advancing their position in the standings from last to fourth by season's end. But the advance-retreat pattern that had characterized the Tigers

throughout much of the 1950s recurred in Dykes's second season, when they stood solidly in sixth spot near the end of July. That was the end of Jimmy Dykes' term in Detroit; he finished the year managing in Cleveland.

## 1960 William Clyde "Billy" Hitchcock

Getting started in major league managing was for former infielder Billy Hitchcock a modest occasion – one game in the middle of the 1960 season. Hitchcock (born on July 31, 1916, in Inverness, Alabama) seized the opportunity and won the game. Two years later he received the chance to prove himself legitimately when he went to the Orioles.

## 1960 Joseph Lowell "Joe" "Flash" Gordon

Released by Cleveland in July, Joe Gordon barely missed managing in a single game when he moved to Detroit and directed the Tigers in their last 57 games in 1960. His 26 wins did not elevate their place in the standings (sixth), however. Gordon was managing in Kansas City when the 1961 season began.

## 1961-1963 Robert Bonden "Bob" Scheffing

Forty-five home runs by Rocky Colavito and 41 by Norm Cash (who also won the league batting title with a .361 average) swept the Tigers to 101 victories in 1961, Bob Scheffing's first year of managing in Detroit. (He had begun his managing career with the Cubs in 1957.) In ordinary years such numbers would mean a pennant, but 1961 was the season when Roger Maris cracked the home run record established by Ruth 34 years earlier, and the Yankees were still getting Olympian performances from Mantle, Berra and Elston Howard. They won 109 and took first place.

**Above:** *Manager Chuck Dressen.*
**Opposite:** *Manager Ralph Houk.*
**Below:** *Martin (l.) and Joe Cronin.*

Scheffing, despite the second-place finish, had achieved the most sensational recovery in Tigers history; the same

players, who had the year before sent two veteran managers packing and had won only 71 games, performed with precision and authority under Scheffing. In his second season with the Tigers, Scheffing continued to win, but not as assuredly, and finished one-half game out of third place. Twenty-four wins in the first 60 games of 1963 plunged the Tigers to ninth in a ten-team expanded league, and Scheffing was forced to leave Detroit. He did not manage in the major leagues afterward. He died on October 26, 1985.

## 1963-1966 Charles Walter 'Chuck" Dressen

To redirect a Detroit team that had two years earlier finished with 101 victories, but had been ambushed during the first two months of 1963 and stood in next-to-last place, Tiger executives procured from Milwaukee a leader of proven competence – Chuck Dressen. He immediately demonstrated his qualifications by reinstating confidence and poise in the team and won a tie for fourth place with Cleveland at the season's end. After winning fourth spot out-

right in Dressen's next two years, the Tigers had won 16 of their first 26 games in 1966 and stood in third place when the manager was forced to leave because of ill-health. Dressen's death in Detroit came barely three months later, on August 10, 1966.

## 1966 Francis Michael "Frank" Skaff

Standing in to fill the gap after the untimely departure of Chuck Dressen, Frank Skaff, who had played the infield briefly for Brooklyn and Philadelphia a quarter century earlier, worked in 79 games to maintain steadiness for a team in danger of losing its focus. Skaff (born on September 30, 1913, in LaCrosse, Wisconsin) performed nobly and directed the Tigers to 40 wins before yielding his post in early August. He did not manage a big league team again.

## 1966 Robert Virgil "Bob" Swift

In his only opportunity to manage in the major leagues, former catcher Bob Swift, a Kansan (born on March 6, 1915, in Salina) closed the 1966 Tigers season after the death of Chuck Dressen. Faced with the demands of maintaining the course of a team beset by trauma, Swift picked up where interim manager Frank Skaff had left off and held the Tigers to their task by winning 32 of their final 57 games for third place. Swift himself died in Detroit that same year, on October 17.

## 1967-1970 Edward Mayo Smith

Mayo Smith had last managed in Cincinnati in 1959. He was brought to Detroit in 1967 and won 91 games, one game behind league-best Boston. In a commanding surge the Tigers won the pennant in Smith's second year by a margin of 12 games. Smith had ended his eight-year hiatus in managing (five years with the Phillies and Cincinnati, three of them partial seasons) when he came to Detroit, but any skepticism about his bona fides vanished when he directed to the front of the league a team whose best hitter (Willie Horton) batted .285 and whose combined batting average ended fourth best in the league. Denny McLain's spectacular 31 wins were by far the league's best, and a league-leading .983 team fielding average reinforced the often-scorned rule that a stout defense can be a formidable force for winning. The Tigers won the Series in seven games from an exceptional Cardinal team. Mayo Smith's Tigers fell out of of the stratosphere the next season and finished second. In his final year in Detroit and in managing, so-so batting and a crippled pitching performance barely kept the team in fourth place in the East Division. Smith died on November 24, 1977, in Boynton Beach, Florida.

## 1971-1973 Alfred Manuel "Billy" Martin

Flamboyance aside, Billy Martin has managed in at least one pennant-winning season for all but one of the several teams he has directed (the exception was the Rangers). The 1970 fourth-place Tigers regained their imposing reputation in the first season under Martin, who had come to them from Minnesota, and finished authoritatively in second spot behind Earl Weaver's Orioles. The next year Martin directed them to the pennant, but lost to Oakland in the League Championship Series, three games to one.

Managing in all but the last 19 games of his last season with the Tigers, Martin left, with the team in third place, to direct the Rangers.

## 1973 Joseph Charles "Joe" "Dode" Schultz

His previous managing experience limited to one season with an expansion team in its maiden year (Seattle), former catcher Joe Schultz completed his managerial career in the major leagues by leading the Tigers in the closing 19 games of 1973. He enabled the team to hold fast to third place by winning nine games.

## 1974-1978 Ralph George "Major" Houck

Missing the pervasive fever which accompanied Billy Martin's high-strung term, the

February 3, 1935, in Eynon), acted as caretaker until the team office secured a name who could recharge the Tigers for the 1980s. Tracewski has not managed in the major leagues since.

## 1979-1988 George Lee "Sparky" Anderson

Few managers in the major leagues today command more regard for their intelligence, craftiness and mastery of winning strategy than Sparky Anderson of the Tigers. Ranking tenth in the major leagues in all-time winning percentage (.576) through 1987, Anderson carries a history of winning. When he came to the Tigers from Cincinnati to complete the 1979 season he had already directed four pennant winners (and one additional division winner) in his first nine years of managing. His poorest year was his first season in Detroit (a partial – only 105 games) when the Tigers finished in fifth place.

As though inexorably, the Tigers began advancing as early as Anderson's first full season. They became pennant-winners in 1984 (Anderson's fifth complete season with the team), and then Alan Trammell and Kirk Gibson helped them bury the Padres four games to one for the World Title. Three years later the Tigers withstood the threats of a persistent Toronto team and again won the East Division, only to take a pasting from the Twins in the League Championship Series.

Always a tactician, as opposed to a showman, Anderson applies principles of discipline and a mastery at playing the game. He practices the theories advanced by Branch Rickey, who emphasized the importance of developing players through an apprenticeship in which they learn the essentials of running, throwing, hitting and fielding. Anachronistically, Anderson has shown no inclination toward buying a team of instant winners, preferring instead to realize the full possibilities of his players.

In 1988 the Tigers clung tenaciously to first place until late in August, when they relinquished it to the Red Sox. Even through September they remained contenders and eventually finished third in a season that concluded with only six and one-half games separating the top five teams.

**Above left:** *Manager Sparky Anderson.*
**Opposite:** *Anderson in an argument.*

---

Tigers drifted into a pattern of inertia during the years that former Yankee manager Ralph Houck worked in Detroit. Signs of trouble began to appear in Houck's first year when the team fell to the bottom of their division, albeit the season's finish was only five games behind fourth-place Cleveland.

The next year, 1975, however, was a nightmare, with a 57-102 performance – the weakest in 12 years and the third worst season winning average in the team's history (.358). Mark Fidrych's 19 wins, 2.34 ERA (league best) and some eccentric behavior on the mound were the only notable performances the next season, 1976, but the Tigers did move up one position to fifth.

One more position up in the standings in Houck's 1977 season with the Tigers would be his best showing in the standings in his

five years in Detroit. His only winning season occurred in his last year, 1978, when the Tigers won 86 games, yet the team ended fifth. Houck returned to managing in 1981, but with the Red Sox.

## 1979 John Lester "Les" Moss

Allowed less than two months to deliver, Les Moss managed in the first 57 games of 1979 and won 27 before Tigers executives replaced him. Moss (born on May 14, 1925, in Tulsa, Oklahoma) did not alter the fifth place the team held at the close of 1978, and he has not managed since.

## 1979 Richard Joseph "Dick" Tracewski

Directing the Tigers to two wins in the three games in which he managed, Dick Tracewski, a Pennsylvanian (born on

# TWINS
Minnesota (1961-    )

### 1961 Harry Arthur "Cookie" Lavagetto

When the Senators moved to Minnesota to become the Twins, Lavagetto went with them as manager, but he didn't stay long. After 74 games in 1961, and with the team in ninth place (29-45), he was fired. He has not managed in the majors since then.

### 1961-1967 Sabath Anthony "Sam" Mele

Mele, born on January 21, 1923, in Astoria, New York, had been an outfielder for several major league clubs. He began his career with the Red Sox (1947-1949), then went to the Senators (1949-1952), the White Sox (1952-1953), the Orioles (1954), the Red Sox again (1954-1955), the Reds (1955) and the Indians (1956). In 1961 he took over as manager of the Twins, with the club in ninth place (29-45), and, by winning 41 and, losing 45, he was able to lift them to seventh (70-90 overall). The next year, 1962, was much better, and he brought them in in second place (91-71). But 1963 saw the club fall to third (91-70), and in 1964 they plunged to sixth (79-83). Then came the exciting year of 1965. Mele brought them in in first place (102-60), and they gave the Dodgers a tussle before submitting four games to three in the World Series. The next year, 1966, was also a pretty good one, with the Twins finishing second (89-73), but in 1967 they fell to sixth (25-25) after 50 games, and Mele was no longer the Twins' manager.

**1967-1968 Calvin Coolidge "Cal" Ermer**

Born on November 10, 1923, in Baltimore, Ermer had played in just one game in the major leagues. In 1947 he appeared as a second baseman for the Senators, going 0 for 3. He inherited the Twins in 1967 when they were in sixth place (25-25), and he brought them in in second place (91-71 overall) by winning 66 and losing 46. But in 1968 the club slipped to seventh (79-83), and Ermer was let go.

**1969 Alfred Manuel "Billy" Martin**

Born Alfred Manuel Pesano on May 16, 1928, in Berkeley, California, Martin had been a peppery, combative, and hard-working second baseman for the Yankees (1950-1953, 1955-1957), Kansas City (1957), the Tigers (1958), the Indians (1959), the Reds (1970), the Braves (1960) and the Twins (1961). The managership of the Twins was his first of many tenures managing major league teams. In his single year with the Twins, he brought the team in in first place (97-65) after a season-long fight against the Oakland A's. They faced the Orioles in the League Championship Series and lost in three straight games – two of them in extra innings. Martin, even though he was a success in Minnesota, was fired because he couldn't get along with the front office. To suggest that this might have indicated a certain flaw in Martin's personality would perhaps understate the case. He appeared as the manager of the Detroit Tigers in 1971.

**1970-1972 William Joseph "Billy" "Specs" "The Cricket" Rigney**

Rigney had been the manager of the Giants (1956-1960) both in New York and San Francisco, of the Dodgers (1961-1964) and of the Angels (1965-1969) before coming to the Twins. In his very first year there he brought the team in in first place (98-64). But then they lost three straight to the Orioles in the League Championship Series. In 1971 the team fell to fifth (74-86), and in 1972, with the Twins in third place (36-34) after 70 games, Rigney was fired. He would turn up managing in San Francisco in 1976.

**Opposite:** *Manager Billy Gardner.*
**Below:** *Manager Billy Martin.*

*Bill Rigney and umpire Ron Luciano having a shouting match – 1971.*

## 1972-1975 Francis Ralph "Frank" "Guido" Quilici

Quilici, born on May 11, 1939, in Chicago, had had a short career in the majors, playing second base for the Twins (1965-1970). He took over when the Twins were in third place (36-34) in 1972, and, by winning 41 and losing 43, he kept them there (77-77 overall). It was then two straight third-place finishes in 1973 (81-81) and 1974 (82-80). In 1975 the team fell to fourth (76-83), and Quilici was gone.

## 1976-1980 Gene William "Skip" Mauch

Mauch had been the manager of the Phillies (1960-1968) and the Expos (1969-1975) before coming to the Twins as manager. After bringing them in in third place (85-77) in 1976, he led them to three straight fourth-place finishes in 1977 (84-77), 1978

(73-89) and 1979 (82-80). In 1980, with the team in sixth place (54-71) after 125 games, he was fired. Mauch later showed up as manager of the Angels in 1981.

## 1980-1981 John Albert Goryl

Goryl, born on October 21, 1933, in Cumberland, Rhode Island, had had a short six-year career in the majors, playing as a utility infielder for the Cubs (1957-1959) and the Twins (1962-1964). He took over the Twins in 1980 when they were in sixth place (54-71) after 125 games and got them up to third by winning 23 and losing 13 (77-84 overall). In 1981 the team had fallen to fifth place (11-25) after 36 games, and Goryl was sent packing.

## 1981-1985 William Frederick "Billy" "Shotgun" Gardner

Born on July 19, 1927, in Waterford, Connecticut, Gardner had been primarily a second baseman for the Yankees (1954-1955), the Orioles (1956-1959), the Senators (1960), the Twins (1961), the Yankees again

(1961-1962) and the Red Sox (1962-1963). He inherited the Twins during the strike-ridden year of 1981, when there was a first-half champion and a second-half champion in each league. With 20 games to go in the first half and with the Twins in fifth place (11-25), he won 6 and lost 14, to bring them in seventh (17-39 overall). The second half was better, and Gardner managed to lead the team in in fourth place (24-29). In 1982 it was back to seventh place (60-102). Then it was fifth place (70-92) in 1983. In 1984, he managed a second-place (81-81) finish, and, with the team in sixth place (27-35) after 62 games in 1985, Gardner was let go. He was to show up as manager of the Royals in 1987.

## 1985-1986 Raymond Roger "Ray" Miller

Miller, born on April 30, 1945, in Tacoma Park, Maryland, had never played in the major leagues when he took over the Twins after 62 games in 1985. The club was in sixth place (27-35), and Miller, by winning 50 and losing 50, was able to raise them to fourth place (77-85 overall). The next year, 1986, Miller was able to do no better than to lead the team to seventh place (59-80) after 139 games, and he was fired.

## 1986- Jay Thomas "Tom" Kelly

Kelly, born on August 15, 1950, in Graceville, Minnesota, had had an extremely short career as a major league baseball player. He had appeared as a first baseman for one game and as an outfielder for two with the Twins in 1975. After inheriting the Twins after 139 games, in seventh place (59-80), he was able to win 12 and lose 11 to up their standing to sixth place (71-91 overall). But 1987 was all his. In his first complete year as a manager he brought the team in in first place (85-77). Not only that, but also he was able to win the League Championship Series by beating the Tigers four games to one. And then this club, with its puny .525 winning percentage during the season, went on to take the World Series from the Cardinals four games to three. In 1988, he brought the team in in second place with a 97-71 record, but was still 13 games back of the Oakland A's.

**Opposite top left:** *Gene Mauch.*
**Opposite top right:** *Billy Gardner.*
**Opposite bottom left:** *Ray Miller.*
**Opposite bottom right:** *Tom Kelly.*

# WHITE SOX
## Chicago (1901-    )

### 1901-1902 Clark Calvin "The Old Fox" Griffith

The American League was formed in 1901, largely through the efforts of Ban Johnson, who had changed the name of the Western League to the American League. Johnson had owned the Grand Rapids club in the Western League, and he moved the franchise to Cleveland. The next step, a crucial one, was to set up a new team in Chicago. For some concessions he convinced the Cubs' general manager, Jim Hart, to allow him to establish an American League ball club on the South Side of Chicago – Hart had figured that the smell of the stockyards would keep fans from patronizing it. In 1900 Chicago native Charles Comiskey gladly packed up his Western League team in St. Paul, Minnesota, and moved back to the Windy City.

Although Hart had stipulated in the agreement that the American League team was not to identify itself as a Chicago club, the canny Comiskey named his team the White Sox, clearly evoking the earlier Chicago National League team, the White Stockings, who later became the Cubs. The new league was ready to go in 1901, with teams in Baltimore, Washington, Philadelphia, Boston, Chicago, Detroit, Cleveland and Milwaukee.

Comiskey chose Clark Griffith as his first manager in Chicago. Born on November

20, 1869, in Clear Creek, Missouri, Griffith, who was elected to the Hall of Fame in 1946, was primarily a right-handed pitcher who had hurled for St. Louis of the American Association (1891), Boston of the American Association (1891) and Chicago of the National League (1893-1900). In 1901 he came in as player-manager of the White Sox and remained until 1902. Then he went on to pitch for the New York Highlanders (1903-1907), the Reds (1909-1910) and the Senators (1912-1914). His career record was 240 wins and 141 losses, and he carried a 3.31 earned run average.

On April 24, 1901, the first game in American League history was played, and the White Sox beat the Indians 8-2. (Three other games had been scheduled, but all of them were rained out.) This contest took only 90 minutes and was played before 14,000 people in the stands at the Chicago Cricket Club.

Griffith brought the White Sox a pennant (83-53) in his – and their – very first year, 1901. Of course there was no World Series in that year, so the Chicagoans had to be satisfied with first place. In 1902 the club slipped to fourth place (74-60), and Griffith was off to become player-manager of the New York Highlanders. He was to continue pitching until 1914.

### 1903-1904 James Joseph "Nixey" Callahan

Callahan, born on March 18, 1974, in Fitchburg, Massachusetts, had been primarily an outfielder (although he did pitch in a total of 195 games) for Philadelphia of the National League (1894) and for Chicago of the National League (1897-1900). He was also to play for the White Sox (1901-1905, 1911-1913). He was able only to bring his White Sox in in seventh place (60-77) in 1903, and in 1904, after 40 games and with the club in fourth place (22-18), he was let go. He returned to playing the outfield, but was to return as White Sox manager in 1912.

### 1904-1908 Fielder Allison Jones

Jones, born on August 13, 1871, in Shinglehouse, Pennsylvania, had played the outfield for Brooklyn of the National League (1896-1900) and for the White Sox since 1901. In 1904 he was called in to become the player-manager of the Sox when they were in fourth place (22-18). Jones was successful enough, winning 67 and losing only 47, and the Sox ended the season in third place (89-65 overall). The next year, 1905, was even better, and the White Sox ended in second place (92-60). In 1906 Jones led them to the pennant (93-58) and into their first World Series. This was the year of the famous White Sox "Hitless Wonders." They had won the pennant with a team batting average of .228, and they had hit only six home runs during the entire season – both records were the lowest in the American League. Their opponents in the Series were their North side rivals, the Cubs, and the White Sox dispatched the National Leaguers four games to one. There was no place to go but down, and

Jones piloted the Sox to two straight third-place finishes in 1907 (87-64) and in 1908 (88-64). Jones was gone, but he was to re-appear later as the player-manager of St. Louis in the Federal League (1914-1915) and then of the Browns (1916-1918).

**Above:** *Manager Kid Gleason.*
**Opposite top left:** *Clark Griffith – the White Sox' first manager.*
**Opposite bottom:** *Manager Fielder Jones.*

## 1909 William Joseph "Billy" Sulivan Sr.

Born on February 1, 1875, in Oakland, Wisconsin, Sullivan was a catcher who had broken into major league baseball with the Boston Beaneaters, catching for them from 1899 to 1900. Traded to the White Sox in 1901, he was asked to take over the reins of the team as player-manager in 1909. He was able to bring them in fourth (78-74), but that was not good enough, and he was relieved of his managerial duties. It was back behind the plate for Billy, and he stayed with the Sox (1910-1912, 1914) for a while and ended up playing for the Tigers in 1916. Sullivan died on January 28, 1965, in Newberg, Oregon.

## 1910-1911 Hugh Duffy

The year 1910 was the year that Charles Comiskey's new ballpark was dedicated. It was a magnificent new playing field, replete with steel and concrete grandstands faced with brick and was no doubt the greatest baseball stadium of the day. After it was built, Comiskey, never a shrinking violet, called it "Charles A. Comiskey's Baseball Palace." But the official name was White Sox Park, and it was not changed to Comiskey Park until later. The first game played there came on July 1, and the Browns beat the Sox 2-0.

Duffy was brought in in 1910 to manage the Sox because he had managed both the Milwaukee club in the American League (1901) and the Phillies (1904-1906). In 1910 he took the club that had finished fourth the previous year and guided them to a sixth-place (68-85) finish. Although he was able to raise them to fourth (77-74) in 1911, that was not enough, and he was fired. Duffy was to show up again as manager of the Red Sox in 1921.

## 1912-1914 James Joseph "Nixey" Callahan

Callahan was brought back to manage the White Sox in 1912 and was able to keep them in fourth place (78-76). But then the slide started. It was fifth (78-74) in 1913 and sixth (70-84) in 1914, and Callahan was out. He became the Pirates' manager in 1916.

## 1915-1918 Clarence Henry "Pants" Rowland

Rowland, born on February 12, 1879, in Platteville, Wisconsin, had had no major league playing experience when he was

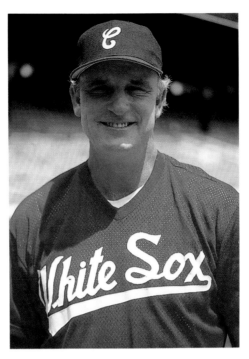

**Above:** *Manager Doug Rader.*
**Opposite:** *Manager Tony LaRussa.*

appointed to be the White Sox manager in 1915. But he did all right, bringing them in in third place (93-61) in 1915 and second (89-65) in 1916. Rowland won the pennant (100-54) in 1917, with excellent pitching, a strong infield and the great Shoeless Joe Jackson in left field. They played the Giants in the World Series and beat them soundly, four games to two. The next year was a disaster, however. The club came in in sixth place (57-67) in 1918, and Rowland was let go. He died on May 17, 1969, in Chicago.

## 1919-1923 William J. "Kid" Gleason

Gleason, born on October 26, 1866, in Camden, New Jersey, had been an all-round athlete on the diamond. Basically a second baseman, he had pitched in 298 games and had played the outfield, shortstop, third base, first base, and had even caught, for the Phillies (1888-1891), the Cardinals (1892-1894), Baltimore in the National League (1894-1895), the Giants (1896-1900), the Tigers (1901-1902), the Phillies again (1903-1908) and the White Sox (1912). He was appointed to be manager of the White Sox in 1919, but had he known what was about to happen, he probably would never have taken the job.

In 1919 the White Sox came back from their 1918 sixth-place finish to win the pennant (88-52) easily under manager Gleason. But no one knew that three of the Sox

players, pitcher Eddie Cicotte, first baseman Arnold "Chick" Gandil, and pitcher Claude "Lefty" Williams had approached gamblers (including the notorious Arnold Rothstein) in New York at midseason to discuss a fix.

The White Sox, unquestionably one of the greatest teams of all time, were hands-down favorites to take the Series, yet they were upset by the Reds five games to three. Obviously there were people who knew the fix was in, since even before the Series started the odds went from 3-1 White Sox to 8-5 Reds.

It was alleged that the prearranged signal from players to the gamblers was to have the White Sox pitcher hit the first batter in the first game. Cicotte performed on cue, and the game turned into a rout, with Cincinnati winning 9-1. There are those who feel that after that first game the Series was played more or less on merit. Nevertheless, Cincinnati won the second game 4-2. The White Sox won the third game 3-0, and there were those who thought that that was because the gamblers were going back on their promise to pay the crooked players $10,000 of the $100,000 total after each game. Cicotte was the pitcher in the fourth game, and the Reds won 2-0 after he made two errors on the mound. Cincinnati won the fifth game 5-0, then the Sox came back in the fifth game 5-4. Cicotte prevailed on manager Gleason to let him pitch in the seventh game and came through this time, 4-1. The eighth game was a disaster for Chicago, as the Reds won 10-5. Thus Cincinnati won the Series five games to three.

It took almost a year for the game-fixing to become general knowledge, although Sox owner Charles Comiskey heard about it after the second game. When he passed the word to John Heydler, the president of the National League, Heydler informed Ban Johnson, the president of the American League. Johnson and Comiskey were feuding at the time, and Johnson passed off the accusation as "the yelp of a beaten cur."

Nothing was known publicly about the fix until the following September, but rumors flew fast and furious. Boxer Abe Attell confessed to being involved in the deal and named eight players on a list of guilty parties. The "Black Sox" on the list were outfielder "Shoeless Joe" Jackson, third baseman George "Buck" Weaver, first baseman Arnold "Chick" Gandil, shortstop Charles "Swede" Risberg,

pitchers Eddie Cicotte and Claude "Lefty" Williams, centerfielder Oscar "Happy" Felsch and utility infielder Fred McMullin. Cicotte, Gandil and Williams were the ringleaders. *The Chicago Tribune* called for a grand jury investigation.

When confronted by Gleason and Comiskey, Cicotte broke down. He, Jackson and Williams then gave the details of how the games were rigged to a grand jury, and Comiskey suspended all eight players, although some argued that Weaver was guilty only by association, for though he had sat in on the negotiations over the fix, he decided not to participate in it. As Jackson was leaving the courthouse after the grand jury hearing, a small boy supposedly came up to him with tears in his eyes, and, as legend has it, cried "Say it ain't so, Joe."

Criminal indictments followed, but by then the players' written confessions had disappeared, and they were all acquitted. According to the letter of the law, they could have been reinstated. But an officer called the Commissioner of Baseball had just been created. Judge Kenesaw Mountain Landis, named for a Civil War battle, took quick and decisive action. "Regardless of the verdict of juries, no player that throws a game, no player that entertains proposals or promises to throw a game, no player that sits in conference with a bunch of crooks and gamblers where the ways and means of throwing games are discussed, and does not promptly tell his club about it, will ever play professional baseball." The scandal of the "Black Sox" seriously undermined the confidence of many in the game that had become the national pastime, but Landis' firm handling of the situation helped mitigate the disaster.

Of course Gleason – who had no part in the fix and no knowledge of it – had the "Black Sox" players back for most of the 1920 season, since the hearing was not held until late in the season, and he managed to guide them in in second place (96-58). But then the nucleus of the great White Sox team was gone in 1921, and it was seventh place (62-92). He led the Sox up to a fifth-place (77-77) finish in 1922, and then it was seventh place (69-85) in 1923, and Gleason was fired. He died on January 2, 1933, in Philadelphia.

**Opposite top:** *The 1919 White Sox.*
**Opposite bottom:** *Hughie Jennings, John McGraw, Kid Gleason.*

*Manager Eddie Collins also played second base while he was the skipper.*

### 1924 John Joseph "Johnny" "The Trojan" "The Crab" Evers
Evers had managed the Cubs in 1913 and 1921, and he was brought to the South Side to manage the White Sox in 1924. The year was a disaster, as the club finished in last place (66-87), and Evers was fired. He died on March 28, 1947, in Albany, New York.

### 1925-1926 Edward Trowbridge "Eddie" "Cocky" Collins Sr.
This Hall of Fame (1939) shortstop was born on May 2, 1887, in Millerton, New York. He had started his career under the name of Eddie Sullivan, playing with the Athletics in 1906. Then, under his own name, he played for the Athletics (1907-1914) and the White Sox (1915-1926). As player-manager of the Sox he was able only to bring them in in two straight fifth-place finishes in 1925 (79-75) and 1926 (81-72). He was let go and finished his major league career in the infield for the Athletics (1927-1930). He died in Boston, Massachusetts, on March 25, 1951.

### 1927-1928 Raymond William "Ray" "Cracker" Schalk
The Sox brought in another future Hall of Famer (1955) to manage in 1927. Schalk, born on August 12, 1892, in Harvel, Illinois, had starred as a catcher with the White Sox since 1912. As player-manager he was able to achieve only a fifth-place (70-83) finish in 1927, and, after 74 games and with the club in sixth place (32-42) in 1928, he was relieved. Schalk then caught for the Yankees in 1929. He died on May 19, 1970, in Chicago.

### 1928-1929 Russell Aubrey "Lena" "Slats" Blackburne
Lena Blackburne was born on October 23, 1886, in Clifton Heights, Pennsylvania, and had played mainly at shortstop, second base and third base for the White Sox (1910, 1912, 1914-1915), the Reds (1918), the Braves (1919), the Phillies (1919) and the White Sox again (1927, 1929). He took over the Sox in 1928 when they were in sixth place (32-42) and was able to raise them to fifth (72-82 overall) by winning 40 and losing 40. In 1929 the team fell to seventh (59-93), and Blackburne's managerial career was over. He died on February 29, 1960, in Riverside, New Jersey.

*Manager Jim Fregosi.*

### 1930-1931 Owen Joseph "Donie" Bush

Bush had been the manager of the Senators (1923) and the Pirates (1927-1929) before he came to the White Sox in 1930. He had a terrible time in Chicago, finishing seventh (62-92) in 1930 and last (56-97) in 1931. In 1933 he was in Cincinnati, managing the Reds.

### 1932-1934 Lewis Albert "Lew" Fonseca

Born on January 21, 1899, in Oakland, California, Fonseca had been a first baseman-second baseman-outfielder with the Reds (1921-19o24), the Phillies (1925) and the Indians (1927-1931). He joined the White Sox in 1931 and became the player-manager of the club the next year. Fonseca was to end his playing career with a .316 batting average. He led the Sox to seventh place (49-102) in 1932, then raised them to sixth (67-83) in 1933. The highlight of that year of 1933 in Comiskey Park had very little to do with the Sox. On July 6 the first major league All-Star Game was played there as a promotion device to go along with the Chicago Worlds Fair – "A Century of Progress." The game, a brainchild of sports editor Arch Ward of *The Chicago Tribune*, was a great success, and it began the tradi-

tion that exists to this day. In the game Connie Mack and the American League stars beat John McGraw and the National League stars 4-2 on Babe Ruth's two-run homer. In 1934, with the team in eighth place (4-13) after 17 games, Fonseca was fired and did not manage thereafter.

### 1934-1946 James Joseph "Jimmy" Dykes

Born on November 10, 1896, in Philadelphia, Dykes was primarily a third baseman-second baseman for the Athletics (1918-1932) before joining the White Sox in 1933. He was to become player-manager of the Sox from 1934 to 1939. In 1940 he gave up playing and remained as manager until 1946, along the way becoming a Chicago favorite. He inherited the team in the eighth place (4-13) in 1934 and, by winning 49 and losing 86, was unable to improve their standing. But it was fifth place (74-78) in 1935, and then came two heady years in third, 1936 (81-70) and 1937 (86-88). A sixth-place finish (65-83) in 1938 was followed by two straight years in fourth, 1939 (85-69) and 1940 (82-72). Dykes raised them to third (77-77) in 1941, and then the Sox slid to sixth (66-82) in 1942. The team was back in fourth place (82-72) in 1943, and then in 1944 came a seventh-place (71-83) finish. After a sixth-place (71-78) finish

in 1945 the club was in seventh place again (10-20) in 1946 when, after 30 games, Dykes was let go. He was to resurface in 1951 as the manager of the Athletics.

### 1946-1948 Theodore Amar "Ted" Lyons

Lyons was born on December 28, 1900, in Lake Charles, Louisiana, and this future Hall of Fame (1955) pitcher was to hurl for the White Sox (1923-1942, 1946) for his entire playing career. He won 260 games for all those miserable teams, led the league in wins in 1925 (21) and 1927 (22), led the league in complete games in 1927 (30) and 1930 (29) and led the league in shutouts in 1925 (5) and 1950 (4). Lyons took over the team in 1946 when it was in seventh place, with a 10-20 mark, and, by winning 64 and losing 60, moved them up to fifth (74-80 overall). But in 1947 they fell to sixth (70-84) and slipped further in 1948 – to last place (51-101) – and Lyons was released. He did not manage in the majors after that and died on July 25, 1986, in Sulpher, Louisisiana.

### 1949-1950 John James "Jack" Onslow

Born on October 13, 1888, in Scottdale, Pennsylvania, Onslow had played only 40 games as a catcher in the big leagues – with the Tigers (31 games) in 1912 and with the Giants (nine games) in 1917. Onslow was able to bring the Sox in in sixth place (63-91) in 1949, but in 1950 the club won eight and lost 22 and was occupying eighth place when Onslow was fired. He died on December 22, 1960, in Concord, Massachusetts.

### 1950 John Michael "Red" Corriden Sr.

Corriden was born on September 4, 1887, in Logansport, Indiana, and had a five-year career as a big league shortstop with the Browns (1910), the Tigers (1912) and the Cubs (1913-1915). He was brought in to finish the 1950 season when the White Sox were in eighth place (8-22). By winning 52 and losing 72 he managed to lift the club to a sixth-place (60-94 overall) finish. He died on September 28, 1959, in Indianapolis.

### 1951-1954 Paul Rapier Richards

Born on November 21, 1908, in Waxahachie, Texas, Richards had been a catcher for eight year in the majors with the Dodgers (1932), the Giants (1933-1935), the

Athletics (1935) and the Tigers (1943-1946). He had one of the canniest minds in baseball and was able to take a mediocre White Sox team to fourth place (81-73) in 1951. Then came two straight years in third place, 1952 (81-73) and 1953 (89-65). In 1954, with the team in third place (91-54) after 145 games, he left the team and was to show up the next year as manager of the Orioles.

## 1954-1956 Martin Whitford "Marty" "Slats" "The Octopus" Marion

Marion had been the manager of the Cardinals (1951) and the Browns (1952-1954) before being brought to Chicago to take over the White Sox. He began in 1954 with only nine games to go in the season. He kept the club in third place (94-60 overall), although they won only three games, while losing six. Marion was able to keep them in third place for the next two years, 1955 (91-63) and 1956 (85-69), but at the end of 1956 his managing career was over.

## 1957-1965 Alfonso Raymond "Al" Lopez

Lopez had done wonders as the manager of the Indians (1951-1956) and was brought to manage the White Sox in 1957. He took over a club that had finished third the year before and led them to a second-place (90-64) record. Another second place (82-72) followed in 1958, and then, in 1959, Lopez won the pennant (94-60), the team's first in 39 years. In winning this pennant, Lopez relied on outstanding pitching, speed and defense, thus beating out his old team, the Indians, by five games. The Sox lost the World Series to the Dodgers four games to two. The Sox fell to third place (87-67) in 1960, and continued to go downhill, finishing fourth (86-76) in 1961 and fifth (85-77) in 1962. Then came three straight years in second place – 1963 (94-68), 1964 (98-64) and 1965 (95-67). After that season he retired but would return in 1968.

## 1966-1968 Edward Raymond "Eddie" "The Brat" "Muggsy" Stanky

Stanky had been a fairly successful manager of the Cardinals (1952-1955). He was brought in to manage the White Sox in 1966 and was able to bring them in in fourth place for two straight years 1966 (83-79) and 1967 (89-73). Then, with the club in ninth place (34-45) after 79 games in 1968, he was let go. Stanky would reappear as manager of the Rangers in 1977.

## 1968 John Lester "Les" Moss

Moss, born on May 14, 1925, in Tulsa, Oklahoma, had been a catcher in the big leagues with the Browns (1946-1951), the Red Sox (1951), the Browns again (1952-1953), the Orioles (1954-1955) and the White Sox (1955-1958). He was brought in as a stopgap manager of the White Sox in 1968, when the club was in ninth place (34-45). He was, in fact, the manager for only two games that year, and he lost both of them. That was all for Moss in Chicago, but he would later return as manager of the Detroit Tigers (1979).

*Manager Jeff Torborg has a conference at the mound.*

## 1968-1969 Alfonso Raymond "Al" Lopez

Lopez was brought out of retirement to finish the year as manager of the Sox. With the team in ninth place (34-47) he didn't improve matters by winning 33 and losing 48, and the team stayed in ninth (67-95 overall). In 1969 he was in fourth place (8-9) when he decided to retire again, this time for good.

### 1969-1970 **Donald Joseph "Don" Gutteridge**

Primarily a second baseman-third baseman, Gutteridge was born on June 19, 1912, in Pittsburg, Kansas. His playing career included stints with the Cardinals (1936-1940), the Browns (1942-1945), the Red Sox (1946-1947) and the Pirates (1948). He took over the Sox in 1969 when they were in fourth place (8-9) and, by winning 60 and losing 85, let them slip to fifth place (68-94 overall). The next year, 1970, was worse, and with the team in sixth place (49-87) after 136 games, he was fired.

### 1970 **Marion Danne "Bill" Adair**

Born on February 10, 1916, in Mobile, Alabama, Adair had had no major league playing experience when he took over the Sox as a stopgap manager in 1970. The team was in sixth place (49-87), and Adair managed for only ten games, winning four.

### 1970-1975 **Charles William "Chuck" Tanner**

Tanner was born on July 4, 1929, in New Castle, Pennsylvania. He had played the outfield for the Braves (1955-1957), the Cubs (1957-1958), the Indians (1959-1960) and the Dodgers (1961-1962). With only 16 games to go in the 1970 season and with the Sox in sixth place (53-93), Tanner was able to win only three, while losing 13, and kept the team in last place (56-106 overall). In 1971 Tanner took them all the way to third place (79-83). It was second place (87-67) in 1972. Then the Sox fell on bad times, finishing fifth (77-85) in 1973, fourth (80-80) in 1974 and fifth again (75-86) in 1975. Tanner was on his way to manage the A's in 1976.

### 1976 **Paul Rapier Richards**

After several years as general manager of the White Sox, Richards, who had earlier (1955-1961) managed in Baltimore, returned as field manager in 1976. But he was not able to do much, and the team finished in last place (64-97). Richards died on May 4, 1986, in his home town of Waxahachie, Texas.

### 1977-1978 **Robert Granville "Bob" Lemon**

Lemon had been a fairly successful manager in Kansas City (1970-1972). He took

over the White Sox in 1977 and was able to lead them to a third-place (90-72) finish. In 1978, after 74 games and with the team in fifth place (34-40), he left to manage the Yankees.

### 1978 Lawrence Eugene "Larry" Doby

Doby, born on December 13, 1924, in Camden, South Carolina, had been the first black man in the American League (and the second black in organized baseball) when he signed with the Indians in 1947. This All-Star outfielder was to play with the Indians (1947-1955), the White Sox (1956-1957), the Indians again (1958), the Tigers (1959) and the White Sox again (1959). Doby took over the Sox in fifth place (34-40) and was unable to improve their standing by winning 37 and losing 50. The club finished in fifth (71-90 overall), and Doby was gone.

### 1979 Donald Eulon "Don" Kessinger

Kessinger, born on July 17, 1942, in Forrest City, Arkansas, had been a slick-fielding shortstop for the Cubs (1964-1975) and the Cardinals (1976-1977) before coming to the White Sox in 1977. He was smart and was a Chicago hero, so it seemed logical to make him the player-manager of the Sox in 1979. He lasted for 106 games, and the Sox were in fifth place (46-60) when he was let go – both as a manager and as a player.

*Left to right: Eddie Stanky, Chuck Tanner, Larry Doby.*

### 1979-1986 Anthony "Tony" LaRussa

Born on October 4, 1944, in Tampa, Florida, LaRussa had been primarily a second baseman for only 132 games in his six-year major league career with the Royals (1963), the A's (1968-1971), the Braves (1971) and the Cubs (1973). This law school graduate took over the Sox in 1979 when they were in fifth place (46-60) after 106 games. He was able to split the remaining 54 games (27-27), but the club still finished in fifth (73-87 overall). It was fifth (70-90) again in 1980, and then came a third-place (31-22) finish in the first half of the strike-torn 1981 season, and a sixth-place (23-30) finish in the second half. In 1982 it was back to third place (87-75), followed by a first-place (99-63) finish in 1983. This was the first time that the Sox had qualified for post-season play since 1959. They went on to lose the League Championship Series to the Orioles three games to one. It was a bad year in 1984, with the Sox finishing fifth (74-88). Probably the only highlight that year came on May 9, when the Sox and the Brewers played eight hours and six minutes in the longest game ever. (The White Sox won 7-6 in the 25th inning.) In 1985 it was a third place (85-77) finish, but in 1986, after 64 games, the Sox were in sixth place (26-38) and LaRussa took off to manage the A's that same year.

### 1986 Douglas Lee "Doug" "Rojo" "The Red Rooster" Rader

Rader had been the manager of the Rangers (1983-1985) before he was brought in to be the stopgap manager of the White Sox. He led the club for two games and split them. But by doing that, he was able to raise the team's standing from sixth place to fifth. Let go at the end of the season, Rader would next resurface as manager of the California Angels in 1989.

### 1986-1988 James Louis "Jim" Fregosi

Fregosi had been the manager of the Angels (1978-1981) and was brought in to finish the 1986 season for the Sox. He inherited a team in fifth place (27-39) and was able only to keep them there (72-90 overall) by winning 45 and losing 51. In 1987 it was yet another fifth-place (77-85) finish. The next year, 1988, was not a good one either, but Fregosi was able to say, when he asked how he felt about making it through two years with the team, "Some baseball jobs last longer than marriages." His didn't last much longer. After bringing the club in in fifth place (71-90) in 1988, he was fired.

### 1989- Jeffrey Allen "Jeff" Torborg

Torborg had managed the Cleveland Indians from 1977 to 1979 before going on to coach for the Yankees in 1988. He was hired to take on the White Sox starting in 1989.

# YANKEES
## New York (1903-    )

Called **HIGHLANDERS** (1903-1912)

### 1903-1908 Clark Calvin "The Old Fox" Griffith

When the American League was established in 1901 the roster of teams went like this: Baltimore, Washington, Philadelphia, Boston, Chicago, Detroit, Cleveland and Milwaukee. The Milwaukee club moved in 1902 to St. Louis. And after one year in fifth place (1901) and another in last place (1902), the Baltimore club moved to New York, calling themselves the Highlanders.

Griffith had been the successful manager of the White Sox (1901-1902) before he was called to New York as manager. In 1903 he led the club to a fourth-place (72-62) finish. The year was made memorable, however, by one highly unusual game. It was a road game played in Columbus, Ohio, on May 17, although Columbus was not in the league: the explanation of this curious state of affairs was that the Indians had to play this home game *away* from home because of Sunday restrictions in Cleveland. And the Indians won it 9-2.

In 1904 Griffith managed a second-place (92-59) finish, but then the team fell to sixth place (71-78) in 1905. In 1906 things looked better, and Griffith had another second-place (90-61) finish. That was the year when the Highlanders set a major league mark that still stands: on September 4 they blanked the Red Sox twice, 7-0 and 1-0, winning their fifth straight double-header. In 1907 it was fifth place (70-78), and, after 56 games in 1908 (24-32), with the club in sixth place, Griffith was let go. He came back as manager of the Reds the next year.

### 1908 Norman Arthur "Kid" "The Tabasco Kid" Elberfeld

Born on April 13, 1875, in Pomeroy, Ohio, Elberfeld had been a shortstop with the Phillies (1898), the Reds (1899) and the Tigers (1901-1903). He had come to the Highlanders in 1903 and was appointed to fill in as player-manager in 1908 after Griffith had gone. He was able to win only 27, while losing 71, and the team fell to last

**Above:** *Manager Clark Griffith.*
**Right:** *Manager George Stallings.*
**Opposite:** *Manager Billy Martin.*

place (51-103 overall). Elberfeld lost his job as manager and went back to being a full-time shortstop. He stayed with the Highlanders through 1909, then went to the Senators (1910-1911) and finally to the Dodgers (1914). He died in Chattanooga, Tennessee, on January 13, 1944.

### 1909-1901 George Tweedy "The Miracle Man" Stallings

Stallings had been the manager of the Phillies (1897-1898) and the Tigers (1901) before he was brought in as manager of the Highlanders. He brought the team in in fifth place (74-77) in 1909, and, with the team in second place (79-61) after 140 games in 1910, he left the club and reappeared as manager of the Braves in 1913.

### 1910-1911 Harold Homer "Hal" "Prince Hal" Chase

Born on February 13, 1883, in Los Gatos, California, Chase had begun his sensational career as shortstop for the Highlanders in 1905. In 1910 he was brought in as player-manager to finish the last 11 games of the season. He won nine and lost two, the Highlanders stayed in second place (88-63 overall) and he was re-hired for the 1911 season. But that was a mistake, and the club finished in sixth place (76-76) that year. Chase was fired as manager but was kept on as a shortstop until 1913. He then played for the White Sox (1913-1914), the Buffalo club of the Federal League (1914), the Reds (1916-1918) and the Giants (1919). He died on May 18, 1947, in Colusa, California.

## 1912 **Harry Sterling Wolverton**

Wolverton was born on December 6, 1873, in Mt. Vernon, Ohio, and played third base for the Cubs (1898-1900), the Phillies (1900-1901), the Senators (1902), the Phillies again (1902-1904) and the Braves (1905). In 1912 he was appointed to be the player-manager of the Highlanders, but he brought them in in last place (50-102) and was fired. He did not manage again. He died on February 4, 1937, in Oakland, California.

## Called **YANKEES** (1913-     )

## 1913-1914 **Frank Leroy "Husk" "The Peerless Leader" Chance**

Chance had been the manager of the Cubs (1905-1912) before he was called in to manage the Yankees in 1913. His was not a great tenure, since he brought them in in seventh (57-94) in 1913, and, with the team still in seventh place (61-76) after 137 games in 1914, he was fired. Chance would show up as manager of the Red Sox in 1923.

## 1914 **Roger Thorpe Peckinpaugh**

Peckinpaugh, born on February 5, 1891, in Wooster, Ohio, was brought in to finish the last 17 games of the 1914 season. He had begun his long career at shortstop with the Indians (1910, 1912-1913) before he was traded to the Yankees. In 1914 he was able to win nine, while losing eight, and the team moved up to sixth place (70-84 overall). Then he was relieved of his managerial duties and went back to playing shortstop for the Yankees until 1921. He was traded to the Senators (1923-1926) and then to the White Sox (1927). In 1928 he became the manager of the Indians.

## 1915-1917 **William Edward "Wild Bill" Donovan**

Born on October 13, 1876, in Lawrence, Massachusetts, Donovan had been a right-handed pitcher with the Senators (1898), the Brooklyn Superbas (1899-1902) and the Tigers (1902-1912). In 1915 he was brought in to be the player-manager of the Yankees. Donovan was able to bring the Yankees in in fifth place (69-83) in 1915, and then it was fourth place (80-74) in 1916. When the club slipped to sixth (71-82) in 1917, Donovan was gone. He pitched for the Tigers in 1918 and was appointed manager of the Phillies in 1921.

## 1918-1929 **Miller James "Hug" "The Mighty Mite" Huggins**

Huggins, "The Mite Manager," stood five feet, four inches and weighed 140 pounds. He had been the player-manager (at second base) of the Cardinals (1913-1917) before coming to the Yankees in 1918. A brilliant man, he was probably the first major league manager to hold a law degree. Comparatively speaking, he had immediate success with the Yankees, bringing them in in fourth place (60-63) in 1918 and in third place (80-59) in 1919.

After the 1919 season a deal was inked that was a turning point in Yankee fortunes. Red Sox owner Harry Frazee received $100,000 and a $300,000 loan from Colonels Jacob Ruppert and Tillinghast

L'Hommidieu Huston, the owners of the Yankees, in return for the 24-year-old Babe Ruth, who had hit a record 29 homers in 1919. Frazee compounded this folly by saying, "Ruth had become simply impossible, and the Boston club could no longer put up with his eccentricities. I think the Yankees are taking a gamble."

Even with Ruth with the club in 1920 the Yankees could do no more than maintain their third-place finish of the previous year by going 95-59. But in 1921 came a pennant (98-55), the Yankees' first. Babe Ruth had hit 59 home runs, had knocked out 204 hits and had batted in 170 runs. The World

**Top:** *Manager Huggins and Babe Ruth.*
**Opposite:** *Miller Huggins (r.).*

To Waite Hoyt
In fond remembrance...
from Miller Huggins

**Above:** *Manager Yogi Berra.*
**Right:** *Manager Lou Piniella.*

Series that year was truly a "Subway Series," since both teams were from New York. But the Giants beat the Yankees five games to three.

Huggins guided the Yankees to another first-place (94-60) finish in 1922. Once again the Yankees were frustrated in the World Series, losing again to the Giants, and they managed only one tie in five games, while losing four games to none. After the Series was over Yankee co-owner Colonel T. L. Huston was so disgusted at the play of the team that he called for the dismissal of Manager Huggins, a move that widened the rift between Huston and co-owner Jacob Ruppert. Ruppert refused to consider letting Huggins go, and over the winter Huston sold out to Ruppert, who became the sole owner of the team.

With the Yankee team and manager now receiving the undivided support of success-oriented Ruppert, the New York club skated to their third straight pennant (98-54) in 1923, finishing a remarkable 16 games ahead of the second-place Tigers. This was the year that Yankee Stadium – "The House That Ruth Built" – was dedicated on April 18. It had cost $2.5 million and was the first three-tiered ballpark ever constructed. Chicago's Wrigley Field, built nine years earlier, had cost a mere $250,000.

*Connie Mack of the Athletics (r.) and Miller Huggins of the Yankees.*

Once again the Yankees met the Giants in the World Series, and this time they won four games to two. Oddly enough, the new Yankee Stadium was not all that lucky for the Yankees – at least as far as this particular World Series was concerned. They won all three games at the Giants' Polo Grounds but won only one of three at the Stadium.

The Yanks fell to second (89-63) in 1924, and then it was a disastrous seventh-place (69-85) finish in 1925. In 1926, however, came another pennant (91-63), but the team lost to the Cardinals in the World Series four games to three.

There are many who characterize the 1927 Yankees as the best team ever in baseball. After all, they had Gehrig, Ruth, Lazzeri, Coombs and other All-Stars on the team. But before the season began, Huggins was worried. "The Yankee pitching staff has reached the stage where I must gamble." But that same pitching staff ended the season with a combined earned run average of 3.20. And four of those pitchers had the best win-loss records in the American League. In fact, the 1927 Yankees were the first team to spend the entire season in first place. They were so hot that there was virtually no pennant race, and they came in first with a 110-44 record, wiping out the Pirates in the World Series four games to none.

It was another pennant (101-53) in 1928, and once again the Yankees won the World Series four games to none, this time beating the Cardinals. In 1928 Huggins, who had become wealthy because of his investments, gave a tip to his players: "If you're in the market, get out. It can't last." Most of the players did and thus dodged the Stock Market Crash of 1929. In 1929, with the team in second place (82-61) after 143 games, Huggins stepped down. This Hall of Fame (1964) manager died before the end of the season, on September 25, 1929, in New York City.

### 1929 Arthur "Art" Fletcher

Fletcher came in to finish the 1929 season with the Yankees. He had been the manager of the Phillies from 1923 to 1926, and with 11 games to go, he won six and lost five, and the team stayed in second place (898-66 overall). It was his last stint as a major league manager. Fletcher died on February 6, 1950, in Los Angeles.

### 1930 James Robert "Bob" Shawkey

Born on December 4, 1890, in Sigel, Pennsylvania, Shawkey had been a right-handed pitcher, carrying a lifetime 3.09 earned run average for his time with the Athletics (1913-1915) and the Yankees (1915-1927). Under him the club sank to third place (86-68), and he was gone, not to manage again. Shawkey died on December 31, 1980, in Syracuse, New York.

## 1931-1946 Joseph Vincent "Joe" "Marse Joe" McCarthy

McCarthy had been the manager of the Cubs (1926-1930) and had been summarily fired in the middle of the season the year after he won Chicago the National League pennant. In his first year with the Yankees he managed to bring them in in second place (94-59). But 1932 was really the year of McCarthy's revenge. At the end of the season the Yanks had won the pennant by 13 games over the Athletics (107-47), and McCarthy thus became the first manager to have won the pennant in both leagues. The Yankees then faced the hated Cubs in the World Series and wiped them out four games to one.

Then came two second-place finishes in 1933 (91-59) and 1934 (94-60). Babe Ruth was traded to the Braves at the end of the 1934 season, and McCarthy (who now had Joe DiMaggio in the outfield) changed the Yankee image from one of Ruthian brute strength to cool, efficient dominance. He not only expected his Yankees to win, he

**Above:** *Manager Joe McCarthy.*
**Below:** *McCarthy, Ruth and Gehrig.*
**Opposite:** *McCarthy (r.) and DiMaggio.*

expected them to be dignified as well. He even got rid of Ben Chapman, a southerner who played the outfield with DiMaggio, because he was too emotional.

It was another second-place (89-60) finish in 1935, and that was as low as the Yankees were going to go for several years.

In 1936 the Yankees had six men batting over .300 and five men batting in over 100 runs. They won the pennant that year (102-51), 19½ games ahead of the second-place Tigers. In the World Series they beat the Giants four games to two. That was also the year when McCarthy began to juggle his pitchers. He later said: "I remember after that Series someone came up to me and said my club was so good it didn't look like anybody was going to beat us for a long time. I'll tell you, that fellow knew what he was talking about."

In 1937 the Yankees won another pennant (102-52) in 1937 and finished 13 games ahead of Detroit. They faced the Giants again in the World Series and beat them four games to one.

McCarthy later called the 1938 Yankees the greatest team he ever fielded. It had so much talent that the American League was dubbed: "Snow White and the Seven Dwarfs." The team won the pennant (99-53), finishing 9½ games ahead of the Red Sox. Once again the Yankees faced the

of the terminally-ill Lou Gehrig. The Bronx Bombers ended the season with 106 wins and 45 losses and a bulge of 17 games over the Red Sox. They met the Reds in the World Series and beat them four games to none – the Yanks' fourth straight world's championship. In those four World Series they had won 16 games, while losing only three .

The Yankees seemed to be on a vacation in 1940, finishing third (88-66). But in 1941 came another pennant (101-53). That was the year that Joe DiMaggio posted his phenomenal record of hitting safely in 56 straight games. New York also set a record by clinching the pennant on September 4, in their 136th game, the earliest date ever. It was a Subway Series between the Yankees and the Dodgers, and the Yankees won four games to one. They had now won their ninth World Series and their eighth in succession.

They won another pennant (103-51) in 1942 – their sixth in seven years. But this time they lost the World Series, falling to the Cardinals four games to one. In 1943 they won their third straight pennant (98-56) and faced the Cardinals again in the World Series. This time they won it four games to one. This gave the Yankees their tenth world's championship and their seventh under McCarthy. It was to be the last for McCarthy.

In 1944 came a third-place (83-71) finish, followed by a fourth-place (81-71) finish in 1945. In 1946, with the Yankees in second place (22-13) after 35 games, McCarthy was gone. He was to resurface in 1948 as the manager of the Red Sox.

### 1946 William Malcolm "Bill" Dickey
This Hall of Fame (1954) catcher was born on June 6, 1907, in Bastrop, Louisiana. He had played for the Yankees (1928-1943) and carried a lifetime batting average of .313. When he was called in to take over the managerial job from Joe McCarthy in 1946, he also caught in 54 games. The Yankees were in second place after 35 games, and Dickey won 57 and lost 48, but the club fell to third place (79-61), and Dickey was let go. It was his last year of playing in the majors, as well as his last year of managing.

### 1946 John Henry "Johnny" Neun
Born on October 28, 1900, in Baltimore, Neun had been a first baseman for the Tigers (1925-1928) and the Braves (1930-

Cubs in the World Series, and once again the Yankees were victorious, humiliating the Cubs four games to none.

In 1939 the Yankees, who had been the first team to win three straight World Series the year before, were again the class of the American League, despite the resignation

**Above:** *Bill Dickey as a player.*
**Top:** *Judge Landis and McCarthy.*

1931). He was called in to finish the last 14 games for the Yankees and won eight, while losing six. The club finished in third place (87-67 overall), and Neun was on his way to manage the Reds in 1947.

## 1947-1948 Stanley Raymond "Bucky" Harris

Harris had been the manager of the Senators (1924-1928), the Tigers (1929-1933), the Red Sox (1934), the Senators again (1935-1942) and the Phillies (1943) before he was called to be the manager of the Yankees in 1947. He immediately won the pennant (97-57) with them and thus became the only manager to win the pennant twice in his first year with a team (he had done it with the 1924 Senators). The Yankees beat the Dodgers four games to three in the World Series, and Harris now became the only manager to win the Series with two different American League clubs (the 1924 Senators was his first). But in 1948 Harris was able only to finish third (94-60), and he was fired. He showed up as manager of the Senators for the third time in 1950.

**Right:** *Bucky Harris (l.), Chuck Dressen.*
**Below:** *Casey Stengel calls a meeting.*

## 1949-1960 Charles Dillon "Casey" "The Old Perfessor" Stengel

Stengel had been the manager of the Dodgers (1934-1936) and the Braves (1938-1943), but he had never finished in the first division with his clubs. Then, after an extremely successful stint as manager of the Oakland Oaks of the Pacific Coast League, a Triple-A club, he was brought to the Yankees as manager in 1949. The possessor of a keen baseball mind, he was often quoted in the press: "The secret of managing is to keep the five guys who hate you away from the five guys who are undecided." Or: 'Pitchers are selfish men."

Stengel immediately changed his whole managerial approach. He eliminated the old utility players in favor of the many young, talented kids he could now platoon. And he turned many long-established baseball conventions inside out. This maverick studied people and situations while many of his opponents followed static guidelines with an almost religious faith. In tight situations Casey astounded the pundits. He used left-handed batters against southpaw pitchers, and vice-versa. The cherished "percentages" may have mandated doing otherwise, but Casey knew better. "People alter percentages," Casey countered in defense of his moves against the book. "Johnny Frederick and Andy High were two left-handed batters with the Dodgers who could wear out a southpaw. And Carl Hubbell, one of the greatest left-handers in history, had more trouble with left-handed batters then he did with the right-handed ones." Stengel pulled things apart and put them together in new exciting forms which effectively devastated a generation of opponents. He knew both his players and his opponents better than anyone else.

In Stengel's very first year with the Yankees, 1949, he took them to the pennant (97-57) – but it took him until the last day of the season. The Yankees had been one game behind the powerful Boston club going into their final two-game series with the Red Sox, but the Yankees won both of the games and finished one game ahead. In the World Series they beat the Dodgers four games to one. In 1950 came another first-place finish (98-56), as the Yanks came in three games ahead of the Tigers. In the Series they beat the Phillies' "Whizz Kids" four games to none.

In 1951 Stengel founded the Yankees' first "instruction school," staffed by a distinguished faculty, including baseball greats Frank Crosetti, Eddie Lopat, Bill Dickey and Ralph Houk. They were assisted by Johnny Neun, Bill Skiff, Steve Souchak and Randy Gumpert. Stengel

**Opposite:** *Yogi Berra changes pitchers.*
**Below:** *Stengel hugs Billy Martin, who won the game clinching the '52 pennant.*
**Bottom:** *Left to right: Mickey Mantle, Ralph Houk, Roger Maris.*

214

delegated the drilling and most of the teaching, although he kept a sharp eye on his students and teachers, overseeing the whole process as well as the details.

Dickey, Houk and Skiff worked with the catchers, Lopat and Gumpert worked with the pitchers and Souchak and Crosetti taught the infielders. The 1951 school was held in Phoenix, Arizona, in the hopes of polishing future superstars quickly in order to move them from the farm system circuit to the majors in the least possible time. The first class included such future stars as Mickey Mantle, Gil McDougald and Tom Morgan. Two American League rookies of the year, Bob Grim (1954) and Tony Kubek (1957), came directly into the majors from Stengel's course of instruction. About Mantle, Stengel said, "My God, the boy runs faster than Cobb." He justified his methods by saying, "If you've got a number of good men sitting around on the bench, you'll do yourself a favor playing them. I've decided I'd never count on one player taking care of one position for an entire season."

The Yankees won another pennant (98-56) in 1951, finishing five games ahead of the Indians; in the World Series they beat the Giants four games to two. Another first-place (95-59) finish came in 1952; this time they beat the Dodgers in the Series four games to three. In 1953 the Yankees rolled over the rest of the League to take an unprecedented fifth straight championship (99-52) under Stengel. It was the easiest pennant of all five, since the Bombers had one 18-game winning streak that all but ended the race. At the beginning of the season Stengel had observed, "I got the players who can execute." He had all of his regulars and his best pitchers back, and he reasoned, "If the players are good enough to win four years they should be good enough to win five." The Yankees won the World Series four games to two against the Dodgers, bringing New York a record-breaking fifth straight World Series.

In 1954 the club slipped to second place (103-51). Actually, the Yankees won more games that year than in any other previous year in Stengel's tenure, but it was not enough. An inspired Indians team broke the American League record by winning 111 games. But then, in 1955, Stengel set the Yankees on the pennant road again with a 96-58 finish. They had put on a remarkable finishing run, winning 15 consecutive

games, to end up three games ahead of the Indians. But this time the Yankees were dethroned by the Dodgers in the Series four games to three.

It was another pennant (97-57), nine games ahead of the Indians, in 1956. The Yankees had taken first place on May 16 and were never headed. In the World Series against the Dodgers, partially helped by Don Larsen's perfect game, they won four games to three. In 1957 the Yankees took over first place on June 30 and ended up (98-56) eight games ahead of the White Sox. But they lost in the World Series to the

Braves four games to three. Another pennant (92-62) followed in 1958, the Yankee's fourth straight and ninth in ten years, with Stengel tying Connie Mack's record of managing nine league champions. The Yankees ended up ten games ahead of the White Sox, and though the World Series against the Braves went the distance, the Yankees won four games to three.

The Yankees slipped to third place (79-75) in 1959. In 1960 they won fifteen straight games toward the end of the season, to finish in first place (97-57), Stengel's tenth pennant in 12 seasons. They faced the

Pirates in the World Series and, although they had scored 55 runs to the Pirates' 27, they lost four games to three.

After the season, the sports community was shocked when Stengel was fired as manager. It might have been because he had lost the World Series, but the official reason given was his age, 70. In any case, he was gone. Arthur Daley of *The New York Times* wrote a tribute. "Casey imparted warmth to a cold organization and gave it an appeal that couldn't be bought for a million dollars. He was priceless. From a public relations standpoint the Yankees have done great damage to themselves. . . . It's a shabby way to treat a man who has not only brought them glory but also has given their dynasty firmer footing than it has ever had. So long, Case, you gave us 12 unforgettable years."

Ever the gentleman, Stengel shrugged it off with "I'll never make the mistake of being 70 again." Fortunately, Casey's age was not a matter of concern to others. In 1962 he became manager of the brand-new Mets.

## 1961-1963 Ralph George "Major" Houk

Houk, born on August 9, 1919, in Lawrence, Kansas, had been an outstanding catcher for the Yankees (1947-1954). But before that he had been a US Army combat officer during World War II. Houk was a clear-headed man, committed to professional baseball and an excellent field manager. The club in his charge was so powerful that no obstacle could stand in its way. He did, however, junk Stengel's strategy of platooning and stuck with a set lineup and a set pitching rotation.

He led the Yankees to the pennant (109-53) in his first year as manager, 1961. This team, considered to be the strongest Yankee club since the awesome 1927 crew, beat the Reds in the World Series four games to one. Houk got them another pennant (96-66) in 1962 and won the Series from the Giants four games to three. The Major did it again in 1963, winning the pennant (104-57), finishing 10½ games ahead, their largest margin since 1947. But this

**Above:** *Manager Bill Virdon in 1975.*
**Top:** *Manager Johnny Kean is dejected as the Yankees go down to another defeat.*

**Above:** *Manager Dick Howser tries on his new uniform.*
**Left:** *A typical scene in the life of Manager Billy Martin.*

time they were blown away by the Dodgers in the World Series four games to none. Houk was then taken into the front office to become general manager of the club. He would return to managing the team in 1966.

### 1964 Lawrence Peter "Yogi" Berra

Berra, also called "The Ugly Duckling," had become famous as a creator of seeming malapropisms, such as "Nobody goes there any more. It's too crowded," "It ain't over 'til it's over," "You've got to be very careful if you don't know where you're going, because you might not get there." But as his old friend catcher-broadcaster Joe Garogiola once said, "If Yogi tells you something about baseball, you can take it to the bank."

Berra, elected to the Hall of Fame in 1972, was born on May 12, 1925, in St. Louis. He was a callow youth when he joined the Yankees as a catcher in 1946, but he immediately established himself as a bad ball hitter. Charlie Dressen was a coach with the Yankees when he said to Berra, "Yogi, *think* when you're up there hitting." Berra struck out in his next at bat without taking the bat off his shoulders. Dressen asked him, "What happened?" Berra replied, "I can't think and hit at the same time."

He played for the Yankees from 1946 to 1963 and was voted the American League Most Valuable Player in two straight years, 1954 and 1955. When he took over as manager of the Yankees in 1964 he said, "My big problem as manager will be to see if I can manage." But manage he did, bringing the Yankees in in first place (99-63), but only one game ahead of the White Sox and two ahead of the Orioles. He lost the World Series to Johnny Keane's Cardinals four games to three. Probably the strangest thing coming out of that Series was what happened to the managers. The day after the Series ended, Keane resigned as Cardinal manager and Berra was fired as Yankees manager. Four days later, Keane was named as Yankee manager, and in November Berra went to the New York Mets as coach. He was to become their manager in 1972.

### 1965-1966 John Joseph "Johnny" Keane

Keane had been the manager of the Cardinals (1961-1964) before being called to the Yankees in 1965. He took a team that had won the pennant the year before and brought them in in sixth place (77-85). The next year, 1966, with the club in tenth place (4-16) after 20 games, he resigned, knowing he was in ill health. He died early the next year on January 6, 1967, in Houston.

### 1966-1973 Ralph George "Major" Houk

Houk came down from the general manager's office to the field manager's office to finish the 1966 season. He inherited the team in tenth place (4-16) and kept them there (70-89 overall) by winning 66 and los-

*Below: Manager Bob Lemon.*

ing 73. He was only able to bring them in in ninth place (72-90) in 1967. Then came two straight years in fifth place, 1968 (83-79) and 1969 (80-81). The Yankees managed a second-place (93-69) finish in 1970, and then it was three consecutive years in fourth place – 1971 (82-80), 1972 (79-76) and 1973 (80-82), and he was gone. He would move to Detroit to become the Tigers' manager in 1974.

### 1974-1975 William Charles "Bill" Virdon

Virdon had been the manager of the Pirates (1972-1973) before he was appointed manager of the Yankees in 1974. That year he was able to bring them in in second place (89-73). In 1975 he had the team in third place (53-51) after 104 games and suddenly left to become the manager of the Astros in Houston.

*Mets manager George Bamberger (l.) and Yankee manager Gene Michaels each try to hold on to the Mayor's Trophy prior to the annual exhibition game between the two teams.*

## 1975-1978 Alfred Manuel "Billy" Martin

Martin had been the manager of the Twins (1969), the Tigers (1971-1973) and the Rangers (1974-1975) before returning to New York to manage the Yankees. He inherited a third-place (53-51) team and kept them in third place (83-77 overall) by winning 30 and losing 26. In 1976 he turned the team around, inspiring the players with his aggressive style, and they came in in first place (100-62), leading the Orioles by 10½ games. The League Championship Series went the full five games, and the Yankees beat the Royals three games to two. They faced the Reds in the World Series, and they lost in four straight games.

Martin led them to another first-place (100-62) finish in 1977. As late as August 7 the Yanks were five games out of first place, but they won 13 of the next 14 games and 38 of their last 51, ending up 2½ games in front. In the League Championship Series they met the Royals once again, and once again won the pennant three games to two. The Yankees took on the Dodgers in the World Series, and they won it four games to two.

Things began to fall apart in 1978. Martin was having trouble with outfielder Reggie Jackson, and when Jackson refused to follow Martin's signals to hit and simply went ahead and tried to bunt, Martin lost his head and quipped to a reporter about Jackson and Yankee owner George Steinbrenner: "One's a born liar, the other's convicted." (The last was a reference to Steinbrenner's having pleaded "no contest" to federal charges of illegal campaign contributions.) On the next day, Martin found himself "resigning." The team was then in third place (52-42) after 94 games. Later that year it was announced that Martin would return as manager the next year.

## 1978 Richard Dalton "Dick" Howser

Howser, born on May 14, 1937, in Miami, Florida, had been a capable shortstop with the Athletics (1961-1963), the Indians (1963-1966) and the Yankees (1967-1968). He had left the team to become the baseball coach at Florida State University and later had rejoined the Yankees as coach. He was made interim manager for one game in 1978, and lost it. Howser would return as manager in 1980.

## 1978-1979 Robert Granville "Bob" Lemon

Lemon had been the manager of the Royals (1970-1972) and the White Sox (1977-1978) before being brought in from Chicago to finish the 1978 season with the Yankees. He inherited a team in third place (52-43), 10½ games behind the Red Sox. But then they began to win. When the Sox lost 14 out of 17 games in September the two teams ended the season tied for first place (99-63 overall). The Yankees won the single tie-breaker game to take over first place.

In the League Championship Series the Yankees beat the Royals three games to one. In the World Series they beat the Dodgers four games to two. Lemon was back in 1979, but after 64 games the Yankees were in fourth place (34-30), and Steinbrenner decided to keep his promise to Billy Martin. Lemon was to return as manager in 1981.

## 1979 Alfred Manuel "Billy" Martin

When Steinbrenner brought Martin back in 1979 the Yankees were in fourth place (34-30). But Martin was unable to improve the standing by winning 55 and losing 41, and the team remained in fourth (89-71 overall). He was fired for the second time and took over the Athletics in 1980.

## 1980 Richard Dalton "Dick" Howser

Howser came back to manage the Yankees in 1980 and was able to last the whole season. He managed a first-place (103-59) finish for the club, but when he lost to the Royals three straight in the League Championship Series, he was fired. Steinbrenner actually implied that he had resigned in order to return to Florida to get into the real estate business, but Howser was really let go. He advised his successor, Gene Michael, to "have a strong stomach and a nice contract." Howser became the Royals' manager in 1981.

219

**Above:** *The George and Billy Show is revived in 1983, as they hold a mock argument at a press conference to announce that Martin has been hired for the third time as manager.*
**Right:** *Manager Bucky Dent.*

## 1981 **Eugene Richard "Gene" "Stick" Michael**

Born on June 2, 1938, in Kent, Ohio, Michael had been a shortstop for the Pirates (1966), the Dodgers (1967), the Yankees (1968-1974) and the Tigers (1975). He was brought in as Yankee manager in 1981 – that strike-divided year in which there were first-half (pre-strike) winners and second-half (post-strike) winners. Michael was able to bring the Yanks in in first (34-22) place in the first half of the season. But in the second half, with the club in fifth place (12-11) after 23 games, he was relieved of his duties. Michael was to return as manager in 1982.

## 1981-1982 **Robert Granville "Bob" Lemon**

Lemon was back in 1981, and, with the Yankees in fifth place (12-11) in the second half of the season, he won 13 and lost 15 and the club ended in last place (25-26 overall). Still, the team had won the first-half championship, and the Yankees were in the Divisional Playoff Series, in which they beat the Brewers three games to two. They went on to sweep the A's in the League Championship Series three games to none and thereby won the American League pennant. The Yanks faced the Dodgers in the Series and lost four games to two. Lemon hung on for a while in 1982, but after 14 games and with the team in fourth place (6-8) he was fired.

## 1982 **Eugene Richard "Gene" "Stick" Michael**

Michael took over the team again on April 25, when they were in fourth place (6-8).

He was able to win only 44, while losing 42, the team dropped to fifth place (50-50) and he was fired again. Michael was to take over the Cubs in 1986.

## 1982 Clyde Edward King

King had been the manager of the Giants (1969-1970) and the Braves (1974-1975). He took over the fifth-place (50-50) Yankees on August 3, 1982, won 29 and lost 33, and the club stayed in fifth place (79-83 overall). He was brought back to the Yankees in 1988 to be the pitching coach.

## 1983 Alfred Manuel "Billy" Martin

Martin was back for the third time in 1983. He was able to manage a third-place (91-71) finish, but because of his off-the-field drunkenness and fighting he was fired for the third time at the end of the season. He would, of course, be back.

## 1984-1985 Lawrence Peter "Yogi" Berra

Berra, who had been the manager of the Yankees (1964) and the Mets (1972-1975), was brought back in 1984. The Yankees had finished third the year before, and Berra kept them in third place (87-75). In 1985, with the team in seventh place (6-10) after 16 games, he was fired. He turned up later as a coach for the Astros.

## 1985 Alfred Manuel "Billy" Martin

It was Martin for the fourth time in 1985. He took over a seventh-place (6-10) club and was able to bring them in in second place (97-64 overall) by winning 91 and losing 54. But his off-the-field behavior got him in trouble and he was fired yet again.

*A worried Lou Piniella muses in the dugout – 1978.*

## 1986-1987 Louis Victor "Lou" Piniella

Born on August 28, 1943, in Tampa, Florida, Piniella had been an outstanding outfielder for the Orioles (1964), the Indians (1968), the Royals (1969-1973) and the Yankees (1974-1984). In 1986 he kept the team in second place (90-72), but in 1987 the Yankees fell to fourth place (89-73). At the end of the season he was moved to the front office to become Yankees' general manager.

## 1988 Alfred Manuel "Billy" Martin

Martin was back for the fifth time in 1988. The Yankees were expected to run away with the American League East, but Martin still had problems and, if anything, seemed more tense and argumentative than ever. He was involved in yet another barroom altercation, this time in a Texas topless bar, where he allegedly lied to policemen. With the team in second place (40-48) co-owner Steinbrenner set a new record by firing Martin for the fifth time.

## 1988 Louis Victor "Lou" Piniella

Piniella left his job as general manager of the Yankees to return to his old field-managing job. The rest of the 1988 season was a struggle, and fired manager Billy Martin didn't help when he said, toward the end of the season, "If I were still managing the Yankees, we'd be in first place, although I don't mean that as a knock at Lou." The fact is, Piniella had a terrible time, with the Yankees, winning only 45, while losing 48. Although the team seemed always on the verge of moving ahead in its division, it gave over first place to the Red Sox on September 5 and never could regain it, finishing a dismal fifth (85-76). As soon as the season ended Piniella was replaced.

## 1989 George Dallas Green

Green had managed the Phillies (1974-1981) and then had served as general manager and president of the Cubs until 1987. In 1989 the Yankees got off to a floundering start, and though they briefly led the AL East in May, by mid-August they had fallen to sixth, and Green was let go.

## 1989 Russell Earl "Bucky" Dent

Former infielder Dent (born in Savannah on November 25, 1951) came in to finish the season. The team was 56-65, eight back, and the prospects looked bleak.